The world's religions

D0813739

The world's religions

**Edited by
Sir Norman Anderson**

Inter-Varsity Press,
Leicester, England

William B. Eerdmans Publishing Company
Grand Rapids, Michigan

Inter-Varsity Press
38 De Montfort Street, Leicester LE1 7GP, England
Wm. B. Eerdmans Publishing Company
255 Jefferson S.E., Grand Rapids, MI 49503

© Inter-Varsity Press 1975
First published July 1950
Fourth edition, completely revised, October 1975

Reprinted, March 1987

All rights reserved. No part of this publication may be reproduced, stored in a retrieval system, or transmitted, in any form or by any means, electronic, mechanical, photocopying, recording or otherwise, without the prior permission of Inter-Varsity Press.

IVP ISBN 0-85111-314-1
EERDMANS ISBN 0-8028-1636-3

Library of Congress Cataloging in Publication Data

Anderson, James Norman Dalrymple, ed.
The world's religions.

Bibliography: after each chapter.
Includes index.
1. Religions.   2. Christianity and other religions.
I. Title.
BL80.A64 1976   291   75-26654
ISBN 0-8028-1636-3

Printed in the United States of America by Eerdmans Printing Company

Inter-Varsity Press is the publishing division of the Universities and Colleges Christian Fellowship (formerly the Inter-Varsity Fellowship), a student movement linking Christian Unions in universities and colleges throughout the United Kingdom and the Republic of Ireland, and a member movement of the International Fellowship of Evangelical Students. For information about local and national activities write to UCCF, 38 De Montfort Street, Leicester LE1 7GP.

Contents

Introduction

This fourth edition of *The World's Religions*, the first edition of which appeared in 1950, is practically a new book, since the majority of the chapters have been re-written, some of them by different authors, and any material retained from the previous editions has been updated and extensively revised. The aim of the book remains the same, however: to summarize the origin and teaching of the main non-Christian religions and to give some idea of what they mean in the thought and lives of their followers. The same basic pattern has been followed, moreover, and the same religions covered: Judaism, Islam, Hinduism, Buddhism, Shinto, Confucianism and the tribal religions here grouped together under the title 'Religions of pre-literary societies'.

It is mainly due to limitations of space that these seven religions have alone been covered, for the line had to be drawn somewhere. Islam and Hinduism were automatic choices, since each claims some 500 million followers. Modern Judaism has, of course, vastly fewer adherents, yet it demanded inclusion as one of the three great monotheistic faiths. Buddhism, Shinto and Confucianism were selected as perhaps the most important of the other great religions which challenge men's allegiance, and a few references to Taoism and Jainism will be found in the sections on Confucianism and Hinduism respectively. Finally, some discussion of the religions of traditional tribal (or pre-literary) societies seemed essential – both because of their intrinsic importance and also because beliefs which are basically 'animistic' in character underlie, and permeate the thought and practices of, many of the more sophisticated religions.

It may well be asked why Christianity is not included in a book on the world's religions. But these studies are intended primarily for students of religion in English-speaking countries, and aim at providing factual information which they might otherwise find it difficult to obtain. As far as the Christian faith is concerned, there is a wide variety of literature available.[1] In the final chapter, moreover,

[1] Three useful introductory books come to mind: *Basic Christianity* by J. R. W.

some reference is made to the distinctive teaching of Christianity
and to the Christian's attitude to other religions.

Similarly, a good case could be made out for the inclusion of an
introductory chapter on comparative religion (or, more accurately,
the comparative study of the world's religions), or even for a discussion of the basic phenomenon of man's religious instinct and the
various theories which have been propounded about how his religious consciousness originated and the different ways in which it
has developed. But again there is already a vast literature on this
subject – most of it of very recent date. For an introduction to a
comparative study of some of the fundamental beliefs of several
different religions, including Christianity, readers may consult
Christianity and Comparative Religion[2] and the bibliography there provided; and for a discussion of the phenomenon of religion in general,
and of the problem whether its history is one of progress from primitive origins, of retrogression from an original revelation, or of a
fluctuating process marked sometimes by progress and sometimes by
retrogression, reference may be made to Robert Brow's paperback
Religion: Origins and Ideas.[3] In any case, the purpose of this present
book is not so much to compare one religion with another as to
describe the great world religions one by one: not so much to theorize
about the phenomenon of religion in general, and its development
and diversification, as to outline how specific religions have originated,
evolved and come to mean what they do today.

This is why each of the following chapters has been contributed
by someone who has not only studied in the abstract the religion
on which he writes, but has also had direct contact with its followers.
The writers have attempted to treat each religion objectively, their
aim being to provide material that is factual and scholarly without
being too technical. No attempt has been made to unify the styles
of individual contributors, and no rigid control has been imposed
on the length or format of the different articles. It is hoped that the
defects of this method will be outweighed by the advantages of
variety and individuality of treatment. Needless to say, each author
is individually responsible for what he has written, for the editor can
claim no detailed knowledge of any non-Christian religion other
than Islam.

The editor and publishers wish to thank those whose advice and
help has been invaluable in the earlier stages of the book's production – whether in providing preliminary drafts, or making criticisms

Stott (Eerdmans, Grand Rapids, Mich., 1957), *Christian Beliefs* by I. H.
Marshall (IVP, Downers Grove, Ill., 1963) and *Mere Christianity* by C. S. Lewis
(Macmillan, New York, 1952). But there are many others.

[2] J. N. D. Anderson, *Christianity and Comparative Religion* (IVP, Downers
Grove, Ill., 1971).

[3] R. Brow, *Religion: Origins and Ideas* (IVP, Downers Grove, Ill., 1966).

and suggestions. Included among these are Mrs Barbara M. Bee, the Rev. T. H. Bendor-Samuel, Dr A. J. Broomhall, Mr Robert Brow, the Rev. R. I. Brown, Miss K. E. Chattock, Mr Chua Wee Hian, the Rev. Dr Kenneth V. Cragg, the Rev. John S. Crossley, the Rev. Eric W. Gosden, Mrs Margaret Gould, Mr Michael C. Griffiths, Dr James D. Holway, Mr Arnold Kellett, Mr Anthony P. Lambert, Mrs J. H. Lewis, Dr William D. Reyburn, the Rev. Basil J. M. Scott, the Rev. N. K. Sonoda, Mr Paul Sudhakar, the Rev. Peter R. Thompson, Mr Andrew F. Walls, Miss Mary Wang, Dr J. Dudley Woodberry. None of these, however, is in any way responsible for the text as it now appears.

J.N.D.A.

CHAPTER ONE

Religions of pre-literary societies

Edward G. Newing*

The African proverb 'a beautiful child has many names' has many applications, even the subject of this chapter! Instead of 'pre-literary' we could have used 'tribal', 'traditional' or 'customary'.[1] Their use in the pages that follow will demonstrate why. On the other hand, other adjectives are frequently found which have not been used here. They are 'primitive', 'primal' and 'animistic'. There are four reasons for this.

First, 'primitive' and 'primal' both carry the idea of priority and with this the sense of purity and simplicity. Since all the religions which come under the umbrella of our title have a long history of development behind them, these concepts cannot be held to apply.[2] Besides this, they have been made suspect by their favoured use within the now discredited evolutionary school of religion.[3] It may be true that the religious activities of present-day tribal folk help us to interpret the evidence available from prehistoric times, but this is not the same as using these activities as data for some theory of primi-

* Edward G. Newing is an Australian who worked as a civil engineer before going to Moore Theological College, Sydney, prior to his ordination in 1959. He has served in parishes in Australia, Tanzania, Kenya and Scotland and was a missionary with the Church Missionary Society of Australia, lecturing in Old Testament and Other Religions at St Paul's United Theological College, Limuru, Kenya until 1973. Since his return to Sydney he has worked as an engineer with the Department of Main Roads.

[1] In, e.g., J. Finegan, Archaeology of World Religions (Princeton University Press, Princeton, New Jersey, 1966); H. von Glasenapp, Non-Christian Religions A to Z (Grosset and Dunlap, New York, 1963), pp. 192-206; M. Eliade, From Primitive to Zen (Harper and Row, New York, 1967). In this chapter we do not deal primarily with pre-historic or historically extinct religions. Our emphasis here, for reasons of space, must be necessarily on extant traditional religions.

[2] E. O. James, Prehistoric Religion (Barnes and Noble, New York, 1961), pp. 147f.

[3] See H. Ringgren and A. V. Ström, Religions of Mankind: Yesterday and Today (Fortress, Philadelphia, 1967), p. 3.

tive religion. This latter activity, so common at the turn of the
century, is now recognized as inadmissible.

Secondly, the terms carry a discordant note to the ears of educated
Africans, Asians and Americans who belong to such societies. They
convey overtones of superiority in the mouths of those who use them
and inferiority in the ears of the hearers. They have become emotive
racial terms in a way which should make us think twice before
using them. It should not be assumed that because a non-literary
tribal society is backward in material culture it is therefore religiously
backward or 'primitive'.[4] In fact, since many originally non-literary
peoples worship one God without any pantheon or intermediary
spirits, it could be argued that, although they have a low materially
developed culture, they are in many respects more advanced in
religious ideas than were, say, the Greeks and Babylonians with their
high civilizations and multiplicity of gods.

Thirdly, 'animism', used merely as a term to show the inter-
connectedness of the world through its animation by personal
will and power, is unobjectionable on the ground that all religions,
even Christianity,[5] may be regarded as animistic in this sense.[6] As a
term to describe a religion, or as a theory to show the origin of
religion, however, it is to be rejected. Pre-literary religions are much
more than a theory about the relationship between the spirit world
and visible world.[7] The closest term which we can find to cover most
of these religions is 'polytheism'.[8] But this would exclude many tribes
which hold to a simple monotheism!

Fourthly, these adjectives are often used to qualify 'religion' as a
singular concept. 'The singular "religion" tends to give the impression
of a homogeneous religion common to all non-literate peoples and
possibly identical with the primal form of religion.'[9] The simple
truth is that we are faced with a multiplicity of religions which
'exhibit such rich variety that it is immensely difficult to select any
traits typical of them all that they do not also share with many of the
religions belonging to the literate civilizations'.[1]

These terms thus exhibit ambiguities that make them unacceptable
as descriptions of the religions discussed in the following pages.

[4] A. P. Elkin, *The Australian Aborigines* (Natural History Press, New York,
1964), pp. 188ff., and E. E. Evans-Pritchard, *Nuer Religion* (OUP, New York,
1956), p. 311.

[5] See, *e.g.*, Exodus 7:3-11:10; Job 37-41; Psalm 29; Proverbs 16:33; Acts 17:28;
Colossians 1:17; Hebrews 1:3.

[6] See G. van der Leeuw, *Religion in Essence and Manifestation* (Harper and
Row, New York, 1963), pp. 83ff. for an excellent discussion of the animistic
theory.

[7] M. Eliade, *Patterns in Comparative Religion* (World Pub., Cleveland, 1963),
pp. 6f., 24f.

[8] E. G. Parrinder, *West African Religion* (Allenson, Naperville, Ill., 1961).

[9] Ringgren and Ström, *Religions of Mankind*, p. 3.   [1] *Ibid.*

Pre-literary societies

Pre-literary societies (PLSs) may also be called traditional tribal societies. Professor H. W. Turner defines such societies as 'a group of people who feel they belong together through sharing a common culture and set of values, a common territory and social organisation, and probably a common language. They differ from our modern societies in lacking a literary tradition,[2] and being undeveloped in scientific knowledge, technological skills, and economic life. They also have a simpler social organisation, are smaller in scale, and very self-contained; some may number only a few hundred people, others a few million. Altogether they account for between two and three hundred million people divided among thousands of tribal groups.'[3] They are to be found to a greater or lesser extent on every major land mass of the world and on thousands of Pacific and Indian Ocean islands.

While the majority of PLSs in existence at the beginning of the nineteenth century have now disappeared or been radically altered by dominant foreign cultures, there are still many who have resisted these pressures and continue in much the same way as their fathers did before them. It is from these existing PLSs that we can by analogy interpret the evidence which is available to us from travellers' notes, letters of missionaries and administrators' reports and descriptions, as well as reinterpret the data collected by earlier writers on these religions. But our main concern must be with the living religions of today. In most parts of the world it is only too easy to discover remnants of past beliefs and practices, survivals of a forgotten past. We should remember that these do not constitute religion as such, just as it is inadmissible to describe some of the ancient ceremonial used today in some European countries as constituting an eighteenth- or nineteenth-century society.

When, therefore, we speak of the religion of a PLS we should keep in mind the fact that we are referring to an integrated and integrating whole. Each PLS expresses itself in its own distinctive religious forms, so that we may say that there are as many pre-literary religions (PLRs) as there are tribes. Each deserves to be studied in its own right by skilled researchers. In addition, it is important to realize that the study of the religion of a PLS demands the study of that society as a whole and not just its religion. Its religious practices and values must be viewed and understood in their social context. It could be said that a PLS does not have a religion. It is itself a religion, or rather a religious community. Practically every activity, both individual and communal, within the PLS has religious signi-

[2] By literary tradition Prof. Turner means written tradition. The PLSs, however, have rich oral traditions for which the term "oral literature" is becoming increasingly used.

[3] Unpublished first-year lecture notes.

ficance. Of course, those who belong to a PLS are not conscious of this. That is simply the way they live. This permeation of life with the sacred is a fundamental characteristic of the PLS and cannot be overemphasized, since we who divide life into sacred and secular, with the emphasis on the latter, by this very fact tend to distort what we see in other societies which are different in quality as well as in quantity from our own.

Each pre-literary religion, then, is distinctive enough in itself to make generalizations quite difficult. But, as long as this is kept in mind, the similarities are such that generalizations of common features are possible over the whole range of the PLSs. It would take a whole book to cover these adequately and to note the variations, so of necessity we have had to be selective. We have chosen three representative examples of PLSs from three continents to illustrate both the distinctiveness and similarity of their religions. Using these as our starting-point we shall then try to summarize the basic features of tribal religions, illustrating them by reference to other PLRs from time to time. But one further word on sources should be given before we attempt this.

Sources of pre-literary religions

We have already mentioned a few sources of data for PLRs: letters, reports, descriptions, notes and books by early explorers, colonial administrators, travellers and missionaries.[4] For most PLRs which have ceased to function these sources are invaluable as our only means of information; on the other hand, we have to handle this material with extreme caution. Often the observations are very superficial, for in most cases they are unrelated to the social context in which they occur or they are distorted by being judged by some Christian or moral yardstick.

Two examples of this should suffice. When Charles Darwin came to Tierra del Fuego in 1833 he believed that he had discovered an aboriginal people with no religion at all. The tremendous impact that his news had on the British people is still being felt today. And this in spite of the fact that fifty years ago a scholar who took the time to live with the Fuegians and to learn their language and customs reported that the idea of God is well developed, and that there is no evidence that there ever was a time when he was not known to them.[5] His name is *Watauinaiwa*, which means Eternal One.

[4] Most of this material may be found in Sir James Frazer's multi-volume *The Golden Bough* (Macmillan, New York, 1958). His uncritical and highly biased use of the material scissored and pasted together to prove his theses fortunately does not in the last resort affect the data itself.

[5] W. Koppers, *Unter Feuerländern Indianern* (Strecker und Schröder, Stuttgart, 1924). See "The Yahgan—The Ona—The Patagonian and Pampean Hunters," *Handbook of South American Indians*, I (Bull. 143, Bur. Amer. Ethnol. Smiths. Inst., Washington, 1946), pp. 102ff.

The second example concerns an explorer who, addressing the Royal Geographical Society about his safari up the Nile through southern Sudan in 1861, said: 'Like all other tribes of the White Nile they have no idea of a Deity, nor even a vestige of superstition; they are mere brutes, whose only idea of earthly happiness is an unlimited supply of wives, cattle and . . . beer.'[6] Yet perhaps the greatest book written on the religion of a PLS has one of these tribes as its subject-matter — *Nuer Religion*, by Professor Evans-Pritchard, first published in 1956. He writes, 'The Nuer are undoubtedly a primitive people by the usual standards of reckoning, but their religious thought is remarkably sensitive, refined, and intelligent. It is also highly complex.'[7]

Even evidence from more recent times, though marked by a good deal more objectivity and impartiality, needs care in its use. This is true for material gathered after a short acquaintance with a PLS through an interpreter, for material too sacred to be communicated fully to comparative strangers,[8] and for material gathered through questions determined by preconceived notions (for example, the animistic theory of religious origins) of what 'primitive' religion should be like.

It is the sort of evidence represented by Evans-Pritchard's *Nuer Religion* that we can rely on and which puts all the other evidence into proper perspective. The most valuable evidence comes from trained field-workers who have spent many years with a particular people gaining their confidence, learning their language, listening and observing. Perhaps among the most privileged people in the world today in this respect are missionaries, for they have opportunities to study PLRs from inside. This privilege is shared also by professional ethnologists and social anthropologists.

At this point it will help us in our understanding of PLSs if we briefly look at the major areas of life in a PLS which yield the data necessary for an evaluation of its religion.

a. Language. To learn the language so as to acquire the full range of religious vocabulary and ultimately to think in it is the chief goal of an investigator. Without it one learns little but the extent of one's own prejudices.

b. Social structure. Behaviour and personal relationships are governed

---

[6] Sir Samuel Baker, "Account of the Discovery of the Second Great Lake of the Nile," *Royal Geographical Society*, xxxvi (1867).

[7] Evans-Pritchard, *Nuer Religion*, p. 322.

[8] Most PLSs have esoteric societies whose secrets are mostly religious. For example, Io, god of the Maoris, remained unknown to Europeans for many years; see Eliade, *From Primitive to Zen*, pp. 14f. Unless one is initiated into such societies or becomes a confidant of a sect leader, their secrets will remain so.

by strict protocol sanctioned by centuries of tradition. The whole range of social relationships has religious meaning. In most cases they cover the ancestral spirits of 'living dead',[9] and sometimes include animals as well.

c. Religious personages. Every PLS has mediators between the seen and the unseen world. Obviously they are important sources of knowledge about religious values and practices.

d. Oral literature. While PLSs have no written literature they still possess an extraordinary range of proverbs, myths, legends, fables, laws and customs which are transmitted by word of mouth. The accuracy of these traditions is not to be doubted. They reveal attitudes to the unseen world, their natural environment, human relationships and so on, all of which have religious value.

e. Prayers. These are of tremendous importance, for they reveal the real feelings of the people to the divine. From them we also obtain divine names, the extent of their power and the religious stance of those who pray.

f. Songs and music. Traditional peoples love to sing, make music and dance. Much of this is religious in character and often expresses itself in their rituals and festivals.

g. Rituals. It is perhaps here more than anywhere else that PLSs have the conviction that to survive they must share in and influence the rhythm of life. There are rites of initiation, cosmological dramas, sacrifices, purificatory ceremonies, burial and funerary rites, to mention a few.

h. Art and sculpture. Religious convictions are also expressed in an astonishing variety of art forms: rock paintings, designs on bark and trees, wood carvings, stone and clay sculpture, body markings, head-dress designs, and paintings and drawings on shields, spears, hut walls and doors, stools and cooking pots are among the many things which demand our attention.

i. Sanctuaries. In the more sophisticated religions, sanctuaries are of a permanent man-made construction. Their absence should not delude us into thinking pre-literate peoples have none. Every PLS has its sacred sites hallowed by tradition as the places where the divine manifests itself. They may be waterfalls, lakes, caves, certain trees or groves, unusually shaped rocks, hills, mountains, places where lightning has struck, or distinctive land formations.

---

[9] A phrase coined by Prof. John Mbiti to designate the ancestral spirits or shades.

j. Tabus. 'Tabu' is a Polynesian word meaning 'what is prohibited'. There are usually all sorts of things which may not be eaten, touched or even seen by either some or all of the PLS. In Africa, for instance, the chameleon is universally tabu. The reason for this is to be found in the African myths which associate it with the introduction of evil into the world. Sanctuaries are invariably forbidden except to the initiated. Sex is always hedged around with sanctions of religious significance.

These are the major areas of investigation but, important as these are, the attitude of the researcher is crucial. It is not enough to know *where* to look. *How* we look also determines what we find. So often we take with us our own prejudices and preconceptions of what we are looking for. As a result we miss what is there because it does not fit into our scheme of things.

Examples of pre-literary religions

As already mentioned, the three examples we have chosen come from three continents and illustrate both the similarities and the differences of such religions.

1. The Ameru of Kenya

To see Mount Kenya is an unforgettable, indelible experience. It stands alone thrusting upwards from the surrounding plains—spectacularly beautiful, awesome, fascinating, compelling. And this sense of wonder grows with the years so that one feels its presence even at night or when it is hidden from sight by the clouds. For the peoples of central Kenya *Kirinyaga* ('Place of Whiteness') has always been there. It is a fact of their existence.

The Ameru live on the eastern and northern slopes of Mount Kenya and spill over the plains and hills to the north-east. The tribe is divided into nine sub-tribes which are territorially, traditionally and dialectally distinct. Despite a good deal of rivalry between these sub-tribes which used to erupt on occasion into violence, they avow that 'the Ameru are one', even though there is no central authority. Each sub-tribe is divided into clans or exogamous lineages.[1] These are the basic social, cultic and political units of the sub-tribe and are ruled over by colleges of elders. There are no chiefs in the original social structure of the Ameru. The elders are themselves classified by both age and wisdom. All share in the government of the clan but it is the *agambi* (speakers) who take the lead and to whom the others look for guidance in making decisions. The

---

[1] "Exogamous" means marrying outside the family, clan or tribe. It is the opposite of "endogamous."

senior elders under the leadership of the sub-tribe's *Mugwe* (prophet-priest) are responsible for offering sacrifices[2] and prayers to *Mulungu* (God) in the sacred grove at times of national calamities such as famine, plague or war, and times of religious and social significance such as the *ntuiko*.[3]

The Ameru are organized, or rather stratified, according to age-sets which are in turn grouped into generation-sets. The information and progress of these sets are marked by *rites de passage*, in particular the initiatory ceremonies of circumcision, and the *ntuiko* ceremony. The former takes place at puberty and covers both male and female, although the male aspect is of greater significance for the clans. The age-set covers a four-year group of initiates, while the generation-set spans seven or eight of these. *Ntuiko* is the ceremony which 'breaks' the authority of one generation-set which then passes over to the next. It is supposed to occur at the fulfilment of a generation-set, *i.e.* every twenty-eight or thirty-two years. The last one occurred in 1938-39 and there will probably never be another because of the rapid western-ization of the tribe. A feature of the *ntuiko*, which lasts for a period of six months or more, besides sacrifices, prayers, instructions, feastings and ritual killings, was the ritual abandonment of all moral restraint and decorum by the elders of the outgoing generation-set for a period of time. This broke their authority and symbolized the chaos which threatened abandonment of tradition and custom. The ritual restoration of order and authority by the incoming set marked the beginning of their term of office.

The Ameru are what we call practical monotheists. How far their understanding of *Mulungu* has been affected and heightened by Christian missionary activity is difficult to determine. As with so many African peoples, there is no doubt that a sharpening of the traditional Ameru concept of God has taken place. But for all that, the traditional view met with by the first Europeans was of a Supreme Being, dwelling alone in the sky or on Mount Kenya. The traditional prayers corroborate this. Here is one example:

'God, you created me and gave me strength.
Everything in its completeness is from God.

[2] Only sheep or goats of one color and without blemish are offered. At the time of the *ntuiko* (see footnote 3, below) a specially prepared black (sacred colour) bull is sacrificed by the religious leader of the sub-tribe who later uses the skin for a mantle.

[3] *Ntuiko* means "breaking." B. Bernardi, *Mugwe, A Failing Prophet* (OUP, New York, 1959), pp. 90ff., describes this ceremony where it coincides with the accession of a new *mugwe*. It is the *rite de passage* from one generation-set to another. (*Rite de passage* is the term used for an initiatory ritual marking the transference of a person from one order of being to another.) I have briefly discussed it above; the account I give is from my own investigations among the Mwimbi peoples.

Give me strength, give me all things (good):
millet, sorghum, beans, and both goats and sheep.
Preserve me from going to rest in a place of shades
for it is the bad shades who call a sleeping man.'

Among the other names for God, *Ngai* is common even though
borrowed from the Maasai. The name of the mountain is also used
(*Kirinyaga*), together with *Nyaga* (Brightness), *Munene* (Lord),
Mwene-into-bionthe (Owner of everything), *Mwene-inya* (Possessor of
power), *Njeru* (Sun), *Baba* (Father), *Mbura* (Rain). In fact all his
activities may be substantized as divine titles, *e.g.* Creator, Protector,
Provider. Unlike many other African PLSs, there are no intermediary
divinities and spirits between God and man. Even today most old
Ameru people who are non-Christians pray on rising, before starting
on a venture and before retiring.

Yet God does not figure largely in the everyday life of the Ameru.
It is the common belief that one should not bother God too much,
otherwise he may get angry. On the whole, however, God is regarded
as the source of all good. The ills of everyday life are ascribed either
to witchcraft or to the *nkoma* (ancestral shades or 'living dead'). As
far as I could determine, there are no 'shades' which do good. The
important thing is to keep them happy and to give them proper
respect by performing the correct rituals on death and after death,
and by feeding them.

When someone does fall sick or if there has been an accident the
mugaa (doctor) is called in to treat the one affected after the cause of
the trouble has been diagnosed by a diviner (*kiruria*). Very often
these are one and the same man. The diagnosis consists of determining
why the person is sick or had the accident. If it is an offended shade
the questions as to who is responsible and what must be done to
'cool' it down are answered. If it is a case of witchcraft, medicines are
prescribed to counteract its effect and efforts are made to find out who
is using it. The rituals involved may last up to a week in length and
involve the whole family. Before starting out on a safari, building
a house, cultivating a new piece of land, getting married and so on,
the diviner and/or doctor is consulted for his advice on the proper
time and the right charms and spells to use to ensure success.

This may be regarded as a right and proper use of the spiritual
power which throbs through the Ameru world. The *arogi* (witches),
however, abuse it and use it for evil ends. The *Ameru* are terrified of
them and their medicines and arts – their *urogi*. Their most powerful
weapon besides that of suggestion is poison. In bygone days when
they were discovered death was administered on the spot. Stoning
and rolling down a hill in a bee-hive[4] were common.

---

[4] Bee-hives in Africa are mostly hollow logs, often large enough to cater for the
human body. African bees are well known for their ferocity and deadliness.

Of all the religious personages of the Ameru, the *Agwe* (plural form of *Mugwe*) are the most important and fascinating. For almost half a century their existence was a closely-guarded secret kept from missionary and administrative officer alike. Not all the sub-tribes have or had *Agwe*. The three who have no tradition of the institution claim, however, that they had prophets who did everything the *Agwe* of the others did! Be that as it may, a *Mugwe* is a king-like figure but without the political authority of a king. Nevertheless his moral and spiritual authority are without question. There is evidence that he is looked on as a divine figure embodying in himself the characteristics of God. Maybe this is because he possesses in a unique way among men the ability to use and control the power of God. Thus his character must be blameless: 1. 'The Mugwe must be a well born person; 2. He should be a pure man all through his life; 3. He should not kill any animal or any man from his childhood to his death; 4. He should be a man of good character; 5. He should follow the correct ancient customs of the Meru; 6. He should not do anything harmful to his people.'[5]

It is no wonder that the very existence of the Ameru is seen to depend on the *Mugwe*, and so his person is carefully guarded. Though Father Bernardi thinks that 'the institution of the *Mugwe* is a fairly recent one',[6] as far as the Ameru are concerned 'he was there from the beginning'. Most of the myths of the genesis of the Ameru connect the first *Mugwe* with the Moses-like figure who brought the people out of slavery when they lived at a place called *Mbwa*.[7] The office is hereditary and passes on to a successor, who has been trained from birth, usually on the death of the *Mugwe*. The badges of office are a judgment seat, a black bull-skin mantle, a staff, a gourd of honey-beer and the *kiragu* (hidden things?). It is this last which gives the *Mugwe* a good deal of his mystique. Very few know what the *kiragu* are and they are sworn to secrecy. After the investiture these are put away until the next time. The tragedy for them is that, in most cases, there will never be a next time.

The work of the *Mugwe* is essentially twofold. First he mediates his people's corporate needs to *Mulungu* (never to the ancestral shades). Secondly, he mediates God's blessings on the people. He does this by sacramentally spraying on them the sacred honey-beer from his mouth and announcing the blessing. The occasions of these prayers and blessings are the great communal festivals of planting, harvest,

---

When a swarm of bees approaches the only escape is to lie on the ground and keep completely still.

[5] Bernardi, *Mugwe*, p. 106, quoting an Igembe elder.

[6] *Ibid.*, p. 75.

[7] "At Mbwa" is translated *Mbwani* which is comparable with the Swahili *Pwani* ("coast"). It is likely the Ameru ancestors were held slaves by the Arabs at the coast. After escaping they came up the Tane River to their present homeland.

initiation and *ntuiko*, the assemblies at the sanctuaries in times of calamity and when raiding parties are sent out. These tasks are essentially priestly and, although the *Mugwe* performs a diviner's work and as a prophet falls into trances and dreams dreams, Father Bernardi's designation of him as a prophet is probably too limited.[8]

We shall conclude this rather inadequate sketch with one of the *Mugwe of Imenti's* prayers:[9]

'*Kirinyaga*, owner of all things, I pray thee, give me what I need, because I am suffering, and also my children and all the things that are in this country of mine. I beg thee for life, the rich abundant life, healthy people with no disease, may they bear healthy children. And also to women who suffer because they are barren, open the way by which they may see children. Give goats, cattle, food and honey. And also the troubles of the other lands, that I don't know, remove.'

2. The Aboriginals of Australia

'The Australian Aboriginal religion possesses a remarkably uniform quality so that . . . it does not consist of several heterogeneous branches functioning side by side and independent of each other. The Aboriginal religion represents in its essentials an organic whole, consisting of the same fundamental concepts of faith which pulsate like an electric current throughout the whole of Australia.'[1] Because of this we shall in this second example describe major features of the Aboriginal religion as a whole and not just those of one tribe's religion.

There were once over 500 tribal groups on the sub-continent of Australia, each with its own language and occupying a tract of country over which religious and hunting rights were claimed by virtue of some supernatural or mythical sanction. Today few of these tribes remain. It has been estimated that about 40,000 pure Aborigines are living on reserves, cattle stations, missions and outskirts of towns. Few have been integrated into the dominant European culture.

Each tribe is divided into various groups such as local descent groups, religious units, clans, hordes (hunting and food-gathering groups) and families. Each tribe is also divided into what are called 'moieties' by social anthropologists.[2] This is important for the under-

[8] Bernardi, *op. cit.*, pp. 136ff.

[9] *Ibid.*, p. 115.

[1] E. A. Worms, "Religion," in W. E. H. Stanner and H. Sheils (eds.), *Australian Aboriginal Studies* (the 1961 Research Conference of Australian Institute of Aboriginal Studies; OUP, New York, 1963), p. 231.

[2] "Moiety" simply means "half". "This system of dual organization . . . provides a clear cut division for social and ceremonial purposes," R. M. and C. H. Berndt, *The World of the First Australians* (Angus and Robertson, Sydney and London, 1964; University of Chicago Press, Chicago, 1965), p. 46.

standing of the Aboriginal society. Briefly it is the system of classifying
every member of a tribe and its neighbours, in fact all natural phenomena, into either one of two divisions. They are exogamous divisions
which, together with the kinship system, govern all social and religious
relationships. Every tribal member knows his or her moiety and
kinship position and this controls their behaviour *vis-à-vis* others in
the tribe. People are thus sorted into categories and all have a number
of kinship names by which they are known. Stanner sets out eleven
categories which indicate 'forms of address and reference; personal
names; nicknames; terms of membership of social divisions; circum-
locutory terms; metaphysical terms, signs and expletives'.[3] The
Berndts comment, 'The kinship system of a particular tribe or
language unit is in effect a shorthand statement about the network
of interpersonal relations within that unit – a blueprint to guide its
members . . . . . We cannot understand or appreciate traditional life
in Aboriginal Australia without knowing something, at least, of its
social organization and structure – of which kinship is the major
integrating element . . . .'[4]

   The basis of Aboriginal economic life is the natural environment of
Australia. Survival comes from their skill in living in harmony with
their surroundings, their knowledge of the bush and their ability to
use the few tools and weapons at their disposal. The bushcraft of the
Aboriginal is legendary. Yet he himself would not put the success of
his survival down to mere ability or training. Elaborate religious
rituals accompany all food-gathering activities. No Aboriginal
would dream of going out on a hunt without ensuring its success by
performing the correct rite.

   The life-cycle of Aboriginals is marked by *rites de passage* which
initiate them into the next stage of manhood or womanhood, though
girls do not have to go through the same prolonged training as boys.
The Berndts' chart of the life-cycle for the Aboriginals of north-east
Arnhem Land is perhaps the best way of demonstrating this.[5]
The initiatory rituals are essential to the continued existence of
tribal life. In them the social and cultural and therefore the religious
traditions of the tribe are transmitted both orally and through
participation in the rituals that accompany the initiation procedure.
By them the male Aboriginal progresses to maturity and finally in
turn becomes the instructor of the next generation.

   Intimately connected with the complicated social system and life-
cycle initiations is a dominant feature of Aboriginal religion, the
'totem'. In the beginning, Aboriginals believe, life was not the same

[3] W. E. H. Stanner, "Modes of Address and Reference in the North-West of the
Northern Territory," *Oceania*, III, 3 (1937), p. 300.

[4] R. M. and C. H. Berndt, *op. cit.*, p. 91. This applies equally to all PLSs.

[5] *Ibid.*, p. 183. Used by permission of the publishers, Angus and Robertson
(UK) Ltd.

Fig. 1 Life-Cycle
North-east Arnhem Land.

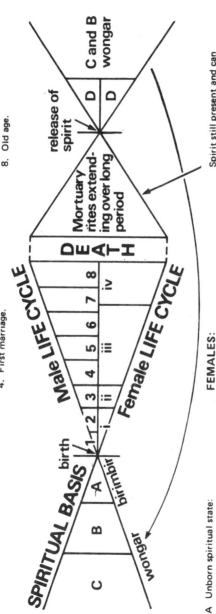

MALES:

1. Infancy and early childhood.
2. First initiation: circumcision: segregation from females.
3. Later initiation.
4. First marriage.
5. Initial parenthood.
6. Further religious revelations.
7. Final religious revelations.
8. Old age.

FEMALES:

i   Infancy and childhood.
ii   Puberty: first marriage.
iii Initial pregnancy: parenthood.
iv   Menopause followed by old age.

A Unborn spiritual state: resident in clan totemic waterholes.

B Direct relationship of A to Ancestral Beings and spirits, from which they are derived.

C Traditional heritage of the group.

D Land of the Dead: one for each moiety; immortality.

Spirit still present and can appear to living: divisible into 'good' (human) and trickster (non-human) or mogwoi spirits. The latter may remain in the bush to haunt the living and eventually be forgotten.

shape and form as we see it now. Personality was a fluid thing which could assume human and animal shapes. An Ancestral Being, for example, may have existed not only as the progenitor of a particular human group but also as the first of a species of animal. It is because of this that human beings today have special relationships with certain animals, for example the goanna, wallaby, dingo, emu and so on. This relationship is termed 'totemic'. The animal is a totem. These relationships pervade the whole of Aboriginal life and are closely tied up with the moiety classificatory system. Professor Elkin's classic definition of Aboriginal totemism deserves quotation. It is 'a relationship between a person or a group of persons and (for example) a natural object or species, as part of nature'. He sees it as a view of nature and life, of the universe and man, which colours and influences the Aborigine's social groupings and mythologies, inspires their rituals and links them to the past. It unites them with nature's activities and species in a bond of mutual life-giving . . . .'[6]

The totemic relationship expresses itself in many different ways. Elkin has classified these under ten broad titles. He further divides them according to whether they serve a cultic or social purpose.[7] The former has to do with those who have responsibility for the sanctuaries of the Ancestral Beings. The custodians must be fully initiated men whose association with the sanctuary is through birth or conception. They have the responsibility of performing the myth-ritual cycles which celebrate the founding of the sanctuary by the Ancestral Beings in their totemic forms. Social totemism, on the other hand, is the more common and all-pervasive type. It defines a person's relationship to others in totemic terms. More often than not it has to do with sexual and marital relationships. For example, one cannot marry a partner from the same totemic group. Nor is a person allowed to eat his or her totem. This is because they come from the same Ancestral Being and therefore are one flesh with each other. None of these characteristics applies to ritual totemism.

Death in an Aboriginal society affects everyone. It is the one completely unnatural event. No-one just dies naturally. Death is usually attributed to the sorcery of someone outside the social group, although a relative who has failed to fulfil kinship obligations may be suspected. All participate in the mourning rites which include chanting, wailing and the cutting of the body with stone knives and pointed sticks. The name of the dead person may not be mentioned and the widow often has to remain silent until after the mourning period is

[6] A. P. Elkin, "Studies in Australian Totemism," *Oceania Monographs*, 2 (Australian National Research Council, Sydney, 1933), p. 133.

[7] A. P. Elkin, *The Australian Aborigines — How to Understand Them* (Angus and Robertson, Sydney and London, 1964), pp. 136ff. Among the many totems are to be found: individual, sex, moiety, section, clan, local, conception, birth, dream, multiple totems.

over. The camp is abandoned or destroyed and close relatives go through special cleansing rites.

A common feature of Aboriginal mortuary rites used to be burial cannibalism.[8] On the whole the rituals of disposal are exceedingly rich and complex. After they are complete the inquest to determine the cause of death is begun. The spirit of the deceased is asked to indicate who killed him. Often only, group responsibility is indicated, though an individual may be accused if evidence of ill-feeling or threats exist. Sometimes parts of the deceased's body are used to ascertain guilt. Revenge expeditions in actual fact are not common because of the fear of either beginning or reinforcing a feud which in the past often proved quite disastrous.

These mortuary rites indicate a widespread and clear belief in personal survival after death. It is of course life on a different level and in a different form. The rituals of death are actually the final initiation which introduces the 'good' soul to the Land of the Dead, returns it to the 'spirit-children' awaiting re-birth or merges it with Ancestral Beings. The important thing is to sever completely its ties with the remaining tribal members and set it free. This is to prevent its assuming its old shape and so causing trouble by seeking its own revenge. As the Berndts point out in their chart,[9] the human, according to Aboriginal belief, also possesses a second, 'trickster', soul or malignant spirit which has independent existence and may remain in the vicinity of the tribal group to haunt the living until it is forgotten.

The Land of the Dead is to be identified with the 'Eternal Dreaming' sphere of existence from which all life comes and to which it eventually returns. This 'Eternal Dreaming' is the pattern for all existence. It is the 'creative period' which has not ceased though its form as a place has changed since it is no longer coterminous with this world as it once was. Eliade calls this mythological era of origins *in illo tempore*.[1] This was the formative period of the world when the Ancestral Beings came into existence and laid down the patterns and laws of life which have to be followed. The Aborigines have a wealth of myths about the Eternal Dreaming, which are enacted and drama-tized in their rituals. This myth-ritual complex enables the Eternal Dreaming pattern to be re-presented and made effective in the lives of the tribal members. By the ritual cycle the life-pattern, its values and goals, as laid down *in illo tempore*, are seasonally renewed. 'As a rule no local descent group, clan, or dialect unit owns a complete myth. Even though at first it may appear to do so, what it has is usually

[8] R. M. and C. H. Berndt, *op. cit.*, pp. 400ff., and A. P. Elkin, *op. cit.*, pp. 153 and 358.

[9] See p. 23.

[1] *In illo tempore* is "at that time" — the mythological period at the beginning of time when all was perfect, heaven was accessible to men and they walked with God.

only a section, dealing with some of the actions of a certain being. The men of the next stretch of country may own the next section . . . and so on, all over the country.' The reason for this is that in the Eternal Dreaming the mythical beings moved across the face of the land on well-defined 'dreaming' tracks performing their creative activities of 'putting water there, meeting other spirits, creating people or other living things, making natural features such as rocks or hollows, naming them, instituting rites, singing songs . . .'.[2]

A number of myth cycles refer to a Supreme Being – an 'All-Father' who is variously named *Nurrundere, Bunjil, Baiame, Nurelli*, and so on.[3] It is probable that he was the first Ancestral Being who retired to the sky where he now lives untouched by and uninterested in human affairs.

Belief in a Rainbow Snake consistently expresses itself in Aboriginal myths. He is always associated with rain and water. The following myth is closely related to the elaborate rituals involving the *ubar* in western Arnhem Land.

'The *ubar*, a long wooden gong in the shape of a hollow log, is one of the most sacred objects. Among the Gunwinggu it is the uterus of the Mother, sometimes identified with Ngajod, the Rainbow. Jurawadbad, a python (sometimes a male Rainbow Snake), is betrothed to a girl named Gulanundoidj, or Minaliwu, but she refuses to sleep with him because she has a young lover, Bulugu, Water Snake. Jurawadbad is angry. He makes an *ubar*, a hollow log, which he leaves lying across a bush track. Then turning himself into a snake, he enters it. In the meantime Gulanundoidj and her mother are out hunting. They come upon the *ubar*. Thinking there may be a small animal inside, the girl kneels down and peers into the aperture but can see nothing there. She calls to her mother, who also tries, but in this case Jurawadbad opens his eyes and she looks right through them to the other side. Gulanundoidj puts in her hand and Jurawadbad "bites" her. Then the mother puts in her hand and is "bitten" too. As they lie beside the *ubar* dying, Jurawadbad emerges, turns himself into a man again, and departs to another place where ceremonies are in progress' (and the myth continues).[4]

The elaborate ritual counterpart to this myth lasts for many days.

Rituals play a substantial role in Aboriginal life. Essentially ritual is the enactment of a myth or myth cycle by initiated tribal members. They are usually associated with sacred sites which in turn, as we have seen, are regarded as having special association with the Ancestral Beings. 'Almost every ritual, like almost every important

[2] R. M. and C. H. Berndt, *op. cit.*, p. 201.

[3] A. W. Howitt, *The Native Tribes of South-East Australia* (Humanities, New York, 1972), pp. 488-508.

[4] R. M. and C. H. Berndt, *op. cit.*, p. 211.

action of every day life, can be referred back to some myth, which provides a sufficient reason for it so there is no need to look further.'[5]

There are rituals covering every aspect of life. The most important are women's love-making rites, for attracting a sweetheart or renewing a husband's affection, fertility cults, for ensuring human and natural reproduction, and hunting rites, for the successful outcome of a hunt.

The Aboriginal 'medicine-man' or 'nature-doctor' is an important personage in the religious structure of the Aborigines. While they are differentiated from sorcerers,[6] the distinction tends to be blurred. Both are looked on as possessing special spiritual powers. They mediate between the spirit world and people. Before qualifying to practise their arts they must pass through special and extensive initiation rites. The essential element or theme of these initiation rites is the symbolic death and rebirth of the candidate replete with all the powers necessary to do his work. They are believed to possess hypnotic power, extra-sensory perception, ability to converse with the spirit world, fly, disappear, change shape, effect cures and kill by merely wishing it. They are, therefore, very much feared and respected. The Berndts list the following examples of beneficent magic performed by native doctors; it 'relates to hunting, food-collecting and fishing; rainmaking, and weather control; love magic; magic of jealousy; curing or healing magic; divination after death; magic to stop quarrels, counteract destructive magic, avert misfortune, evade enemies, keep away snakes and so on'.[7]

'Pointing the bone' is the most common act of sorcery practised in Australia. A special prepared bone is pointed at a victim in a pointing rite. Either the spirit of the bone is believed to enter the victim or the victim's soul is captured through the bone. In all cases the victim's death is inevitable. Only by counteracting the sorcery with a stronger magic prepared by a native doctor can a cure be effected – and this is not always certain.

'Sacrifice' and 'prayer', in the usual senses of the words, are marked by their absence. In a recent article on Aboriginal religion by Father E. A. Worms of Sydney the point is made that this is probably due to our too narrow definition of these terms. He believes that, in Aboriginal terms, both these religious practices are to be found and calls for 'a thorough investigation by a student of Australian Religion',[8] before all the evidence disappears.

3. The Quechua[9] of South America

The highland region of the Andes along the west coast of South America through Equador, Peru and Bolivia has the largest in-

[5] *Ibid.*, pp. 217ff.

[6] Elkin, *op. cit.*, pp. 308ff.

[7] R. M. and C. H. Berndt, *op. cit.*, p. 259.

[8] Worms, *op. cit.*, p. 246.

[9] The Quechua are the descendants of the Inca peoples whose great and vastly

digenous population in the Americas. It is difficult to find accurate statistics, but a conservative figure would be about six or seven million. The Quechua language is spoken throughout the area divided into seven distinct dialects.

This outline of their religion is based on information gathered in southern Peru in the mountain valleys around Cuzco and on the high plateau towards the Bolivian border. In this region there is a high concentration of Indian people, chiefly the Quechua, but there is also a considerable number of Aymara living on the 'altiplane', whose language is different but whose culture is practically identical with that of the Quechua.

From the air the snow peaks of the two main ranges of the Andes can be seen stretching as far as the eye can see, while below the vast panorama of magnificent scenery unfolds itself before one's eyes. Roads wind round the hills connecting the towns and hundreds of trails lead to villages and rural communities. The people who live in these small communities know the ritual name of every mountain and hill, river and lake, and believe them to be places where spirits dwell who demand their reverent acknowledgment.

The Quechua are agricultural people, living at altitudes ranging from 6,000 to 13,000 feet above sea level. In the valleys they are occupied chiefly in cultivating the land and in the higher altitudes in the herding of llama, alpaca and sheep. At best life is hard and the struggle for existence is a constant battle against the elements.

The *ayllu*, or community, is the basic social unit and tends to be endogamous. This creates a strong group identity and is looked upon as a defence against the possibility of losing their land. Religious activities are to be seen throughout the whole range of social life, although there is no awareness that what they practise is religion as such. It is an inseparable part of their way of living and essential to community welfare. To break with custom means to break with the community and would result in disaster.

There are no written records, but traditions are handed down from father to son. One man put it: '. . . as my father and mother did, so do I; in the same manner as they made their offerings, so do I.'

The Quechua Indian is extremely sensitive to the natural forces that surround him; his universe is populated by spirit beings who exercise a powerful influence over every aspect of his life. Chief in his pantheon is the 'Earth Mother', *Pachamama* – the source and sustainer of life. She is followed by the *apu*, the spirits of the snow peaks and high mountains. These are the lords and owners of

---

rich empire (*c.* 1150-1550) was crushed by the Spaniards in the sixteenth century. The following account was supplied by Leslie Hoggarth of St. Andrews University and the Glasgow Bible Training Institute. *Cf.* B. Miskin, "The Contemporary Quechua," in J. Steward (ed.), *Handbook of South American Indians*, II (Bur. Amer. Ethnol. Smiths. Inst., Washington, 1946), pp. 462ff.

different regions. The *auki* are the spirits indwelling the nearby hills. They are addressed as 'father' and, though it may appear to be a contradiction, seem to be representatives of *Pachamama* and guardians of her interests. Lesser but highly significant divinities inhabit the thunder and lightning, mountain passes, curiously shaped rocks, springs, fire, wind, rain and rivers. Each member of the pantheon has his or her special name. For the Indian, everything has 'life' which he calls *kausay*. This life force can be used by men to influence events.

The divinities, especially *Pachamama*, exercise their *kausay* chiefly by giving or withholding it in the production of crops, in animal fertility and in the health of the people. The divinities can be angry, hungry, capricious, demanding. Permission must be obtained from them to travel, build or embark on a business venture. They have to be served and propitiated with offerings, libations and sacrifices, each with its own complicated ritual. If such service is inappropriate or incomplete, the offended spirit may punish the offender by handing him over to some 'wind' that causes illness, or to thieves, or may even demand his life. The hill nearest the community and household is known as the *Uywaq* and is looked upon as the special guardian, intimately involved in the social and economic life of the inhabitants.

Today little reference is made to the sun-god who once dominated the Inca religion. In some places a prayer is addressed to him at sunrise or early morning: 'Sun Father, care for me this day with your glorious light until darkness falls. You are the one who cares for us . . . the clothing of the poor.'

When tragedy or sickness strikes, the people turn to the *Paqo*, or *shaman*,[1] to interpret the mind and desires of the offended spirit. The *Paqo* has been chosen by the spirits, supposedly by surviving being struck by lightning, and is given their authority and power. The term used to designate the *Paqo* after his initiation is *diospa wawan*, or 'child of God'. There are different categories of *Paqo* corresponding to the hierarchical order of spirits. Interpretation is sometimes by direct communication with the spirit or through divination. A Quechua text tells of the visit of a *Paqo* to a sick man, how he ascertains the cause of the sickness and prescribes what the offering should be. In this particular case, it was 'the blood of the vicuna, the foetus of a pig and of a guinea-pig, corn, cocoa, and animal fat, to be taken by two men and offered as a burnt offering, because this is what the lord *Apu* demands'.

It is impossible here to give full details of the ritual of animal fertility rites, sowing rites, ritual drinking, the practice of tabus, magic, and other aspects of this very involved religious culture, but a brief look at some ritual prayers may give us a little insight into the religious thinking of the Quechua.

---

[1] A *shaman* is a medicine-man, priest and prophet; see further, below, p. 44.

This prayer is said to *Pachamama* in the spring of the year:

'This is your due I serve you in August at the beginning of the year. You, the one who nurtures me, receive this offering. You, the one who feeds me as a mother giving the breast, as a bird that feeds its young, receive this kindly and from all things defend me; from illness, cause it to be removed far from me, may I be free of all trouble, may I live happily for another year.'

This one is addressed to the highest snow peak in the district:

'Father *Ausangate* bless – breathe on my animals. In the month of August I am offering what is your due. Receive this my offering as I serve it to you with all my heart.'

Here is a prayer for money:

'O, Owner of all silver, bless my money that it might be plentiful and never ending. I am offering this to you at the beginning of the year in August, receive now this offering.'

After prayers and offerings have been made, to make sure that no spirit or divinity has been offended or left out coco leaves, animal fat and maize are served as an offering and forgiveness is asked.

It can be seen that the religious life cannot be divided from the secular. These practices permeate the whole of everyday life and have a considerable hold on the individual. This is well substantiated by the fact that, although the influence of the Roman Catholic Church has now been felt for more than 400 years, traditional beliefs have persisted until today.

It may be of interest to the reader to contrast the above account of a PLR with what we know of it when it was the religion of the great Inca Empire. The following represents the bare bones of Inca religion as described by H. Trimborn.[2]

a. Spirit beings. The Supreme Being (*Huiracocha*) was represented by a golden idol. He was remote and his authority was delegated to nature-gods. The sun, moon, stars, sea, earth and weather were worshipped as gods. *Huacha* or spirits were believed to dwell in places and things and offerings were made to these when encountered. Important *huacha* were souls of dead rulers and nobles.

b. Sacred places. Temples and shrines were used mainly to store images of the gods and paraphernalia of worship. Worship itself was carried on in the open air. The Temple of the Sun at Cuzco was the

---

[2] H. Trimborn, "South Central America and the Andean Civilizations," in W. Krickerberg *et al.*, *Pre-Columbian American Religions* (Holt, Rinehart and Winston, New York, 1969), pp. 114-146.

most significant of the sanctuaries. Local shrines were set up by the people and attended to by themselves.

c. Sacred persons. There was a high priest at the head of a hierarchy of officials who cared for the sun temples. Female attendants were also known. There were certain *Mama-Kona* set aside in perpetual chastity from among the Chosen Women. The high priestess was regarded as wife of the sun. Diviners and healers played important religious roles especially in the ancestor cults. The Incas were much concerned with life after death. The ruler of the Incas was considered to be son of the sun and his person was sacred. After death he was paid divine honours. His wives and servants were buried with him.

d. Sacred actions. The official cult was governed by a calendar of twelve lunar months. Ceremonies were held seasonally and monthly and sacrifices were offered to all the spirit beings by both officials and laymen. Llamas were the main victims – brown ones to *Huiracocha* and specially cared-for white ones to *Inti*, the sun. Children of the Chosen Women were offered at times of dire crisis.

Prayers were offered both silently and audibly in a standing bowed position with arms outstretched. Purificatory ceremonies were of special significance. Confession, penance and ritual bathing in rivers were the main features of these rites. Confession was made to a priest who used divination to determine whether the penitent had confessed all his sin. Abstinence from pleasures such as sexual intercourse, eating salt, meat and so on was a major means of individual piety. Divination affected life in all its forms. Each enquiry was accompanied by sacrifice. Much store was set on dreams.

Underlying principles of pre-literary religions

Having glimpsed the religions of three PLSs we are now better equipped to understand and appreciate the principles which characterize and underlie these religions – or better still the religious world of the PLSs. These principles will in turn make it easier for us to evaluate and comprehend the features and characteristics of PLRs which we deal with in a synoptic manner in our final section.

1. Holistic

The world of the PLS man is holistic, *i.e.* it is much more than the sum of the parts of the visible world he sees around him. His world is a rhythmic whole pulsating with vital spiritual forces. Everything is interconnected so that every activity from birth to death and beyond is interpreted as belonging to a whole – a religious whole. The whole of life is a religious phenomenon. Moreover, the individual parts cannot be extracted from the whole and examined *in themselves* as religious phenomena. This is why labelling PLSs and their religions as 'animistic', 'dynamistic', 'fetishistic', and so on, is inappropriate to say the least. It was doomed to failure from the outset because it took a part, and not always the most significant part, of the religious phenomena and used it to label the whole.

We who live in the modern world of the steel and concrete jungle have lost to a large extent this way of viewing life. We used to share it, but now we fragment and departmentalize life and look out on the world as observing aliens with a view to controlling it. Not so the PLS man. He has 'a sense of affinity, a mysterious knowledge of the relationship between men and the living world'.[3] He lives his life in a relationship of expanding ripples of community both within the seen and unseen world. This can be seen both in the extended family system of interdependence and community, and in the inclusion of the 'living dead' in the family, clan and tribal circle. The PLS man's life is a strange mixture of awe and dread on the one hand, and a sense of oneness and contentment on the other, *vis-à-vis* his environment. In spite of this ambivalence in his attitude to the spirit world which we shall have cause to note later on, his reverence for the totality of life, his feeling of oneness with it and his awareness that he is a participator in the rhythm of being mark off and characterize the PLS man in his religious world.[4]

2. Spiritual

People brought up in a PLS look at happenings and see in them the working of spiritual forces which permeate their environment. This is not to say that they have no understanding of the normal sequence of events which we describe as cause and effect.[5] But in the event of injury, sickness, death, dreams, a hunt, sowing, building, journeying, indeed any activity whether successful or unsuccessful, the primary

[3] W. Müller, "The 'Passivity' of Language and the Experience of Nature: A Study in the Structure of the Mind," in J. M. Kitagawa *et al.* (eds.), *Myths and Symbols. Studies in honor of Mircea Eliade* (University of Chicago Press, Chicago, 1969), p. 234.

[4] *Cf.* V. Mulago, "Vital Participation: The Cohesive Principle of the Bantu Community," in K. A. Dickson and P. Ellingworth (eds.), *Biblical Revelation and African Beliefs* (Orbis Books, Maryknoll, New York, 1971), pp. 137-158.

[5] L. Levy-Bruhl, *The Primitive Mentality* (Beacon Press, Boston, 1966) put forward a theory of pre-logical corporate thinking among primitive peoples. He postulated that primitives saw no logical, objective, causal relationships between events as we do. Evans-Pritchard's criticisms of Levy-Bruhl are decisive *(Theories of Primitive Religion*, OUP, New York, 1965, pp. 78ff.). So-called primitive peoples do see causal relationships between events, *e.g.* when a man is killed by an elephant. But another dimension is added: the spiritual. These two explanations supplement each other and are not exclusive.

factor to be considered in any chain of causation is the spiritual forces which control the outcome. If, for instance, an Ameru child contracts pneumonia the parents do not ask 'How?' but 'Why?'. They will not blame themselves for being neglectful or the child for being foolish. They will go to their *mugaa* to determine the cause of the illness. This cause will be understood in spiritual, not medical, terms. Has the child been bewitched? If so, who has bewitched him? If not, has one of the 'living dead' been offended? Which one? What must be done to appease the offended 'shade'? Unless the harmony of spiritual forces is restored death will inevitably result. This spiritual-istic interpretation of their world dominates the thinking of pre-literary men and women.

They live in close relationship with a world inhabited by an infinite variety of spiritual beings. The universe throbs and pulsates with sacred life. The fact of this spirit-dominated world is never disputed. It is taken for granted. We who have been raised in modern technologically-orientated societies find this difficult to grasp. Even those of us who are Christians and who believe in a God who 'upholds all things by his powerful word' (Hebrews 1:3) are conditioned by the scientific revolution set in train by Newton. The mechanical view of the universe and the physical basis of life were the inevitable results of his theories. Few serious attempts have been made to find an alternative.[6] When, therefore, we come face to face with a thoroughly spiritual and personal interpretation of the phenomena of life we should tread softly. Given the premises of the PLSs it can be seen as an acceptable interpretation of life.

When we grasp this spiritual principle of PLSs we can begin to appreciate many of the activities which modern man so often dis-misses as superstitious, magical or just plain pagan. We begin to understand the place of the diviner, medicine-man, the seer and the sacral king and to differentiate them from the witch and the sorcerer. We begin to have some insight into the paralysing fear that accompan-ies the activities of these last, the necessity for medicines and charms which protect the wearer from these evil forces and the rituals of purification, initiation, restoration, appeasement, and so on.

There is no doubt that the world of the PLSs is a fearful one. Fear plays an important role in their life: dread of the spirit-filled night – none goes out alone at night; terror of the witch and his witchcraft –

---

[6] I think of two: Goethe in the eighteenth century and Teilhard de Chardin in this century. The former's aim was "to recognize living forms *as such*, to see in context their visible and tangible parts, to perceive them as manifestations of *something within*, and thus to master them, to a certain extent, in their whole-ness through a concrete vision". (Quoted by E. Heller, *The Disinherited Mind*, Barnes and Noble, New York, 1971, p. 12.) Teilhard de Chardin's *The Phenom-enon of Man* (Harper and Row, New York, 1959) has been hailed by many Christians, but its metaphysical basis makes it unacceptable to most empirical scientists as a serious work of "science".

death is normally ascribed to witchcraft; horror of offending an ancestral shade or some divinity – their capricious behaviour makes this an everyday possibility.

Something should be said here about what is called 'magic' and 'superstition'. These are distinctions made by Western observers and not by the members of pre-literary societies. Thus the distinction between religion and magic is essentially an academic question and of little use in the description of PLRs. In all levels of these cultures religion and superstitions or magical practices are closely intertwined. In fact it would be a brave man who imagined he could differentiate them. There is a distinction, however, which we should observe, and that is the one made by PLS peoples themselves. In their minds 'black magic' and 'white magic' are quite distinct, though the word 'magic' in each of these phrases hardly means what we mean by it. The former refers to those practices intended to bring harm, *e.g.* bewitching, while the latter is intended to bring about well-being and harmony to either individual or community, *e.g.* rain-making ceremonies, preparation of good-luck charms, *etc.*

In connection with the spiritual principle of PLSs we should note that there is a difference between the sacred and the profane. Some writers tend to talk of the total sanctity of the PLS world and ignore the distinction.[7] This does not accord with the facts. The spiritual-sacred is not always present in uniform intensity. Much of the PLS environment is in fact spiritually neutral. But everything is potentially sacred. The divine may break through into the visible-profane world at any moment and at any time in what are technically termed hierophanies, theophanies or kratophanies.[8] Perhaps the best meter available for reading off this differential is the fear and awe exhibited by members of a PLS when they come into contact with the sacred.

3. Mythical

By 'mythical' we do not mean 'unreal'. Far from it! By means of myths all the great moments of life and death are given meaningful expression and interpretation. For the people of a PLS the origins of their world, how they came to be in it, their relationship to God and/or the gods as well as the origin of evil and death – all these fundamental beliefs are set out in mythic forms. Myth is the means by which a community expresses its faith in the reality of life. It is in actual fact, as Plato and C. S. Lewis have said, the only satisfactory

---

[7] *Cf.* J. V. Taylor, *The Primal Vision* (Fortress Press, Philadelphia, 1964), p. 72.
[8] These words are technical terms of Greek origin. *Theophany:* manifestation of god; *hierophany:* manifestation of the sacred; *kratophany:* manifestation of power. For Eliade these epiphanies of the divine world are the phenomenological data for the study of comparative religion (*op. cit.*, pp. 26ff.).

way of doing this in a universally understandable and emotionally satisfying manner.

'Every myth, whatever its nature, recounts an event that took place *in illo tempore* and constitutes as a result a precedent and pattern for all actions and "situations" later to repeat that event. Every ritual, and every meaningful act that man performs repeats a mythical archetype; and . . . this repetition involves the abolition of profane time and placing of man in a magico-religious time which has no connection with succession in the true sense, but forms the "eternal now" of mythical time. In other words, along with other magico-religious experiences, myth makes man once more exist in a timeless period, which is in effect an *illud tempus*, a time of dawn and of "paradise", outside history.'[9]

The purpose of myth and its accompanying re-enactment in dramatic rites of mime, song and dance is to keep before PLS members the ideal it embodies and recounts – but more, it catches them up into the actuality re-presented so that the people once more live *in illo tempore* and share in the life of the divine.

The use of myth in PLSs permeates their language and thus their ways of thinking. It explains 'the deviousness of the savage', his refusal to come straight to the point, his delight in verbal obliqueness, and most importantly it explains actions, mostly ritual, which to us appear as barbaric, immoral and superstitious but which have to be viewed in their total context to be understood.[1]

4. Ritualistic

The myths of PLSs express themselves chiefly in the rituals of the tribe. There are rituals, however, which are not connected to myths even though perhaps they once were. In all the great moments of life, and in most of the trivial, rituals are observed: birth, puberty, marriage, war, sickness, divorce, eating, cooking, planting, reaping, herding, house-building, departing and arriving, entering and leaving a house, buying and selling and so on. There are rituals performed only by men, those acted out by women alone, those in which

---

[9] Eliade, *From Primitive to Zen,* pp. 429f. For a brilliant discussion of myth and its place in society see M. Eliade, *Myths, Dreams and Mysteries* (Harper and Row, New York, 1967).

[1] I refer primarily to the rituals of violence, conflict and abandonment which used to, and occasionally still do, characterize PLSs. Inter- and intra-tribal and clan wars and raids, ritual slaughters on a chief/king's death, human sacrifice, cannibalism, ritual indiscriminate sexual intercourse and so on must be viewed from within the myth-sanctioned, socio-religious structure of PLSs. It is interesting to note that Prof. J. S. Mbiti, in his work *African Religions and Philosophy* (Praeger, New York, 1970), omits any reference to these things.

both sexes share together and those involving children. Some rituals are peculiar to particular sacred sites. The myths tell the reason why a site is sacred. The rituals enact the myth which in turn explains and interprets the ritual. Word and act belong together so that one may say that PLSs are sacramental in their religious expressions.

Perhaps the most important of the rituals found in practically all PLSs are the fertility rites. By these a PLS ensures the continuance of its life. For people dependent on the natural elements for their survival, the coming of the rains or the passing of the winter is of urgent necessity. These events are seen as dependent on the spiritual forces which govern the seasons. As we have seen, impersonal natural laws have no place in the PLSs' world. Experience has taught them that the gods (*i.e.* the nature gods or spirits) are not consistent in bringing about the seasonal variations which make life possible. Through the fertility rites the myths portraying the triumph of life over death are enacted in the belief that this will make certain the coming of the rain or the return of the sun. This is not an attempt to control their environment. It is a recognition of their dependence on the spirit world. Through the ritual they link themselves with this world and through sympathetic action ensure light and life, fire and water. Thus the harmony of their world is maintained, the spiritual and mythical beings are not offended and disaster does not befall the PLS through famine or plague. If, however, tragedy does strike a community in spite of the correct observance of these rites, there are rituals designed to cope with such emergencies and to restore the balance and rhythm of life.

5. Rhythmic

In the previous pages the words 'rhythm' and 'rhythmical' have been continually cropping up. This is because PLSs are governed by the seasonal cycle of seed-time and harvest, wet and dry season, winter and summer. A rhythmic beat is induced in the communal pattern of existence by this cycle and on it is superimposed the individual and generational themes of the human life-cycle with its many variations. And so a syncopated rhythm is experienced as these two cycles make their presence felt in a PLS's existence. The life-patterns of both individual and community adjust to harmonize with this rhythm and all life-events are seen in relationship to its pulsations.

An important aspect of the rhythmic principle is the PLS's view of time. A common criticism of Africans heard among Europeans is that they have no sense of time. This is not surprising, since time as we know it does not exist in the PLS world. Since the invention of the clock and the development of the cult of efficiency in the West we experience time as movement towards some 'future' moment or event and we are conscious of its continuous flow. But it was not always like this and remnants of our former event- or experience-orientated life is still with us when time 'drags' or 'races'. Even so, time for us is primarily a linear process and not a cyclic one, as it is for the PLSs. For them the seasonal clock is their time-piece, with the sun, moon and stars as reference points. But more important are the events and the experience of the events which take place regularly, rhythmically, cyclically within the seasonal pattern. What is significant for PLSs is the right response to the ever-recurring events on which the life of the tribe depends. In this the past, as remembered events which provide the way of response in the present, is far more important than the non-existent future on which we place so much store.[2]

Rituals are the time-markers on the rhythmic cycle of season and life. There is no rush, no schedules to keep. Lateness and impatience are unknown. The PLSs fit themselves into and accept the givenness of their situation. They live according to the rhythmic pattern laid down by their life-situation and as interpreted by the traditions and customs of the ancestors.

These five principles of the wholeness of life, the spiritual foundation of life, mythically-expressed life-meanings, the ritual domination of life-events and the rhythmic pattern of life provide the essential background to our summary of the major religious themes in pre-literary societies.

An outline of major religious features

In outlining these features the reader should remember that we are not describing any one religion. This is merely an attempt to highlight the main characteristics of PLRs and as such it is an abstraction which can be of use only if it is recognized as one and used accordingly as a tentative framework of reference.

1. The unseen world

a. Power or mana. In all PLSs a spiritual power or life-force is recognized as permeating the universe of their experience. The Melanesian word *mana* has been adopted by scholars to describe this sacred power. It is never worshipped but it is recognized as the given fact of life. The Nilotic peoples of East Africa and the Sudan term it *jok* which, like *wakan* of the Sioux and *manitou* of the Aloquin Ameroindians, is also the name of the Supreme Being. Among other PLSs God simply possesses power in a highly intensive form.

Mana may concentrate itself in certain things such as stones, plants, trees, animals and people with varying degrees of intensity. 'All success and all advantage proceed from the favourable exercise of this *mana*.'[3] A man's position in the community depends on the amount

[2] R. H. Codrington, *The Melanesians* (Midway, Ann Arbor, 1891), p. 119.
[3] *Ibid.*

he possesses. Its manipulation is the main function of the religious experts. Charms, medicines, rites, *etc.* contain this power for the benefit of the wearer or user.

It has been argued[4] that in its uncontrolled form it is simply Fate, the irreducible surd[5] of existence on which all things, including the Supreme Being, depend. It is the 'metadivine' existing above and ultimately outside the control of man and gods alike. It can be highly dangerous and therefore the PLSs protect themselves against its abuse by a system of tabus.

b. Supreme Being. Most, if not all, pre-literary people have a belief in a Supreme Being which most scholars call a High God[6] to distinguish him from the lesser divinities. It has been argued that 'Pagan peoples have a clear notion of a high god *now*, as fulfilment of a hazy idea before'[7] because of the impact of Christian missions. This may be true in certain cases, but on the whole most PLSs' concept of God was quite clear and well formed before the arrival of the missionaries. True, in the majority of instances he takes very little interest in the affairs of men, contenting himself to play the part of a disinterested observer; yet it is interesting to note that among some of the most backward peoples of the world clear and high ideas of God are to be found.[8] W. Schmidt of Vienna was so impressed by this that he built up a whole theory on it: that the original religious concept of man in his primeval state was monotheism which later became corrupted into polytheism.[9]

In general the Supreme Being is a sky-divinity. He is the Creator, or Originator of the creation. He is not often worshipped and shrines to him are rare. When all else fails, however, he is appealed to since he possesses power more than any other spirit or man. To trouble him too much, most Africans believe, is only to ask for trouble. For ordinary everyday matters the living dead, nature-gods and manipulation of the *mana* are of far greater importance.

c. Divinities. We have already noticed that neither the Australian

---

[4] Y. J. Kaufmann, *The Religion of Israel*, ed. Moshe Greenberg (University of Chicago Press, Chicago, 1960), pp. 23f.

[5] A surd is a mathematical and philosophical concept signifying the minimal givenness of a situation which cannot be overcome or explained away. It is the irrational something which defies ultimate explanation by man. Evil, *e.g.*, is a surd to all philosophical and theological systems.

[6] J. S. Mbiti, *Concepts of God in Africa* (Praeger, New York, 1970) and E. B. Idowu, "God," ch. 1 in Dickson and Ellingworth (eds.), *Biblical Revelation and African Beliefs*, pp. 18ff., both scorn this term.

[7] Monica Wilson, unpublished lecture notes.

[8] *E.g.* the Bushmen of the Kalahari, the Pygmy tribes of the Congo and the tribes of Tierra del Fuego.

[9] W. Schmidt, *The Origin and Growth of Religion* (Cooper Sq., New York, 1972).

Aborigines nor the Ameru of Kenya have divinities. This is true for most Bantu-speaking peoples of Africa, the Melanesians, and one or two other groups. The PLSs of West Africa, the Americas, Asia and Polynesia, however, believe in multitudes of gods other than the Supreme Being. The Incas, for instance, from whom the Quechua descended, had a fantastic array of nature-gods and goddesses – personifications of the powers of nature. Among the Yoruba of Nigeria 1,700 such divinities are acknowledged as controlling, or at least responsible for, every conceivable natural phenomenon and human activity. The earth, sun, moon, thunder, lightning, water, sea, rivers, lakes, waterfalls, rain, war, fire – each is seen as expressions of a god's work or the god himself.

Among the Bushmen of the Kalahari only one other divinity besides the good Creator-God is believed in. He seeks to disrupt God's creation and wilfully and vindictively to work evil among men. An interesting feature of North American hunting-tribes' religion is a belief in an Owner of animals who cares for them as the Great Spirit cares for men.

d. Spirits. The boundary between divinities and spirits is hard to draw, but we may say as generally true that all PLSs believe in both capricious, malevolent spirits and good spirits, whether they possess divinities or not. As to the former, in many places they are regarded as either forgotten 'living dead' or the 'trickster' souls of the dead. They dwell in all sorts of places such as trees, rocks, caves, mountain passes, river crossings, animals, insects and so on. They are quite unpredictable and people are always most careful not to offend them and to pay them proper respect by making small offerings of food when they pass by their supposed dwelling-places. Demons take on various shapes to terrify people and all PLSs have innumerable stories about them. Among the good spirits are the clan and tribal ghosts who watch over the welfare of the people.

Totemic spirits form an important group under this heading. We have already discussed totemism among the Australian Aborigines. In North America also it was an important part of religious beliefs. Many Indian clans trace their ancestry back to totem animals. Dancing around the totem-pole, which was primarily a clan emblem, was part of the totemic ritual. Individual totemism was widespread. It was associated with the young brave's search for a visionary experience. Ascetic practices and a long period of solitude led to a vivid dream or vision of his guardian spirit from whom he learnt a personal spirit song. The spirit usually was a bird or animal which became the brave's individual totem. Among the Dakota and Sioux the seeking after revelations was associated with the great Sun Dance which was aimed at renewing the fertility of the earth and involved sacrifices of the dancers' own blood and visions induced by self-torture.

e. Ancestral spirits or the 'living dead'. All PLSs without exception believe in an existence after death of the spirit or spirits of the human being. The fact that a person once dead is believed to be both in the Land of the Dead and able to cause mischief to those whom he has left behind is most often due to a common belief in a multi-spirited human personality. We noticed this about the Australian Aborigines, but it is widespread throughout the world. The Land of the Dead is thought by the North American Indians as a happy hunting-ground stocked plentifully with game. For most Africans it is a shadowy existence under the ground – beneath the village, homestead, or cattle corral – somewhat similar to the Hebrew Sheol and the Greek Hades.

In most PLSs mortuary rites are of the greatest importance because the connection of the soul of the deceased with what he or she knew and was accustomed to must be broken completely, otherwise the soul may return and cause harm to the kin. The proper rites are also believed essential for speeding the soul to the Land of the Dead. They involve mourning, purifications, destruction of the deceased's dwelling in most cases, proper disposal of the remains, sometimes ritual intercourse with the deceased's wives and feastings. In times past chiefs and kings were often sent on their way by the ritual slaughter of their household, servants and warriors who would be able to serve them adequately in the Land of the Dead. Death is nearly always regarded as the result of witchcraft, so an essential factor in the mortuary rites is the determination of the source of the witchcraft. Second and even third burials are found among some PLSs in order that the living dead may be given their proper respect.

For most pre-literary peoples there is a continuing relationship between the living dead and the living. In few societies are the living dead regarded as the source of blessing for the clan or family. In most instances the living dead are feared as a source of arbitrary and irrational evil. This is why, in addition to the mortuary rites, offerings of food and drink are regularly made to them. There is no formality in these offerings and they can hardly be called 'ancestor-worship' unless the term 'worship' is reduced to mean 'respect'. They are looked upon as rather irresponsible old men who play tricks on their surviving relatives if they do not get the respect age demands.

This then is the hierarchy of the spiritual forces recognized by most PLSs. We may represent it diagrammatically (see p. 41) by a series of concentric spheres submerged in a sea of power which inter-penetrates the whole. The personal will or wills of the respective spheres can affect directly those enclosed by it or them. But those in the inner spheres can affect the outer only by manipulation of the *mana* in which they all share to varying degrees.

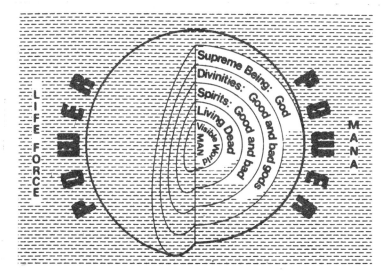

2. The seen world

Man lives in community in a world in which he feels at home and into whose rhythm he fits. But it is also a world which brings terror and fear. In order that he may continually enjoy the good – long life, many children, much food and wealth, great respect – and ward off evil – sickness, barren wives, locust plagues, disrespect from the young, witchcraft – man must know the secrets of power or be able to consult those who have special skill in its manipulation for good or evil.

a. Prohibitions or tabus. It is dangerous to come too near to the sacred world. Where *mana* is concentrated in a particular person or thing it is considered dangerous – it becomes tabu. This has its source essentially in the fear of the unknown, the unusual and abnormal, contact with which may bring upheaval in the human life-pattern, even death. A whole range of people, things and places are thus prohibited: sacred persons who are in close contact with the divine or who are able to manipulate the sacred power are tabu; the dead and all that belongs to them; birth, menstruation and sex; war; sickness; sanctuaries and their paraphernalia; all these and many others are hedged round with myriads of tabus for the protection of the communities and their members.

b. Sacred places. Every PLS has sanctuaries where response is made to the sacred world. These are places where the divine power is believed to be especially present and available. The Australians situated their totem centres most often in a sacred group of trees. In Kenya the

Ameru and the Kikuyu offered sacrifices to the *Mwenenyaga* in sacred groves formed by certain trees and regarded certain hills and mountains as his special province. Trees seem to be of particular importance in the location of sacred places by PLSs. The stone too played a significant part, for we often find sanctuaries located in a clump of unusually shaped stones or rocks. Water, in all its permanent manifestations in pools, falls, lakes, rivers and seas, provided another ingredient for the location of a sanctuary by many tribal groups. Usually associated with the sanctuary are myths and their accompanying rituals which celebrate the divine manifestation at that place. It is tabu to the uninitiated and usually it is served by specially trained and consecrated persons.

Mircea Eliade sees in these sacred places a microcosm reflecting the whole – the universe of life.[1] In the more developed societies they grew into the temple with its stylized representation of heaven and earth as they were *in illo tempore*. It is the centre of the world where is to be found the Tree of Life, the River of Life and the Sacred Mountain. Its rites are reproductions of life as it was and as it should be, and by them men escape from the mundane into the sacred for renewal and blessing.

c. Sacred things. For members of PLSs a whole host of objects are looked on as possessing power and are therefore potentially or actually dangerous. Stones are commonly regarded as having sacred value, probably because of their instrumental value and later because of their use as emblems of dignity, strength and everlastingness. They are used especially in connection with the burial of the dead among some tribes who see the stones as containing the spirits of the dead and of special use in bringing rain and fertility. The earth is especially sacred to all PLSs, so much so that among many she is divinized as Mother Earth. Certain plants, animals and insects may also be venerated or regarded as tabu because of their sacred character. In our own Anglo-Saxon society the ancient maypole ceremony is a vestige of the belief in the fertilizing powers of the sacred tree ritually burnt and scattered on the field at the beginning of spring. Masks and body decorations are universal features of pre-literary religious rituals. These are often quite elaborate and highly colourful. Their purpose is to represent more vividly to the minds of the participants the state of the world *in illo tempore*. Images of divinities are not as widespread as many people think. The Bantu, Bushmen and Pygmy and Nilotic tribes of Africa, the Australians, the Melanesians, the Aboriginal tribe of Asia and the North American Indians make no images of the divinity or divinities, though graphic representations are common. In ancient Polynesia, Central and South America, plastic and carved representations were widespread and in West

[1] Eliade, *Patterns in Comparative Religion*, p. 367.

Africa they still are. In most cases it is believed that the divinity indwells the image and so it is given the respect and honour it would receive if the image was the divinity's own body—in fact it is regarded as the body of the divinity.

d. Sacred actions. We have already looked at the importance of myth and ritual in the life of traditional peoples. Burial and initiation rites have been referred to. We shall deal here more with offerings and sacrifices. Worship of the Supreme Being, though non-existent among many PLSs, does play a part among others, especially in times of communal need such as famine or plague. This worship consists of the sacrifice of some animal or animals, the offering of praise and the making of supplications. Among the Maoris of New Zealand the worship of *Io* was confined to the priests who jealously guarded the secrets of his identity. The elders of the Kikuyu of Kenya alone had the privilege of sacrificing to *Ngai* and there too the cult was essentially esoteric. For those who acknowledge nature-divinities, the offerings of food to gain their patronage at the multitudinous shrines are the main feature of their worship. Human sacrifice and ritual cannibalism were fairly widespread in days gone by. Human sacrifice was mainly used in agricultural communities to ensure the success of the harvest. It was also used in times of national calamity to ward off the impending doom. The ritual eating of human flesh was indulged in probably to gain access to the *mana* of the dead person. Cannibalism for its own sake was also practised, of course, as part of the staple diet, but on the whole this was uncommon.

In PLSs omens play an extremely important part in daily life. To see, for example, certain types of reptiles or animals may cause the postponement of a venture and/or the consultation of a diviner or oracle for advice and remedy against its evil effects. Signs in the heavens are carefully watched. A series of misfortunes may indicate either bewitchment or warnings from the world of the sacred.

e. Sacred words. Besides the many myths recounted in a PLS, oaths curses and blessings are commonly encountered – words charged with sacred power especially if they are uttered by someone of importance such as an elder, doctor or chief. Such words are regarded as possessing a *mana* of their own to effect what their speaker intends in much the same way as words are regarded in the Old Testament.[2] Prayers are perhaps the most important sacred words of PLSs. On, the whole these prayers refer to material needs as we saw in two of our earlier examples; but there are occasions when we come across hymns of great beauty:

---

[2] See, *e.g.,* Genesis 27; Isaiah 55:10f.

'Great Spirit!
Piler up of rocks into towering mountains:
When thou stampest on the stone,
The dust rises and fills the land.
Hardness of the precipice;
Waters of the pool turn
Into misty rain when stirred.
Vessel overflowing with oil!
Father of Runji,
Who seweth the heavens like cloth;
Let him knit together that which is below.
Caller forth of the branching trees:
Thou bringest forth the shoots
That they stand erect.
Thou hast filled the land with mankind,
The dust rises on high, O Lord!
Wonderful One, thou livest
In the midst of the sheltering rocks,
Thou givest rain to mankind:
We pray thee,
Hear us, Lord!
Show mercy when we beseech thee, Lord.
Thou art on high with the spirits of the great.
Thou raisest the grass-covered hills
Above the earth, and createst the rivers,
Gracious One.'[3]

f. Sacred persons. The misunderstanding of pre-literary peoples by Westerners is no better exemplified than by our use of the word 'witch-doctor' to describe the sacred specialist in those societies. Its use can have arisen only out of prejudice and ignorance. The sooner it is dropped the better.

Our three examples show us that we can divide the mediators (for that is what they are) into two groups, the good and the bad. Besides the diviners, medicine-men, prophets and priests we have already met with, we need to take note of two sacred persons who appear in two distinct areas of the world: the *shaman* and the sacred king. The word *shaman* has been borrowed from the Tungus of Central Asia to describe a religious personage found in many PLSs of Asia, Oceania and the Americas. He 'is medicine man, priest and psychopompous, that is to say, he cures sickness, directs the communal sacrifices, and he escorts the souls of the dead to the other world'.[4] He succeeds to his position, is elected to it by super-

---

[3] Translated by F. W. T. Posselt and quoted by E. W. Smith, "The Idea of God among South African Tribes," in E. W. Smith (ed.), *African Ideas of God*, revised by E. G. Parrinder (Lutterworth Press, London, 1962), p. 127.

[4] Eliade, *Patterns in Comparative Religion*, p. 423.

natural beings or, as in North America, a man seeks after the ecstatic experience which will enable him to fill the role of *shaman*. A man is accepted as *shaman* only after he has successfully passed his initiations and received the necessary secrets of the job. In essence he is a new order of being, having died to the old life and been re-born into the realm of the divine.| A characteristic of the *shaman* is his ability to leave his body and observe events in distant places.

In Africa and Polynesia the sacred king is the important religious functionary in many tribal societies. Monica Wilson's study of the Wanyakusa of Northern Malawi reveals how sacred the personality of the king is regarded as representative of the well-being of the people. The Wanyakusa believe the *kyungu* is divine. He is chosen by the nobles from one of two royal clans. His life is surrounded by tabus.

'He must not fall ill, or suffer a wound, or even scratch himself and bleed a little, for his ill health, or his blood falling on the earth would bring sickness to the whole country . . . . Great precautions were taken to preserve his health . . . . When the Kyungu did fall ill he was smothered by the nobles who lived around him at Mbande, and buried in great secrecy, with a score or more of living persons – slaves — in the grave beneath him, and one or two wives and the sons of commoners above . . . . The living Kyungu was thought to create food and rain, and his breath and the growing parts of his body . . . we believed to be magically connected with the fertility of the Ngonde plain . . . . His death was kept a secret . . . and one of the nobles impersonated him wearing his clothes. After a month or two when the nobles had decided whom to choose as the new Kyungu, the luckless man was summoned to Mbande: "Your father calls you". . . . To insult Kyungu was not only treasonable, it was blasphemous, and the whole plain was believed to be cursed with drought or disease in reply. An "insult" might mean any neglect of the obligations of the chiefs and nobles and commoners of the plain to their lord . . .'[5]

Professor Noel Q. King speaks of the court ceremonial of the Bunyoro kings,[6] in the following terms; it 'was detailed and complicated enough to have satisfied a Constantine Porphyrogenitus whose book of Byzantine ceremonies still makes one gasp'. Among the Baganda, who are neighbours of the Bunyoro, the king is regarded as the personification of his predecessors. On his death his jaw-bone and umbilical cord are preserved in a shrine attended by guardians. There his spirit is consulted by his successors.

There is little to add to what we have already seen with respect to

---

[5] M. Wilson, *Communal Rituals of the Nyakyusa* (OUP, New York, 1959), pp. 40ff.
[6] N. Q. King, *Religions of Africa* (Harper and Row, New York, 1970), pp. 50f.

those who practise 'black' magic and mediate the evil effects of the unseen world into the lives of individuals and communities.

g. Sin, morality and the after-life.[7] Good and evil within a PLS are judged by a very simple rule – whether or not it does harm to the well-being of the community or threatens its members' health. Religion and morality, contrary to what many scholars say, are connected – not as we connect them in our Christian tradition but in the sense that, as most activities of a PLS may be interpreted to be responses to the sacred, in order to preserve the harmony of life and ensure the blessings of the divine, all actions which threaten harmony are seen to be evil and therefore must be eliminated as contrary to the original will of the Creator-Spirit. It is true that sometimes the moral sense of some pre-literary peoples may appear to us to be faulty. For example, the Semang of Malaysia believe that their god *Karei* allows them to kill a man not of their own tribe, but not to mock a helpless animal; but they *have* a very real moral sense in relation to other members of their community. We cannot blame them when, as so often happens, their social structure is broken up through the impact of Western technology and values, and they then appear to act irresponsibly and selfishly. The same thing has happened in our own society. I have yet to meet a PLS person living in his own environment and according to his inherited values and customs who has not shown kindness, generosity and friendliness. People tend to act otherwise only when they feel threatened or after their traditional world has been shattered.

What really marks off pre-literary peoples from the so-called ethical religions is that, except in a few isolated instances, a man's actions in this life do not affect his eternal destiny. Yet even this statement must be qualified. To a large extent immortality and one's happiness in the Land of the Dead depends on the care and respect shown after death by one's relatives. If one is banished from the tribe or is killed for threatening the community, he becomes effectually extinct, since he is unremembered and the proper rites are impossible to perform. He is obliterated from the clan 'register' of the living dead. In addition the uninitiated of the PLS appear to have no real existence after death. They are not full persons and have no real personality to survive. Those who have an assured place in eternity are those, such as warriors and chiefs, who, through their exploits and positions within the society, will be for ever remembered.

[7] *Cf.* R. R. Marett, *Faith, Hope and Charity in Primitive Religion* (Blom, New York, 1972).

Bibliography

For a fuller bibliography see H. Ringgren and A. V. Ström, *Religions of Mankind*. Books marked * are recommended for beginners.

1. *General*

*S. G. F. Brandon (ed.), *Dictionary of Comparative Religion* (Scribner's Sons, New York, 1970).

*M. Eliade, *From Primitive to Zen* (Harper and Row, New York, 1967).

M. Eliade, *Patterns in Comparative Religion* (Meridian Books, New York, 1963).

E. E. Evans-Pritchard, *Theories of Primitive Religion* (OUP, New York, 1965).

E. O. James, *Prehistoric Religion* (Barnes and Noble, New York, 1961).

G. van der Leeuw, *Religion in Essence and Manifestation* (Harper and Row, New York, 1963).

H. Ringgren and A. V. Ström, *Religions of Mankind: Yesterday and Today* (Fortress, Philadelphia, 1967).

2. *Africa*

E. E. Evans-Prichard, *Nuer Religion* (OUP, New York, 1956).

J. S. Mbiti, *African Religions and Philosophy* (Praeger, New York, 1969).

E. G. Parrinder, *West African Religion* (Allenson, Naperville, Ill., 1961).

*E. W. Smith (ed.), *African Ideas of God,* revised by E. G. Parrinder (Lutterworth Press, London, 1962).

J. V. Taylor, *The Primal Vision* (Fortress, Philadelphia, 1964).

3. *Americas*

W. Krickerberg *et al., Pre-Columbian American Religions* (Holt, Rinehart and Winston, New York, 1969).

P. Radin, *Indians of South America* (Greenwood, Westport, Conn., 1942).

*R. M. Underhill, *Red Man's Religion* (University of Chicago Press, Chicago, 1966).

4. *Asia*

M. A. C. Czaplicka, *Aboriginal Siberia* (OUP, New York, 1914).

M. Eliade, *Shamanism: Archaic Techniques of Ecstasy* (Princeton University Press, Princeton, New Jersey, 1964).

*D. G. E. Hall, *A History of South East Asia* (St. Martin's Press, New York, 1968).

M. MacDonald, *Borneo People* (Jonathan Cape, London, 1956).

N. G. Munro, *The Ainu, Creed and Cult* (Columbia University Press, New York, 1963).

5. *Australia and Oceania*

R. M. and C. H. Berndt, *The World of the First Australians* (University of Chicago Press, Chicago, 1965).
R. H. Codrington, *The Melanesians* (Midway, Ann Arbor, Mich., 1891).
*A. P. Elkin, *The Australian Aborigines* (Natural History Press, New York, 1964).
E. S. C. Handy, *Polynesian Religion* (Kraus Repr., Millwood, New York, 1971).

6. *Europe*

R. Bosi, *The Lapps* (Thames and Hudson, London, 1960).

CHAPTER TWO

Judaism

H. D. Leuner*

At a time when a good deal of political and theological discussion is engendered by the Jewish State in the Middle East and when Departments of Jewish Studies are an established part of many universities in Europe and America, a treatment of Judaism in a book such as this is a matter of course. Looking for a working definition of the Jewish religion, we find, in an article by the Director of Studies of the Institute of Jewish Studies in London, Raphael James Loewe, the following description: 'A complex of faith and social ethics, of universal significance and possibly universal relevance, resting upon the sanction of uncompromised and absolute monotheism.'[1] The last words make it perfectly plain where Judaism differs from its daughter religions, Christianity and Islam, for 'absolute monotheism' allows neither for the dogma of the Trinity nor for the affirmation of Muhammad as being *the* Prophet. And both Christians and Muslims would have to agree that the Old Testament, a treasure to all three religions, calls no-one but Israel 'the chosen people', or 'the property' of the very God in whom they all believe. It must, therefore, be stated *a priori* that Judaism is not just another non-Christian religion, but a system of faith and worship inseparably linked, on the one hand, with the idea of God as accepted (to some extent) by Christians and Muslims and, on the other hand, with the existence of a particular people. Not only the Jew, but the followers of Jesus and Muhammad as well would assert that the

---

* H. D. Leuner was born in Breslau, the son of conservative Jewish parents. He worked as a journalist until he had to flee from the Nazis and went to Prague, where he became a believer in the Messiah through reading the Bible. He studied History and Theology, was ordained as a minister in the Church of Scotland and has become recognized as an international expert in the field of Jewish-Christian relations. From 1950 until 1973 he served the International Hebrew Christian Alliance as full-time Secretary for Europe.

[1] R. J. Loewe, in *The Jewish Journal of Society*, VII. 2, December, 1965.

Old Testament was somehow a way of life and an approach to God, but only the Jew will make it the centre of his doctrinal edifice.

For all that, it would be incorrect to identify Judaism with Old Testament religion, and overlook post-biblical teaching which forms a large part of present-day Jewish religion. Again, it would be equally fallacious to assume that the Judaism of the post-biblical period was the kind of religion most widely practised among Jews today. Judaism is a conglomeration, the result of a long process of religious development. It has been influenced by ideas which cannot be traced back to the Old Testament, and has also appropriated some teaching which cannot be found in the literature of the *Talmud*, that encyclopaedic body of Jewish religion and mentality compiled between the third and the sixth centuries of the Christian era, whose instructions are accepted as scarcely less important than those of the Old Testament.

There is another basic difficulty which faces the student of Judaism. Christianity has its Apostles' and Nicene Creeds; Islam has its *Kalima* (*cf.* p. 118). But there is no such formal summary of Jewish doctrine that would be recognized as absolutely binding by all and sundry. This does not mean that no attempts have been made to systematize and formulate the tenets of Jewish religion. Scholars and philosophers have endeavoured repeatedly to work out a confession of faith and their products are occasionally used to this day. But none of them has ever enjoyed the official sanction of a supreme ecclesiastical organization. This absence of an authoritative creed will become understandable only as we proceed to show that Judaism and Jewry, religion and people, are almost completely identical, so that race and birth are of greater importance than a profession of certain dogmas. The fact of Jewishness derives from one's being born of a Jewish mother.

Origin and early development

Abraham, the Hebrew (*i.e.* from the other side of the river), is the first of the patriarchs from whom the Jews trace their descent. He came from Ur, in Chaldea, and obeyed a divine call to leave his home and proceed to the land of Canaan (Genesis 12). He was promised that his descendants should live there as a great nation and play a unique part in the history of the human race. This covenant was repeated to Isaac and Jacob, whose family eventually settled in neighbouring Egypt. It was there that, in the course of centuries, the Children of Israel (*B'ne Yisrael*) rose from a small clan to be a people considerable in numbers, were turned into Pharaonic serfs, and set to labour at those gigantic works and monuments which have remained the wonder of posterity. One Israelite, Moses, became alive to the slavery which crushed his kith and kin, and when a divine voice recalled to him God's purpose in the promise to the patriarchs and bade him lead the people of Israel out of Egypt, he obeyed.

The exodus from Egypt became the most far-reaching event, and has always been considered as the central incident, in the political and religious history of the Jews.

After Yahweh (Exodus 6:2, 3) had proved to be the Redeemer and Liberator of his people, he revealed himself at Sinai as the Lawgiver and entered into a covenant with Israel. They were to become his holy nation, living according to his instruction, guidance and teaching. All this is covered by the Hebrew term *Torah*, whose English translation as 'law' is more a matter of convenience than of accuracy. The corner-stone of Torah was provided by the Ten Words, or 'Decalogue' (see Exodus 20), that proclaimed the unity and incorporeality of God and a moral law. The Torah also ordained rites and observances which were meant to strengthen the national consciousness. Other outstanding features were the sacredness and moral purpose of human life and the equality of all without distinction, including the foreigner and the slave, before the law. The Torah demanded personal holiness as well as justice and righteousness in social relations. We ought not to overlook that Judaism through its Torah confronted the world not merely with a religious revolution, but even more with a reversal of social values. Judaism entered into the world as a proclamation on behalf of all the poor, deprived, oppressed and needy people.

Under the leadership of Joshua, the successor of Moses, the Israelites invaded Canaan. Their divisions and tribal jealousies produced a new kind of leader, known by the title of 'judge'. The last and greatest of the judges was Samuel and it was against his advice that the Israelites asked for a royal ruler who would lead them to war and judge them in times of peace. The first king, Saul, proved a talented military leader but succumbed to private troubles and was followed by David, who exercised a magnetic influence on his people and conquered Jerusalem, which he made the eternal city of the Jews. David's son, Solomon, became the most important king of his day between the Euphrates and the border of Egypt and endeared himself to his subjects by building a national Temple of remarkable splendour on Mount Moriah in Jerusalem (973 BC). On his death, the kingdom split into two: the southern kingdom of Judah with Jerusalem as the capital, and a northern kingdom of Ephraim, or Israel, with its capital, Samaria.

From the beginning both kingdoms were threatened by the larger empires of Assyria and Egypt and in 721 BC Assyria captured Samaria, only to be overrun in its turn by Babylon, whose forces took Judah between 597 and 587. Jerusalem was stormed and razed to the ground in 586, the most important groups of the people being carried away into exile.

Judaism after the exile

The Jews of Babylonia grew into a flourishing community, united by their distinctive religion. Deprived of the centralizing Temple with its animal sacrifices, the exiles in the various places of their dispersion established houses of prayer (synagogues) where God was worshipped without sacrifices and priests. The reading and exposition of the Torah of Moses gradually became a fixed institution. In 538 BC Cyrus, the ruler of conquering Persia, permitted the return of the exiles and the rebuilding of the Temple in Jerusalem, but the response was very meagre. Under Ezra, associated with, and supported by, Nehemiah, the returning exiles founded a new theocratic society in which the God of Abraham, Isaac and Jacob was the only God. In this they followed closely the teaching of the great prophet, Isaiah.[2] It was only now that Jewish monotheism blossomed out. There is only one God in the universe and he is the God of Israel. Israel's suffering is not merely punishment; it is sermon and object-lesson, and it is a means of redemption to the whole world.

Again, it was in the post-exilic Jewish community that the individual assumed a place of ever-growing importance. Even the ideas of life after death, and of the love of God that could not possibly stop when physical life ends but would have to continue on the other side, only now matured. Similarly, the hope of the coming of the Messiah (God's Anointed), the concept of the Day of the Lord, which would not be a time of Israel's triumph but a day of judgment, and similar trends only now became dominant ideas. And while it is true that during the time between Malachi, the last of the prophets, probably contemporaneous with Nehemiah, and the appearance of John the Baptist no major work of religious literature was produced, we must understand that it was centuries before the spirit of the prophets had really permeated all strata of society and had become the common property of the people. The varied writings contained in the Hebrew Bible were sifted and settled by the scribes and religious authorities. In those days the so-called 'Men of the Great Synagogue' (sometimes called the Great Synod), a body of somewhat uncertain composition and duration, applied themselves to the solution of the new spiritual problems which arose with the ever-changing needs of the Jewish people. As recognized authorities on the text and interpretation of the Scriptures, they began to formulate the oral Law, that part of the divine revelation to Moses which is not recorded in the Five Books of Moses but was transmitted by oral tradition. It often differed from, and modified as well as exceeded, the written Law. Most of it was later committed to writing in the *Mishnah*, which, together with rabbinic comments on it called the *Gemara*, formed the Talmud.

[2] See especially Isaiah 43-45.

It was during that same period that Judaism came in contact with other parts of the world, its religions and peoples, and especially with Greek thought. But it would be a mistake to attribute the 'Wisdom Literature', to be found both in the Old Testament and in the Apocrypha, to Hellenistic origins only. It was based on the praise of Wisdom as the quintessence of human perfection and virtue and is represented in the Old Testament by the books of Proverbs, Job and Ecclesiastes, as well as by what are known as the 'didactic' Psalms (for example, Psalms 1, 15, 37, 112). Even if the existence of a Hellenistic element in those books is allowed, the majority of its material is certainly Jewish and leaves no doubt that piety and the fear of the Lord are the beginning of all wisdom. Even during this period of intensification of Judaism and onwards, the Jews still had to fight the danger of polytheism. To this day one can see in a synagogue in Beth Alpha in the Emek, the plain stretching from the Mediterranean at Haifa to the Jordan valley, a mosaic floor which dates back to the fourth century after Christ and which shows a design representing the sun god in his chariot.

But the spirit of prophetic Judaism proved too strong to be suppressed for any length of time. Its distinctiveness over against Hellenistic philosophy has found profound expression in the writings of Abraham Joshua Heschel.

> 'The god of the philosophers is all indifference, too sublime to possess a heart or to cast a glance at our world. His wisdom consists in being conscious of himself and oblivious to the world. In contrast, the God of the prophets is all concern, too merciful to remain aloof to His creation. He not only rules the world in the majesty of His might; He is personally concerned and even stirred by the conduct and fate of man. "His mercy is upon all His work" (Psalm 145:9). These are the two poles of prophetic thinking: the idea that God is one, holy, different and apart from all that exists, and the idea of the inexhaustible concern of God for man, at times brightened by His mercy, at times darkened by His anger. He is both transcendent, beyond human understanding, and full of love, compassion, grief or anger. . . . He is the father of all men, not only a judge; He is a lover engaged to His people, not only a king. His love or anger, His mercy or disappointment is an expression of His profound participation in the history of Israel and all men.'[3]

The unique feature of Jewish monotheism as displayed in Judaism just before the birth of Christ is that the national God becomes the expression of the highest, purest and most sublime thought as well as of the most intimate religious sentiment, without in the least losing his personal qualities. Only in a nation which in its history

[3] A. J. Heschel, "The Concept of Man in Jewish Thought," in *The Concept of Man*, edited by S. Radhakrishnan and P. T. Raju (Johnsen, Lincoln, Nebraska, 1966), pp. 124f.

had experienced the power of that God as Deliverer, Lawgiver and Father was such a development possible. But even the best and loftiest prophet could not attain to a universalism that would overcome all barriers of nationality. What the Jews presented to other nations was not so much an individualistic and universal religion that thought little of all national and tribal frontiers, but rather their own national religion which had achieved an ethical and theological summit. They hoped that others would turn to that type of religion and thereby acknowledge the sovereign reign of Yahweh by whom they had been chosen as a peculiar people, as privileged priests, and as a holy nation (Exodus 19:5f.).

The synagogue and the Pharisees

Little is known of Jewish life from the end of Nehemiah's activity until the time when Alexander of Macedon swept like a gale through Asia Minor and the Persian Empire collapsed (331 BC). The process of Hellenization engulfed Palestine as much as the other surrounding states and the Jewish revolt against idolatry and the worship of foreign deities had, under the Maccabees, only transient success, though it was fully recorded in the apocryphal books of the *Maccabees*. The process could be fought only by the revival of personal and corporate piety in the services of the synagogue. The time between the Alexandrian conquest and the Christian era saw the rise of rabbinic Judaism, most clearly represented by a group of men who saw in the strictest observance of both written and oral Law the only hope for survival, and separated themselves from all others in order to carry out their hard task. They were soon called *Pharisees* (from the Hebrew *Perushim*, *i.e.* 'the Separated') and had the largest following amongst the democratic, urban laity, whereas the opposite body of aristocratic people of the ecclesiastical party came to be known as *Sadducees* (from Zadok, Solomon's High Priest).

Pharisaism is not to be viewed as one solidly uniform section of Jewry. The Talmud knows six unpleasant types of Pharisee and one type dear to God, men who serve him out of love. Wholesale condemnation of the Pharisees has found its way into dictionaries and popular language, but is not warranted even on the strength of the Gospel records, and Jews of all sections rightly resent it. There are, in fact, passages in the New Testament which show a different type of Pharisee, one who is patient and understanding (see, *e.g.*, Acts 5:38f.; 23:9), and it deserves mention that, according to the Gospel records, no Pharisee took part in the trial of Jesus. The Pharisees not only produced a school of famous rabbis such as Hillel and Shammai (who lived just prior to the birth of Jesus), but developed the doctrine of immortality,[4] introduced those translations of the

---

[4] Readers of the New Testament may remember the argument between Pharisees

Scriptures into the vernacular Aramaic which are known as *Targumim* (from *Targum*, *i.e.* 'translation'), and fostered the establishment of synagogues wherever Jews had settled in the dispersion of the Mediterranean civilization.

The significance of the destruction of Jerusalem and its Temple in AD 70 has often been exaggerated. It was neither the end of Jewry nor the closing chapter of Judaism. Ever since the flower of Judah's inhabitants was taken into Babylonian captivity, Jews had gradually strayed from Babylon to all parts of the classical world. Long before the Christian era, Jews were found in Egypt and all along the Mediterranean coast, and when St Paul undertook his missionary journeys throughout the Roman Empire, more than twenty years prior to the fall of Jerusalem, he found Jewish communities and their synagogues everywhere. Nevertheless, Judaism seemed to have lost its centre when the Temple went up in flames. But one man, Rabbi Jochanan ben Zakkai, had foreseen the doom and had persuaded Vespasian to grant him the gift of Jabneh, a coastal town with an already famous school. Here he established a spiritual centre with a new Sanhedrin modelled after the Supreme Council of pre-Maccabean times. Its president became in course of time the nation's accredited representative before the Roman authorities.

It is noteworthy that the synagogue was both a place of worship and a communal centre. It was designed to bring religion to the masses of the people, and was accordingly called the 'house of prayer' as well as the 'people's house'. It proved to be one of the principal means of keeping Judaism alive when both the Temple and the national life of the Jews were lost. With the destruction of the Temple, the system of sacrifices had come to an end and the Sadducees disappeared, thus leaving the field to their opponents, the Pharisees. This meant that, henceforth, the Law became the pivot of Jewish religion. Its 613 commandments were divided into 248 positive injunctions and 365 prohibitions, and the whole was surrounded by a large number of interpretative regulations. This oral Law gradually became recognized as divinely inspired.

Torah and Talmud

The entire body of written and oral Law is known as the *Torah*, and represents to the Jew the whole mystery and tangible expression of God. Its application extends to the deepest emotions, the very heart of the Jew. In the words of *The Encyclopedia of the Jewish Religion*:

'Unlike wisdom, which is shared by all nations, Torah is the exclusive possession of the Jewish people and shall (Joshua 1:8) "not depart from thy mouth, but thou shalt meditate on it day

---

and Sadducees as to whether or not there was a resurrection (Mark 12:18).

and night". The rabbinic passage enumerating those things, the fruit of which man enjoys in this world while the main reward is reserved for the World to Come, concludes: "but the study of the Torah is equivalent to them all". The idea that the Torah is the source of life of the Jewish people, is expressed in many rabbinic parables and homilies, but particularly in the liturgical blessings recited by the person called to the synagogal reading of the Five Books of Moses, and in the daily morning prayer.'[5]

The discussions and decisions of scholars and rabbis in the matter of Torah, covering not only legal and ethical but also homiletic and didactic questions, were eventually gathered up in that monumental work called *Talmud*, which absorbed the prophetic conception of the close interconnection of religion and life. The Talmud consists of the *Mishnah* which became invested with a large body of commentary material, the *Gemara*. Between them, they represent the scholastic activities of the rabbis from the beginning of the third to the close of the fifth century AD. There is an earlier compilation, the Palestinian Talmud, and a later recension, the Babylonian, published about 500 years after the crucifixion. The influence of the Talmud upon Jewish life can hardly be overestimated. It has kept the Jew mentally and theologically alert, it has been his refuge in the long and dreary centuries of persecution and ghetto life when he was debarred from secular studies, and it still exerts considerable influence upon Jewish teaching today, although it is practically unknown to the average Jew. Its vast dimensions can be gauged from the fact that the English translation, edited by Isidore Epstein and published in London between 1935 and 1952, takes up 34 volumes plus an Index volume. Without going into details, we may distinguish between the *Halakhah*, the abstract formulation of Jewish law, and the *Aggadah* (or *Haggadah*), the non-legal contents, including ethical and moral teaching, legends, folklore, and expressions of Messianic faith and longing.

But not even the Talmud tried to summarize Judaism in a creed or confession of faith. The first definite attempt to produce a formula against which doctrines and principles could be measured was made by Moses Maimonides in the twelfth century. He worked out Thirteen Articles which are listed to this day in the Authorized Prayer Book of most Jewish congregations, and laid down the following fundamental axioms, the denial of which cuts a man off from Israel:

1. Belief in the existence of a Creator and Providence.
2. Belief in his unity.
3. Belief in his incorporeality.

5 *The Encyclopedia of the Jewish Religion* (Holt, Rinehart and Winston, New York, 1966), p. 387.

4. Belief in his eternity.
5. Belief that to him alone is worship due.
6. Belief in the words of the Prophets.
7. Belief that Moses was the greatest of all Prophets.
8. Belief in the revelation of the Lord to Moses at Sinai.
9. Belief in the immutability of the revealed Law.
10. Belief that God is omniscient.
11. Belief in retribution in this world and the hereafter.
12. Belief in the coming of the Messiah.
13. Belief in the resurrection of the dead.

The creed as sketched out by Maimonides came in for severe criticism by many Jewish authorities in the following centuries. Among the more interesting attacks was one by Rabbi Joseph Albo in the fifteenth century, who pointed out that even within the body of the Law there were certain contradictions and discrepancies, so that it was not safe to claim, as Maimonides had done in his ninth article, that the Law will never be changed. Albo further relegated belief in the coming of the Messiah to the level of a secondary principle of the Jewish faith.

In the course of the last five or six centuries various and often differing doctrinal statements have been issued by leaders of different groups in Judaism, such as the Orthodox, the Conservative, and the Progressive; and if all of these formal summaries were put down as authoritative explanations of what Judaism means, the average reader would be completely at sea. But as all of them somehow or other refer to the Talmud, we may take some of the doctrinal utterances of the Talmud to guide us in our search for the essence of Judaism.

One of the basic parts, the *Sayings of the Fathers*, contains in its six chapters statements such as the following: 'Moses received the Torah on Sinai, and handed it down to Joshua; Joshua to the Elders; the Elders to the Prophets; and the Prophets handed it down to the men of the Great Synagogue. They said three things: be deliberate in judgment, raise up many disciples, and make a fence round the Torah' (I, 1). 'Hillel and Shammai received the tradition from the preceding. Hillel said, Be of the disciples of Aaron, loving peace and pursuing peace, loving thy fellow-creatures, and drawing them near to the Torah' (I, 12). 'If I am not for myself, who will be for me? And being for my own self, what am I? And if not now, when?' (I, 14). 'Shammai said, Fix a period for thy study of the Torah; say little and do much' (I, 15). 'Rabban Simeon, the son of Gamaliel, said, By three things is the world preserved: by truth, by judgment and by peace' (I, 18). 'Hillel said, Separate not thyself from the congregation. . . . Judge not thy neighbour until thou art come into his place' (II, 5). 'The more Torah, the more life; the more schooling, the more wisdom; the more charity, the more peace. He who has acquired for himself words of Torah, has acquired for himself life in the world to come' (II, 8). 'Rabbi Tarphon said, The day is short, the work is great, the labourers are sluggish, the reward is much, and the Master of the house is urgent. It is not thy duty to complete the work, but neither art thou free to desist from it' (II, 20f.). 'Rabbi Eleazar (in the second century) said, He whose wisdom exceeds his works, to what is he like? To a tree whose branches are many, but whose roots are few; and the wind comes and plucks it up and overturns it upon its face . . . But he whose works exceed his wisdom, to what is he like? To a tree whose branches are few, but whose roots are many, so that even if all the winds in the world come and blow upon it, it cannot be stirred from its place' (III, 22).[6]

The resemblance to passages in the sayings of Jesus is as obvious as the influence of Old Testament ideas. This influence is seen as well in the following quotation from the last chapter of the same work, which is also a good example of the interpretative manner of the Talmud: 'In the hour of man's departure neither silver nor gold nor precious stones nor pearls accompany him, but only Torah and good works, as it is said, "When thou walkest it shall lead thee; when thou liest down it shall watch over thee; and when thou awakest it shall talk with thee" (Proverbs 6:22):—"When thou walkest it shall lead thee"—in this world; "when thou liest down it shall watch over thee"—in the grave; "and when thou awakest it shall talk with thee"—in the world to come, and it says, "The silver is mine, and the gold is mine, saith the Lord of Hosts" (Haggai 2:8)' (VI, 9). In brief, it is to the Torah that the work of sanctification is ascribed which in Christian theology is attributed to the Holy Spirit indwelling the believer. The strict observance of the Torah is, therefore, one of the most distinct features of Judaism, making for the separation of the Jew from his fellowmen.

The central doctrines

Bearing in mind the difficulty of finding authoritative statements which would be generally accepted as absolutely binding, we must now try to examine the Jewish teaching on certain central doctrines of religion.

1. God and man

To the Jew, God is a full personality, free from all limitations and imperfections, pure Spirit, and the life of the universe. While Judaism admits that nature and all its phenomena point to the existence of a

[6] *Authorized Daily Prayer Book* (Eyre and Spottiswoode, London, several editions).

Creator, and that philosophy and science may provide an indirect knowledge of God, it insists emphatically that only religion reveals a direct, personal and complete knowledge of the divine character, will and purpose. Though the revelation to Moses, which means the Torah, is the foundation-stone on which Judaism rests, revelation has not reached its completion at any particular point of history, but is considered to be gradually unfolding. The *Encyclopedia of the Jewish Religion* declares:

> 'The view that revelation was essentially the manifestation of a Divine Law, since reason itself was sufficient for insight into the principles of religious truth and ethics, was still held by Moses Mendelssohn (1729–86). Liberal and Reformed theologians speak of revelation as a subjective mode of experience or as a growing (and increasingly refined) perception of the Divine creative power and of moral values in human history. Hence the notion of a progressive revelation rather than that of revelation as a distinct, objective, and supranatural event.'[7]

Man is to see in God his heavenly Father and Companion who is concerned in his fate and does not leave him alone in an apparently friendless universe. As man is made in the image of God (Genesis 1:26), it follows that all human beings are creatures of the same Creator and meant to live as brothers. All have a share in God's eternal spirit. A. J. Heschel, the outstanding voice of Judaism at present, has this to say on the God-likeness of man:

> 'Nothing is said about the intention or the plan that preceded the creation of heaven and earth. The creation of man, however, is preceded by a forecast: "And God said: Let us make man in our image, after our likeness". It is the whole man and every man who was made in the image and likeness of God. It is both body and soul, sage and fool, saint and sinner, man in his joy and in his grief, in his righteousness and wickedness. The image is not in man; it is man.' And to drive home the all-important fact of the sacredness of all human life, he continues: 'The Bible does not say, God created the plant or the animal; it says, He created different kinds of plants and different kinds of animals. In striking contrast, it does not say that God created different kinds of man, men of different colours and races: it says, He created one single man. From one single man all men are descended.'[8]

Neighbourly love, as enjoined in Leviticus 19:18 (and repeated by Jesus in Matthew 5:43; 19:19; 22:39 and Luke 10:27), is stressed as an altogether Hebrew thought, for as nature knows only fear and defence, primitive religions are ignorant of divine revelation and

[7] *Encyclopedia of Jewish Religion*, p. 332.
[8] Heschel, *op. cit.*, pp. 126, 131.

cannot propagate the dignity of human relationship, nor can they postulate love as the basis of such relationship.

Just as God is considered as perfect unity, so man's body and soul are seen as a unit which knows no opposition between spirit and matter. The correlation of psychological phenomena with bodily conditions, expressed in modern parlance as 'psychosomatic unity', is taken for granted. Equally vehemently is the idea denied that there might be a cosmic force of evil. 'There is no loss of the God-likeness of man, or of his ability to do right in the eyes of God,' said Joseph Hertz, the Chief Rabbi of the British Commonwealth from 1913 until 1946, in his *Commentary on Genesis*, 'and no such loss has been transmitted to his latest descendants'.[9]

Christian theology speaks of 'original sin', the state in which humankind has been held captive since the Fall, because, through Adam, sin entered into the world (Romans 5:12–21). Over against that doctrine of original sin, Judaism puts its emphasis on original virtue and righteousness which, according to the Jewish doctrine of 'the merits of the Fathers', are the common heritage of every member of the congregation of Israel. Roy A. Stewart, in his *Rabbinic Theology*, explains:

> 'Sin began, the Rabbis would declare, with the disobedience of Adam to the divine commandment, and it has continued historically ever since. The usual view is that men are given a clean sheet at birth, and that if they allow it to become dirty, they are themselves responsible. . . . The principal theory offered is that every person is born with an impulse or inclination towards evil, the *yetzer ha-ra*, which enters into his nature the moment he emerges from the womb. This is more or less equivalent to what the Christian would call the power of temptation. It is, or should be, counterbalanced in the Jew by the good inclination, the *yetzer ha-tobh*. Victory in the struggle is by no means assured, for the enemy is insidiously strong (Genesis 8:21).'[1]

Judaism takes sins (in contrast to the Christian concept of sin) very seriously and returns to the subject in every century. Here is Heschel's view:

> 'Together, image and dust express the polarity of the nature of man. He is formed of the most inferior stuff in the most superior image. . . . Yet while the duality of human nature may not imply an eternal tension, it does imply a duality of grandeur and insignificance, a relatedness to earth and an affinity with God. The duality is not based on the contrast of soul and body. The contradiction is in what man does with his soul and body. The contradic-

[9] J. H. Hertz, *Genesis* (OUP, London, 1940), p. 60.
[1] R. A. Stewart, *Rabbinic Theology* (Oliver and Boyd, Edinburgh, 1960), pp. 76-81.

tion lies in his acts rather than in his substance. Being the master of the earth, man forgets that he is the servant of God.'[2]

While recognizing definite sins, Judaism does not acknowledge sin as such, and accordingly sees no cause for admitting a sense of personal unworthiness. This has a profound bearing on the question of atonement, as the next section will make clear. Jews believe that a relationship exists between man and God according to which God looks favourably on man and desires his well-being. That relationship is disturbed when man fails to act in accordance with the will of God. Atonement is the means by which it is re-established.

2. Atonement

There is but one teaching regarding atonement among all groups of theologians, however widely they may differ on other points. Repentance, prayer and active kindness achieve perfect reconciliation. To quote from the writings of Dr Hertz:

'Note that the initiative in atonement is with the sinner (Ezekiel 18:31). He cleanses himself on the Day of Atonement by fearless self-examination, open confession, and the resolve not to repeat the transgressions of the past year. When our Heavenly Father sees the abasement of the penitent sinner, He sprinkles, as it were, the clean waters of pardon and forgiveness upon him.'[3] And again: 'On the Day of Atonement the Israelites resemble the angels, without human wants, without sins, linked together in love and peace. It is the only day of the year on which the accuser Satan is silenced before the throne of Glory, and even becomes the defender of Israel. . . . The closing prayer (on the Day of Atonement) begins: "Thou givest a hand to transgressors, and Thy right hand is stretched out to receive the penitent. Thou hast taught us to make confession unto Thee of all our sins, in order that we may cease from the violence of our hands and may return unto Thee who delightest in the repentance of the wicked." These words contain what has been called "the Jewish doctrine of salvation".'[4]

As in the late Dr Hertz's pronouncement, so elsewhere much prominence is given to the belief that human initiative takes the first step which eventually leads to perfection. The second sentence of the Credo worked out by Professor M. L. Margolis, an outstanding Hebrew scholar, underlines that basic doctrine: 'I believe that man possesses a divine power wherewith he may subdue his evil influences and passions, strive to come nearer and nearer the perfection of God,

---

[2] Heschel, *op. cit.*, p. 141.

[3] J. H. Hertz, *The Pentateuch and the Haftorahs* (Soncino Press, London, 1938), p. 484.

[4] *Ibid.*, pp. 523f.

and commune with Him in prayer.' There is a definite note of optimism implied in these statements. A hopeful view is taken of man and his progressive development. The student of Judaism will frequently be struck by the similarity that exists between Jewish teaching and the evolutionary theories concerning the progress of mankind, a phenomenon which is particularly obvious in the doctrine of the Messiah.

3. The Messiah

Few Jews of today would explicitly subscribe to the Twelfth Article of Maimonides's Creed, for the meaning of the term Messiah (God's Anointed) has undergone a radical change in the course of the centuries. There was a time when the idea carried with it the belief in a divinely-appointed person who would deliver Israel and bring about the consummation of the divine plan with its corollary of peace, freedom and justice. Thus the Authorized Prayer Book contains a prayer going back some eighteen centuries and closing with the words: '(Lord our God) Who rememberest the pious deeds of the patriarchs, and in love wilt bring a redeemer to their children's children for thy name's sake.'[5] But in modern Jewish thought this conception is as good as abandoned, and we read in the most recent *Encyclopaedia Judaica* published in Jerusalem in 1972 (sixteen volumes): 'Jewish messianism has been and continues to be an activist element in world culture. For Jews it has retained the life force of charisma, and the binding spell of Jewish statehood and kingship to be realized through God's will, through the passion and devotion of His people.'[6] In talmudic writings, says Roy A. Stewart,

> 'The messianic age is regarded as an era in this world, quite distinct from the world to come . . . underlined by the repeated statement that Old Testament prophecy related only to the mundane era, and not to that which is to follow. Messiah is depicted as bringing only a limited improvement to the existing order of things: Israel will be released from bondage to foreign powers. There is the resurrection of the dead, the cessation of physical death, an age of peace. The power of temptation over the human heart will be finally broken. The main weight of evidence inclines to an era radically different from the existing one, though still mundane. There will be special divine protection for Israel, those buried in the Holy Land will be the first to enjoy resurrection, and the divine blessings lost through Adam's sin will be restored. Israel will enjoy a delicious reversal of circumstances, and a rich revenge on all those who have insulted or persecuted her.'[7]

[5] *Authorized Daily Prayer Book*, p. 44.

[6] Article "Messiah" in *Encyclopaedia Judaica*, Vol. II, Col. 1427.

[7] Stewart, *op. cit.*, pp. 50f.

To all of which may be added the concluding lines on 'Messiah' in *The Encyclopedia of the Jewish Religion*: 'Reform Judaism has tended to reject the concept of a personal Messiah substituting for it the optimistic faith in the advent of a messianic era or "the establishment of the kingdom of truth, justice, and peace".'[8]

The blending in Judaism of political and religious ideas, to which reference has frequently been made, appears in its most modern form in an address given by David Ben Gurion at the Zionist General Council held in Jerusalem, in July 1957:

'The suffering of the Jewish people in the Diaspora, whether economic, political, or cultural, has been a powerful factor in bringing about the immigrations to the Land of Israel. But it was only the Messianic vision which made that factor fruitful and guided it towards the creation of the State. Suffering alone is degrading, oppression destructive; and if we had not inherited from the prophets the Messianic vision of redemption, the suffering of the Jewish people in the Diaspora would have led to their extinction. The ingathering of the exiles, the return of the Jewish people to their land, is the beginning of the realization of the Messianic vision.'[9]

4. The future life

A Jew inherits heaven by right through the divine covenant with Abraham. Professor Dr H. J. Schoeps, of Erlangen, declares: 'In Isaac all Jews have become as the seed of Abraham (i.e. Children of the Promise), and they can all return to Abraham's bosom.'[1] Concerning the resurrection, *The Encyclopedia of the Jewish Religion* has this to say:

'Belief in resurrection began to develop toward the end of the Biblical Period, possibly under Persian influence, and is referred to in the Book of Daniel (12:2). By the end of the Second Temple Period it had developed into a fundamental dogma of the Pharisees, who declared it heresy to deny, as did the Sadducees, that the doctrine possessed Mosaic authority. Resurrection is one of the few dogmas expressly stated in the liturgy, where it is the subject of the second paragraph of the statutory daily Prayer: "Blessed art thou, O Lord, who makest alive the dead." Since rabbinic times it has been accepted as a fundamental doctrine of Judaism, and is commonly associated with the Messianic Era. . . . Reform

[8] *Encyclopedia of Jewish Religion*, p. 260.
[9] Isidore Epstein, *Judaism: A Historical Presentation* (Penguin, Baltimore, 1959), p. 321. Rabbi Epstein was Principal of The Jews' College, London.
[1] H. J. Schoeps, *Jüdisch-Christliches Religionsgespräch in 19 Jahrhunderten* (Atharva Verlag, Frankfurt/Main, 1949), p. 150.

Judaism has denied the literal concept of bodily resurrection and the Conservatives tend to identify it with the doctrine of the immortality of the soul. This belief almost wholly denies the doctrine of resurrection, the belief that some part of the human personality is eternal and is freed from the body at death to enjoy a separate existence in the celestial spheres.'[2]

As to the principles which are to guide retribution, and as to the mode of the judgment to come, very little is said in the textbooks, the matter being left to God in his infinite wisdom.

5. The Scriptures

When we come to study Jewish teaching on the authority and inspiration of the Holy Scriptures, we must understand that not all parts of the Old Testament are considered to be of equal value. The arrangement of the books of the Hebrew Bible differs from that familiar to Christian readers. There is first of all the *Torah*, *i.e.* the Pentateuch or Five Books of Moses, regarded as the most authoritative group. This is followed by the second group of books, the *Prophets*, which are divided into Former and Latter Prophets. The first division consists of the books of Joshua, Judges, 1 and 2 Samuel, 1 and 2 Kings; the second division comprises Isaiah, Jeremiah, Ezekiel, and the so-called Book of the Twelve, known to Christians as the Minor Prophets. The last group bears the title *Writings* and is divided into three parts. Part one is composed of the Psalms, Proverbs, and the book of Job; part two consists of the 'Five Scrolls', viz. Ruth, Song of Songs, Ecclesiastes, Lamentations and Esther; part three is made up of the remaining books, Daniel, Ezra, Nehemiah, and 1 and 2 Chronicles.

The arrangement is all the more important as it reflects the varying degree of authority attached to the different sections by Jews. Among observing Jews, the Torah is regarded as so absolutely and fully inspired that every letter and phrase bears the mark of its divine origin. Inspiration to a slightly lesser degree is attributed to the Prophets, and to a still lesser degree to the Writings, though it has to be stated that the authority of the Scriptures has never been seriously questioned in Judaism. The care with which they were passed on from generation to generation, the reverence and awe in which they were held, and the courage and sacrificial love with which they were defended, are without parallel in human history.

This applies especially to the Torah, out of loyalty to which innumerable martyrs have laid down their lives. *Martyrdom* means, in the Hebrew idiom, death for the Sanctification of the Name of God and was looked upon as a supreme act of faith and the Jew's willingness to 'love the Lord with all thy soul' (Deuteronomy 6:5).

[2] *Encyclopedia of Jewish Religion*, pp. 331 and 199.

During the Middle Ages whole communities committed suicide as a public demonstration of loyalty to the Torah rather than submit to baptism. It was Spinoza (1632–77), the Dutch Jewish philosopher, who, through the influence of Descartes, was led away from traditional orthodoxy and in his *Tractatus Theologico-Politicus* ushered in the beginning of modern biblical criticism and Jewish scholarly investigation. His critical analysis of the Bible led some later Jewish scholars to pursue the so-called documentary theory and in the last century to embrace the higher criticism of men such as Graf and Wellhausen. But today the new trend in biblical studies is towards greater conservatism.

6. Good and evil

The problem of good and evil has exercised Jewish minds as incessantly as it has the sages of Christianity and Islam, for it cannot be evaded in monotheism. *The Encyclopedia of the Jewish Religion* tackles the subject as follows:

> 'The problem of good and evil is inherent in the doctrine of monotheism. Dualism or pluralism can attribute good to one divinity and evil to another. A monotheistic faith, however, is faced with the difficulty that God, in apparently permitting the existence of evil, is either imperfect or not omnipotent. As far as the Bible is concerned the view expounded in Genesis seems to be that everything created by God is good (1:31) but man's being endowed with freedom of will and the fact that "the inclination of man's heart is evil from his youth" (8:21) cause evil in the world, thus thwarting the Divine plan. . . . The Talmud also gives only general indications. . . . The rabbis affirm the existence of evil and are also exercised by the problem of the prosperity of the wicked and the suffering of the righteous which runs counter to their belief that evil is the wages of sin. . . . According to Judaism the motive determines the good or evil nature of an action.'[3]

No-one has stressed the power and reality of evil in the world more strongly than Heschel who writes:

> 'Just because of the realization of the power of evil, life in this world assumed unique significance and worth. Evil is not only a threat; it is also a challenge. It is precisely because of the task of fighting evil that life in this world is so preciously significant. True, there is no reward for good deeds in this world; yet this does not mean that the world is a prison. It is rather a prelude, a vestibule, a place of preparation, of initiation, of apprenticeship to a future life. Life in this world is a time for action, for good works, for worship and sanctification, as eternity is a time for retribution. . . .

[3] *Ibid.*, p. 162.

More frustrating than the fact that evil is real, mighty, and tempting is the fact that it thrives so well in the disguise of the good, and that it can draw its nutriment from the life of the holy. In this world, it seems, the holy and the unholy do not exist apart but are mixed, interrelated, and confounded; it is a world where idols are at home, and where even the worship of God may be alloyed with the worship of idols.'[4]

'The pious man knows that his inner life is full of pitfalls. The ego, the evil inclination, is constantly trying to enchant him. The temptations are fierce, yet his resistance is unyielding. And so he proves his spiritual strength and stands victorious, unconquerable. Does not his situation look glorious? But then the evil inclination employs a more subtle device, approaching him with congratulations: What a pious man you are! He begins to feel proud of himself. And there he is caught in the trap.'[5]

'Empirically, our spiritual situation looks hopeless: "We are all as an unclean thing, and all our deeds of righteousness are as filthy rags" (Isaiah 64:6). Even the good deeds we do are not pleasing but instead revolting. For we perform them out of the desire of self-aggrandizement and for pride, and in order to impress our neighbours. . . . Should we, then, despair because of our being unable to attain perfect purity? We should if perfection were our goal. Yet we are not obliged to be perfect once for all, but only to rise again and again. Perfection is divine, and to make it a goal of man is to call on man to be divine. All we can do is to try to wring our hearts clean in contrition. Contrition begins with a feeling of shame at our being incapable of disentanglement from the self. To be contrite at our failures is holier than to be complacent in perfection. It is a problem of supreme gravity. If an act to be good must be done exclusively for the sake of God, are we ever able to do good?'[6]

Heschel goes on to answer himself in the form of a parable that comes very near Christian ideas:

'A stork fell into the mud and was unable to pull out his legs until an idea occurred to him. Does he not have a long beak? So he stuck his beak into the mud, leaned upon it, and pulled out his legs. But what was the use? His legs were out, but his beak was stuck. So another idea occurred to him. He stuck his legs into the mud and pulled out his beak. But what was the use? The legs were stuck in the mud. . . . Such is exactly the condition of man. Succeeding in one way, he fails in another. We must constantly remember: We spoil, and God restores. How ugly is the way in which we spoil, and how good and how beautiful is the way in

[4] Heschel, *op. cit.*, pp. 148ff.   [5] *Ibid.*, p. 151.   [6] *Ibid.*, p. 153.

which He restores! And yet, Judaism insists upon the deed and hopes for the intention.'[7]

7. Religion and morality

One of the main tenets of Judaism is the inseparable link between religion and morality. Faith is meaningless unless it is translated into action, and there are some specifically Jewish terms which require elucidating as they express ethical consequences of religious beliefs. The word *tsedakah* (literally, 'righteousness') has gathered up the inter-relationship between faith and action in an utterly untranslatable way, covering, among many more meanings, charity, social justice, and the giving of tithes in support of the whole spiritual and social work of the synagogue. Relief is a matter of legal rightness, and kindness to those in need is at once presupposition and evidence of the correct attitude to the Torah. Another Hebrew term, *rachmanut* (literally, 'mercy'), has almost been raised to the level of a religious postulate demanding of the Jew very nearly indiscriminate charity towards those in distress, irrespective of their religion.

Jewish distinctiveness

From the very outset it has been pointed out time and again that in Judaism the spiritual and national ideas coalesce. If the exodus constitutes one focal point of Jewish doctrine, Sinai constitutes the other, and between them they have conditioned not merely the rigid monotheism of the Jew, but his distinctiveness among the nations of the world and his attitude to other people and religions.

When a Jewish boy reaches the age of thirteen he becomes a 'Son of the Commandment' (*Barmitzvah*) and is called up to the reading of the Torah on the sabbath following his birthday. On that occasion he recites the words: 'Blessed art Thou, O Lord our God, King of the Universe, who hast chosen us from all peoples, and hast given us Thy Torah.' And every Jew is supposed to reiterate three times daily the words of the following prayer: 'It is our duty to praise the Lord of all things, to ascribe greatness to Him who formed the world in the beginning, since He has not made us like the nations of other lands, and has not placed us like other families of the earth, since He has not assigned to us a portion as unto them, nor a lot as unto all their multitude. For *we* bend the knee and offer worship and thanks before the supreme King of Kings, the Holy One.'[8]

For while all peoples and nations are God's creatures through Adam, the Jew only is his elect child through Abraham, and continues, in the words of Professor Margolis, to be 'chosen by God as His

---

[7] *Ibid.*
[8] *Authorized Daily Prayer Book,* pp. 68, 76.

anointed servant to proclaim unto the families of mankind His truth. . . . until there come in, through him (that is, the Jew), the Kingdom of Peace and moral perfection'.[9] It follows that Israel and non-Jews cannot be equals. The biblical records of the missionary period in Israel's history (Isaiah, Jonah, Malachi) show that even in those efforts to win the outsider, the national character was retained, for Israel was to be the leader and master.

Missionary efforts seeking to proselytize non-Jews, therefore, would mean a contradiction of one of the principal dogmas, for they could not become sons of Abraham. This explains why missionary efforts have never been made on any large scale, not because it might run counter to the Jewish idea of tolerance, but because it could not be reconciled with the distinctiveness that goes with the idea of the 'Chosen People'. Judaism looks upon itself as a redeemed community, its members being the covenanting partners of God. That is the principle underlying its view, already described, of such doctrines as the atonement and the life hereafter.

This physical character of Judaism has been expressed times without number, but one of the clearest definitions has been provided in the writings of Professor Schoeps.

> 'The election of Abraham's seed brings the result that he who has been born an Israelite is already in the Covenant by his physical descent. So the seed of Abraham has become "holy seed". . . . Jews have been elected by God ever since the day that the reception of Abraham's complete devotion (in the offering of Isaac) has been fixed in the covenant with him, so that even a Jew who has turned away from his faith requires, on his repentance, only to turn back into that relation to Abraham which he received by birth.'[1]

Circumcision which was enjoined by God upon Abraham and his descendants (Genesis 17:10–12) has always been regarded as the supreme obligatory sign of loyalty and adherence to Judaism. As the sign of the Covenant (*Berit*) 'sealed in the flesh', circumcision came to be known as *berit milah* or the 'covenant of our father Abraham'.

Judaism is at once a religion and a people, and the very core of all its doctrine is this conception of the '*bene Yisrael*', the Children of Israel, as the people of God who cannot withdraw his benediction given once for all. A Jew may become completely secularized; he may have embraced atheism; but he is and remains a son of the promise because he is of Abraham's seed, irrespective of his attitude to religion. Isaac Deutscher, a self-confessed atheist, has tried in his book, *The Non-Jewish Jew*,[2] to show that famous Jews, such as Spinoza,

---

[9] J. H. Hertz (ed.), *A Book of Jewish Thoughts* (Bloch, New York, 1965), p. 14.

[1] Schoeps, *op. cit.*, pp. 149ff.

[2] I. Deutscher, *The Non-Jewish Jew* (OUP, New York, 1968).

Karl Marx, Sigmund Freud and Leon Trotsky, betrayed in their thinking plenty of Jewishness though they repudiated the Jewish religion. He wrote:

'What then makes a Jew? Religion? I am an atheist. Jewish Nationalism? I am an Internationalist. In neither sense am I, therefore, a Jew. I am, however, a Jew by force of my unconditional solidarity with the persecuted and exterminated. I am a Jew because I feel the Jewish tragedy as my own tragedy; because I feel the pulse of Jewish history; because I should like to do all I can do to assure the real, not spurious, security and self-respect of the Jews.'

This conviction of the physical or biological concept of Judaism, a repercussion of which may be seen in the two genealogies of Jesus as given in the Gospels of Matthew and Luke, is the ultimate reason for the rejection of a Messiah who not only claimed to be the Saviour of the Jews, but had come to admit the outsider on the same terms as the sons of the promise. Jesus' first sermon in the synagogue of Nazareth (Luke 4:16–30) meets with no opposition or resentment until he points out that Elias was sent to the widow at Sarepta and that Elisha healed the Syrian Naaman, the meaning being that the non-Jewish outsider was not excluded from God's redeeming love that does not stop at any racial or national frontier.

In the most extensive treatise ever written on the subject of Jesus by a Jewish authority, the author, a Professor in the Hebrew University of Jerusalem, said:

'Judaism is not only religion and it is not only ethics: it is the sum-total of all the needs of the nation, placed on a religious basis. It is a national world outlook with an ethico-religious basis. . . . Judaism is a national life, a life which the national religion and human ethical principles embrace without engulfing. Jesus came and thrust aside all the requirements of the national life . . . he ignored them completely. In the self-same moment he both annulled Judaism as the life-force of the Jewish nation, and also the nation itself as a nation. For a religion which possesses only a certain conception of God and a morality acceptable to all mankind does not belong to any special nation, and, consciously or unconsciously, breaks down the barriers of nationality. This inevitably brought it to pass that his people, Israel, rejected him.'[3]

There is a logical consistency in that attitude which can hardly be questioned.

For the moment we are not concerned with the general attitude of Judaism to Jesus, which will be the subject of a later paragraph. The matter under discussion is the national character of the Jewish

---

[3] Joseph Klausner, *Jesus of Nazareth* (Beacon Press, Boston, 1964).

religion which determines the view Judaism takes of other peoples and religions. Once we realize the distinct superiority which Israel claims above all others, we must expect to find those others relegated to the position of spiritual subordinates, however carefully that position may be paraphrased in order to eschew the appearance of haughtiness.

There are certain religious demands Judaism makes upon others as a prerequisite of their partnership in the realization of their plan. Non-Jews cannot become children of Abraham. Judaism is out of reach for most of them, although individuals are admitted if there are good reasons, as, for example, where there has been a mixed marriage. The 'religion of humanity' is, then, the condition upon which partnership is granted to others, and which constitutes the role assigned to the nations. It is based on the seven precepts which, according to rabbinical teaching, were given to the sons of Noah, and has been termed 'Noachism'. The precepts consist of prohibitions against 1. blasphemy; 2. idolatry; 3. sexual immorality; 4. murder; 5. robbery; 6. eating a portion of a living animal; and an injunction concerning 7. the administration of justice, which includes the entire range of social legislation. Rabbi Dr Isidore Epstein, in his book *Judaism*[4], emphasizes:

> 'From an early date Rabbinic Judaism differentiated mankind into those who did and who did not obey the Noachian Laws. The one who observed these laws was accepted as "proselyte of the Gates" (*ger toshaw*) and was included among the pious of the nations of the world who have a share in the world to come as an Israelite.'

This is the missionary programme of Judaism for the nations, whether they be Christians, Muslims, or adherents of some other creed. It is significant that in the 118 pages of *A Guide to Jewish Knowledge*[5] neither Christianity nor any other religion is mentioned, which is, of course, absolutely consistent with the view held in normative Judaism that all other religions transgress at least against either the first or the second Noachian precept. Nor can we overlook the eschatological implications of Noachism which are underlined by a quotation from the writings of Maimonides: 'Whosoever accepts the seven precepts and is careful in the observance of them is of the pious among the nations of the world and has a share in the world to come.'

Observers of Jewish life are occasionally puzzled over the phenomenon that even a Jew who has turned atheist is still regarded as a Jew, whereas one who has become a Christian is looked upon

[4] Epstein, *Judaism*, p. 143.
[5] C. Pearl and R. S. Brookes, *A Guide to Jewish Knowledge* (Taplinger, New York, 1958).

immediately as a traitor and apostate. But there is nothing in-consistent in such an attitude, as anyone who has followed the argument will easily understand. By accepting, through Jesus, the universal validity and applicability of redemption, election, grace, eternal life, *etc.*, a Jew has left the covenant, has deserted the host of the Chosen People, has thrown away his election and cut himself off from the redeemed community. But, to the same extent as the religious side of Judaism is taking a back seat and the national-physical component is gaining predominance among Jews, some of the age-long detestation of the convert to Christianity is slowly disappearing, provided that the 'apostate' continues to emphasize his loyalty to Jewish peoplehood and maintains his support of the Zionist cause. Even *The Encyclopedia of the Jewish Religion* makes the concession, that 'with the emergence of the State of Israel, and the corollary idea that Jewishness is a national and not a religious concept, a small movement of Jewish Christians is trying to establish itself in Israel'.[6] But nobody can in fairness expect that a negative attitude, traditional throughout many centuries, is likely to be abandoned in a hurry.

The practice of Judaism

Official Jewish circles in Britain and the USA make no secret of the deplorable religious situation in which Judaism finds itself due to the ever-growing influence of secularism, the belief that religious influence should be restricted and in particular that education and morality should be independent of religion. In *Confrontations with Judaism*, 'a book by Jews on Judaism', Raphael James Loewe states blandly

'that the twentieth century is not an age of significant response to theological thought-patterns, and agnosticism, plus or minus materialism, is now an attitude endemic as much within Jewry as in the wider world . . . The typical Jewish secularist is usually a person in search of a philosophy of Judaism that will permit him to maintain certain traditional Jewish ethical, social and aesthetic values whilst discarding the Deity as their sanction, and substitu-ting for the Deity some alternative acceptable to his own intellec-tual self-respect. He is, in other words, replacing Judaism by Judaicity and Jewish Culture. Judaicity is living a "Jewish" life but repudiating God and could be as much an idol as materialism or the nation-state.'[7]

Loewe also notices 'the replacement of theology by archaeology as a

---

[6] *Encyclopedia of Jewish Religion*, p. 212.

[7] P. Longworth (ed.), *Confrontation with Judaism* (Bloch, New York, 1967), pp. 36, 38f., 47

foundation for a faith in "Judaism", but the only positive Jewish element demonstrably reflected in Jewish archaeology is seen to be a theologically orientated element'. But he realizes that the assertion that the present age is unreceptive to religious values requires qualification

> 'by the phenomenon of a small yet significant minority of Jews, many of them young intellectuals, who revert from a Jewishly indifferent background to a rigorous and generally exclusive and intolerant form of Jewish traditionalism. What proves attractive to such recruits, as also to certain converts to Catholicism, though they may but rarely realize it, is not in fact dogmas or ceremonials. It is rather the accents of authority in which Jewish orthodoxy (and also the Catholic Church) claims the right to direct the day-to-day lives of its adherents in accordance with a detailed regimen. It nevertheless remains true that what has prompted their renewals of practical allegiance has been the search for something immovable as a basis of confidence with which to face conditions of change, uncertainty, and the ever-present threat of global war.'

David Singer, writing in *Commentary*, which is published by the American Jewish Committee, says pointedly: 'The truth is that the large majority of American Jews are far less Jewish than they wish to believe.'[8] Experts of life among Jewish students on both sides of the Atlantic have discovered that there are three types; the first group will find in Zionism the most exciting form of Jewish activity; a second type will devote their time to the Talmud, 'imagining that they will thus immunize themselves against ideas current in the universities'; while a third type may be interested and involved only in issues such as pacifism, non-violence, human rights, freedom from hunger, liberty of conscience, and the like.

But although it is an undisputed fact that the observance of the practices, rites and religious customs of Judaism has most markedly declined, no survey of the Mosaic religion would be complete without a description of some of the more important features of that practice. It is true enough that only a small minority now observes what in the past would have been considered the barest minimum, but it is equally necessary to add that there are, and always will be, people of Jewish faith to whom the faithful attendance at Jewish worship, the regular perusal of the Prayer Book, and the celebration of festivals mean everything. In this connection it is worth mentioning that Martin Buber (1878–1965) stopped all religious practices at the age of fourteen because they had lost their meaning for him. That may have been the reason why his influence has been felt more strongly outside than inside traditional Judaism. A. J. Heschel (1907–72), on the other hand, in many ways Buber's successor, was

[8] *Commentary*, Vol. 57, No. 3, March 1974, p. 86.

an observant Jew, ordained rabbi, professor at several Jewish theological colleges, and guest lecturer at many non-Jewish universities in America. The literary output of both was enormous, but Buber's was mainly in German while Heschel mastered German, English, Yiddish and Hebrew equally well, though most of his books appeared in English.

1. Services

Compared with the study of the Torah, prayer is of secondary importance to the Jew, although it is regarded as superior to the sacrifices once offered in Jerusalem. Prayer now takes the place of offerings, and the set times of morning, afternoon and evening worship correspond to the hours of the Temple sacrifices. Jews keep their head covered at prayer and other religious exercises as a mark of piety, though there is little basis for the habit in Jewish law. It is, in the words of *The Encyclopedia of the Jewish Religion*, 'an outstanding example of custom assuming the force of Law', and may have its origin at the time when most Jews lived in countries under the rule of Islam. Reform Jews have abolished the custom. At morning worship and on festivals the male worshipper wears the *tallit*, a cloth of white silk or wool with blue or black stripes at the end and fringes (*cf.* Numbers 15:37 ff.). Another biblical injunction (Exodus 13:9) is observed by putting on, at morning prayers, the *tephillin* (phylacteries), which consist of two small leather boxes (containing passages from Scripture) which are fixed on the forehead and left forearm and connected by a leather strap. The principal prayer at all services is the *Amidah*, which may well be as ancient as the books of Ezra and Nehemiah, and is made up of eighteen blessings expressing, in turn, eulogy, petitions and thanksgiving. The Amidah is preceded by the *Shema* (Deuteronomy 6:4), often considered the most significant part of the Jewish liturgy as it contains the whole dogma in the opening sentence: 'Hear, O Israel, the Lord is our God, the Lord is *One*!' Jesus called it the first of all commandments (Mark 12:29).

The services are conducted by the Reader (*Chazzan, i.e.* 'overseer'), as distinct from the Rabbi who gives a discourse and is the head of the community. The Reader also attends to the public recitation of the Pentateuch, which is divided into a large number of portions to make up an annual or triennial cycle. The Reading from the Law is a conspicuous part of the service and it is followed by a portion from the Prophets, including certain passages from Isaiah, but leaving out 52:13–15 and the whole of chapter 53. A fixed selection of Psalms is embodied in the Prayer Book, but does not contain, among others, Psalms 2, 22, 31, 45, 69 and 110.

2. The Sabbath

There are more elaborate services on the Sabbath which is celebrated in memory of the creation as well as of the exodus, both of which form the central idea of the *Kiddush*, a series of prayers and blessings read in the home by the master of the house. A cup of wine and two loaves are partaken of to symbolize joy and plenty, and hymns and table songs are prescribed which show the twofold character of the Sabbath as a religious and socio-ethical festival with a definite Messianic connotation as it typifies peace and brotherhood to come.

'On this day the conforming Jew will abstain from all kind of work, labour, or business for the Sabbath is a "Holy Day", a day of inwardness and moral regeneration, a day to attend to the claims of his relation to God and his fellow-man. The end of the Sabbath, like its entry, is marked by a special benediction, in praise of God for the distinction between the Sabbath and the six working days of the week.'[9]

3. The festivals

Three feasts serve to keep alive the memory of the pilgrimages that used to be undertaken three times a year in order to offer sacrifices in Jerusalem. They coincided with the three main crops of the Holy Land: Passover being held at the time of the barley harvest, Pentecost at the gathering of wheat, and Tabernacles at the season of fruit.

Passover (Hebrew, *Pessach*) is by far the most important of the three, for it commemorates God's intervention on behalf of his people, the exodus from Egypt. All traces of leaven must be removed from Jewish homes as this is the Feast of Unleavened Bread, the *Matzot*, in memory of the exodus when the Israelites in leaving Egypt could not wait until their dough leavened (Exodus 12:39). The most significant part of the service is held in the home. The story of the divine deliverance from Pharaoh is related in all its details, and accompanied by many symbols, *e.g.* a roast shank-bone to remind the participants of the paschal lamb which was slain and whose blood was sprinkled on the doorsteps so that the angel of death, walking through the country and killing the first-born of the Egyptians, would recognize the Jewish homes and 'pass over' them. At one point the master of the house breaks a cake of unleavened bread and says:

'This is the bread of affliction which our ancestors ate in the land of Egypt. Let all those who are hungry enter and eat thereof, and all who are in distress, come and celebrate the Passover. At present we celebrate it here, but next year we hope to celebrate it in the land of Israel. This year we are accounted aliens here, but next year we hope to be children of freedom in the land of Israel.'

[9] Epstein, *Judaism*, pp. 170f.

This blessing is in the Chaldee language and probably dates from the pre-Christian era.

Pentecost (Hebrew, *Shavuot*) follows seven weeks after Passover (Leviticus 23:15) and the synagogue is decorated with plants and flowers in memory of the pastoral origin of the feast. In rabbinical tradition it was associated with the giving of the Law at Sinai, which converted a company of runaway slaves into a national as well as a religious body of free men and women.

Tabernacles (Hebrew, *Succot*, *i.e.* booths) is a typical autumn festival (Exodus 23:16 and Deuteronomy 16:13) with prayers for rain and for the dead. Its last day (*Simchat Torah*) is an occasion of rejoicing, especially among the young, and marks the point at which the annual reading of the Torah is commenced anew.

Apart from these festivals there are two holy days, both of which are full of most solemn meaning. Many a Jew who would not come near a synagogue throughout the year would not like to be missed there on those two occasions, one of which is the New Year, the other the Day of Atonement.

Rosh Hashanah (*i.e.* the 'head of the year') commences the secular calendar, whereas Passover marks the beginning of the religious year. It is viewed as a day of judgment on which individuals and nations are entered in, or struck off, the divine Book of Life. To quote from the liturgy of the New Year's service: 'On this day sentence is pronounced upon countries – which of them is destined to the sword and which to peace, which to famine and which to plenty; and each separate creature is visited thereon, and recorded for life or for death.' It is also a day of remembrance (Leviticus 23:24 f.), and God is asked to forgive the petitioners on account of the faith of their ancestors who have laid up a store of righteousness upon which the present generation may draw. It is the day of the trumpet, the *Shofar*. This is a ram's horn which has always been blown as the signal for important occasions of a religious and national character.

A dramatic climax of genuine devotion and emotion is reached on the highest of all holy days, the Day of Atonement (*Yom Kippur*), described in Leviticus 23:32 as 'a sabbath of solemn rest', with its abstention from food and drink. To put it in the words of the liturgy: 'Thou hast given us in love, O Lord our God, this Day of Atonement for pardon, forgiveness, and atonement, that we may obtain pardon thereon for all our iniquities; an holy convocation, as a memorial of the departure from Egypt.' Four times throughout the day a catalogue of twenty-four definite transgressions is recited, followed by a further enumeration of those sins for which certain sacrifices were offered in the days of the Temple. There is also the narration of the ancient ritual of the scapegoat upon which the nation's sins were symbolically placed, and which was then driven to the wilderness or cast from a precipice. No-one who has attended the services on that day can possibly forget the note of urgency and the passionate yearning for forgiveness that are present throughout the prayers and prostrations, and are perhaps best summed up in these two passages from the liturgy: 'What shall we say before Thee, O Thou who dwellest on high, and what shall we recount unto Thee, Thou who abidest in the heavens? Dost Thou not know all things, both the hidden and the revealed? May it then be Thy will, O Lord our God, and God of our Fathers, to forgive us for all our sins, to pardon us for all our iniquities, and to grant us remission for all our transgressions.' The sevenfold proclamation of God's Oneness, taken from the story of Elijah's triumph over the prophets of Baal on Mount Carmel (1 Kings 18:39), and one blast of the Shofar close the day, whose doctrinal significance has been dealt with elsewhere (p. 61).

There is, however, an ancient and widespread custom which shows that the lack of a vicarious sacrifice constituted a serious problem to many a Jew who felt that prayer could not altogether take the place of the scapegoat of old. A fowl is taken and waved three times around the head of the penitent. The bird is then slaughtered and given to the poor. 'Though the rabbis opposed the practice, the weight of opinion and tradition have caused it to be continued in observant circles.'[1]

4. The semi-festivals

To the major holy days some later festivals have been added on which work is not prohibited. *Purim* commemorates the deliverance of the Jews of the Persian Empire as is recorded in the biblical book of Esther. In Israel, Purim constitutes a carnival period, while in the Diaspora the festival is celebrated with a certain amount of levity and popular amusement. *Chanukkah* (Dedication) is observed in memory of the rededication of the Second Temple by Judas Maccabeus, in 165 BC. Talmudic legend relates that it was instituted for eight days because the pure oil found in the temple, though sufficient for one day only, miraculously burned for eight days. The kindling of the eight-branched candelabrum (*Menorah*) forms the main feature. The Chanukkah candelabrum has been an important object of Jewish art as its shape was modelled on the seven-branched candelabrum used in the temple and carried away to Rome by Titus in AD 70. At the establishment of the State of Israel the Menorah became part of the official coat of arms.

5. Other practices

Reference has already been made to the ceremony of *Barmitzvah* (p. 67). It is a rite devoid of ancient authority or sanction, though generally observed since the fifteenth century. The comparable

---

[1] *Encyclopedia of Jewish Religion*, article "Kapparot," p. 222.

ceremony for girls, *Batmitzvah*, is of fairly recent date and will not be permitted by orthodox Jewry, which looks askance at any participation of females in the synagogue service. In Britain, however, Batmitzvah met with the approval of the late Dr Hertz and has become a widespread custom.

As has been seen, certain practices are incumbent upon male members of the community. No prayer meeting, no synagogue service, no marriage ceremony can be held unless there are ten male Jews above the age of thirteen, for that is the quorum required for the divine presence. No number of women can make up the deficiency as woman does not count. The opening part of the daily morning service contains the injunction: 'Men say, "Blessed art Thou, O Lord our God, King of the Universe, who hast not made me a woman." Women say, "Blessed art Thou, O Lord our God, King of the Universe, who hast made me according to Thy will." ' In orthodox and conservative synagogues, men and women are strictly separated and female worshippers do not take any official part in the service.

Among progressive Jews, women are accorded equal rights with men. But it would be most fallacious to infer from the above that the status of the Jewess in ordinary life was somehow inferior to that held by other women. The truth is that Judaism takes an exceptionally high and lofty view of the true vocation of womanhood, which is seen to be in home and family. Judaism does not believe in asceticism and celibacy. On the contrary, its teaching emphasizes that only through married life can sanctity and purity be realized.

A custom going back to Mosaic legislation, and most likely to be noticed by anyone visiting a Jewish home, concerns the *Mezuzzah* (Deuteronomy 6:9), a small case of metal or wood, containing the words of Deuteronomy 6:4–9 in Hebrew, which is affixed to the doorposts. There is, finally, another custom in which Judaism differs notably from other religions. It concerns the burial, which among Jews is a matter of the greatest simplicity. Irrespective of their calling or station in life, the richest and the poorest are given the same plain wooden coffin and the same simple hearse. The anniversary of the death of a near relative is regularly observed by lighting a candle or lamp on the eve of the day and keeping it burning until sunset of the next day.

6. The dietary laws

Biblical ordinances and rabbinical precepts prohibit certain foods from the diet of the Jews. The regulations apply mainly to animal foods. Quadrupeds permitted for consumption are enumerated in Leviticus 11:3 and Deuteronomy 14:4ff., but ritual slaughter is obligatory. The eating of pork is strictly prohibited, as is the eating of the blood of beasts and birds. Only fish that have both fins and scales and clean birds are allowed to be eaten. Food prepared with milk and food in which meat is an ingredient should not be eaten at the same meal. As a consequence of the barrier which the deeply-rooted observance of the dietary laws has formed around the Jews, they have never been fully absorbed in the surrounding population. Many Jews who no longer restrict themselves to ritually-slaughtered meat will nevertheless refrain from eating pork. In Reform Judaism, the dietary laws have been renounced on the ground that they are mainly 'ceremonial' and not religious or moral precepts. Conservative Judaism, on the other hand, accepts them in principle but allows a certain latitude in practice.

Modern trends

Judaism, as has been pointed out before, is not a static religion and has been affected by many tendencies which, although they became movements within Judaism, originally arose through its contact with the surrounding world. Jewish emancipation, *i.e.* the setting free from bondage or disability of any kind, was first achieved in the USA, then by the French Declaration of Human Rights (1789), and eventually carried victoriously through Europe and the rest of the world. In its wake, various sections of Jewry began to establish themselves without repudiating the main tenets of the faith. Dr E. L. Ehrlich of *B'nai B'rith* ('Sons of the Covenant'), a fraternal organiza-tion including representatives of every shade of Jewish belief and practice, has given what may be termed a present-day formulation of Maimonides' Articles, something all Jews will nowadays subscribe to:

1. *Ahavat Yisrael, i.e.* love for the Jewish people as a corporate unit of religion and peoplehood,
2. *Ahavat Torah, i.e.* love for the Torah in its written and oral forms, though varying in the degree of acknowledgment,
3. *Ahavat Erets Yisrael*, the love for the Holy Land, promised to the Fathers and regained in our time,
4. *Ahavat Briyot*, the love for mankind as all men were created in the image and likeness of God,
5. *Ahavat Adonai*, the love for God in fulfilment of Deuteronomy 6:5.[2]

We speak of Orthodox, Conservative and Progressive Judaism, but these are not always separated by rigid borderlines. Also the terms used to denote them do not always have the same meaning in every place. For example, Conservative Judaism on the European Conti-nent is usually contrasted with Progressive Judaism; in America, however, it suggests, rather, a modified form of Orthodoxy.

[2] In *Religiöse Strömungen im Judentum Heute* (Flamberg Verlag, Zürich, 1973), p. 28.

1. Orthodox Judaism

Orthodoxy is a modern designation for the strictly traditional section of Jewry. There is no proper Hebrew equivalent for Orthodoxy; 'orthopraxy', *i.e.* the upholding of the Law, would be a more appropriate term. *The Encyclopedia of the Jewish Religion* puts it this way:

'Though Orthodoxy is widely diversified among its many religious groupings and nuances of belief and practice, all Orthodox Jews are united in their belief in the historical event of revelation at Sinai, as described in the Torah; in their acceptance of the Divine Law, in its Written and Oral forms, as immutable and binding for all times; in their acknowledgement of the authority of duly qualified rabbis – who themselves recognize the validity of the Talmud and all other traditional sources of the Halakhah — to interpret and administer Jewish Law.[3]

In its contacts with non-orthodox Jewish communities, Orthodoxy is rigorous and unbending and exhibits a marked reluctance to co-operate with them, not merely in religious areas but even in sporting events. Football teams of Orthodox congregations in England are known to have been forbidden to meet teams of Reform communities. Orthodox Jews remain consciously within the bonds of legalism and particularism.

2. Conservative Judaism

Early in the nineteenth century pleas for modification of ritual were heard and taken up, especially in America. Midway between Orthodox and Progressive Judaism, Conservative Judaism has on the one hand taken over some external modes of worship of Reform Judaism, such as prayers said in the vernacular. Many of its synagogues employ the organ. On the other hand Conservatives claim to accept the entire structure of rabbinic tradition, although they do permit themselves to interpret the Law in accordance with modern needs and convictions. The three principal objectives of Conservative Judaism are: the fostering of the unity of universal Israel; the perpetuation of Jewish tradition; and the cultivation of Jewish scholarship. The rest can take care of itself. Conservatism refuses to commit itself to a definite platform of principles and dogmas, and allows considerable latitude in matters of practice and belief among its constituent groups.

3. Progressive (*i.e.* Liberal and Reform) Judaism

Influenced by the enlightenment of the eighteenth century, a movement in favour of the grammatical and historical exegesis of the Bible started among the Jews on the continent of Europe in opposition

[3] *Encyclopedia of Jewish Religion,* p. 293.

to the dialectic school of Talmudism. Scientific research was made the yardstick of biblical interpretation, the dietary laws were considered obsolete, and only the ethical injunctions came to be regarded as obligatory. The movement came to be called 'Liberal Judaism'. Dr Claude Montefiore, its protagonist in Britain, summarized its programme as follows:

'It modifies or enlarges the doctrines of the past so as to make them consistent with each other and in harmony with the highest conceptions of truth to which it can attain. It deliberately aims at universalism and universalization. It sets out to emphasize the "prophetic" elements in Judaism, and to minimize or negate the "priestly" elements. It gives up all praying for the restoration of the Temple and of animal sacrifices. It sets the Prophets above the Law.'[4]

Similar forces were at work in what was known as 'Reform Judaism', which demanded the subordination or elimination of the references to Zion, to a personal Messiah, and to the restoration of the sacrificial system. The abolition of certain ceremonies was followed by making phylacteries and dietary laws optional. Not surprisingly, the two sections formed, in 1926, a World Union for Progressive Judaism. There are now more than 600 congregations in many countries joined together in the Union, with a growing emphasis on Hebrew and traditional customs. The most startling reversal in its policy occurred when it urged its members to participate in the rebuilding of the Holy Land and to realize that Jews were bound to each other not only in a religious faith but as a people with a common history and faith.

4. Chassidism

It was, however, neither Conservative nor Progressive Judaism which shook the foundations of Orthodoxy, but the secularism and indifference of modern man, who does not believe what he cannot handle. This conflict is still going on and the only group in Judaism that has emerged victoriously from that battle is the mystical movement of Chassidism which began as a reaction against the dry legalism of Orthodox Judaism. The term *chassidim* ('the pious ones') had been used before but, as a revival movement, Chassidism originated in Poland and the Ukraine in the eighteenth century and spread to other parts of Eastern Europe and then to the United States and Israel. After being long connected with the poorer, uneducated mass of Eastern Jewry, it gradually won respect and admiration among the learned. Here was a direct approach to God, based on personal experience and prayer rather than on dogma and ritual. The founder of Chassidism, Israel Baal Shem-Tov (c. 1700–60), taught that

[4] C. Montefiore, *The Old Testament and After* (Books for Libraries, New York, 1972), pp. 557f.

zeal, prayerful devotion and humility were more acceptable to God than intellectualism. Its great textbooks go back to the *Kabbalah*, a mystical Jewish philosophy that exerted a far-reaching influence on European thought at the time of the Reformation. One of the Kabbalah's earliest components was the *Sefer Yezirah* ('Book of Creation'), whose ideas were revived in Chassidism. Another sourcebook was the *Zohar* ('splendour'), a kabbalistic, mystical commentary on the Pentateuch. Both works were essentially Jewish although they show distinct traces of Hellenistic, Gnostic and Christian influences. Chassidism is characterized by a genuine piety and humility that are the outcome of an intense life of prayer, combined with cheerfulness and great enthusiasm. It has had its moments of ecstasy and wild extremes when thousands were carried away by miracle-working 'holy men', who thrived on superstition. But it can also claim to have produced distinguished writers and scholars. The greatest representative of Chassidism, and doubtless the intellectual leader of his generation, was Martin Buber, at once mystic, theologian, scholar and philosopher. His book, *I and Thou*, has been praised by Berdyaev, the Russian philosopher who turned from scepticism to the church, as one of the most eminent manifestations of the religious thought of Europe. It certainly showed an unusual insight into the mind of God.

5. Zionism

We turn now to consider a movement which cuts right across all divisions and groups and is known as Zionism.

We have repeatedly alluded to the drift from the synagogue so typical of Judaism today, irrespective of the country or social class to which the individual belongs. It is, of course, perfectly correct to say that, in forsaking his religion, the Jew only copies his neighbour. But we are not concerned here with the question as to how far the religious poverty of the Jews reflects the low spiritual state of their environment. In this connection it must be remembered that, after the ruthless annihilation of some six million Jews in Europe by the Nazi regime, about one quarter of Jewry now lives in countries dominated by Communism. It is, however, not so much the deified materialism of Marx that claims most of those Jews who have given up their faith, but the fashionable, pseudo-religious systems of humanitarianism, spiritism, Christian Science, *etc.*, or sheer indifference to anything that savours of human recognition of a power outside oneself.

Some Jewish leaders had cherished the hope that the terrible persecution of European Jewry would result in a great religious revival, a solemn return to the faith of the Fathers. But while a few have sought refuge in the old traditions, the majority have found a way out of their indifference by throwing themselves into the arms of Zionism as the new faith.

Deeply religious and completely secular ideas converge in this movement, which has swept Judaism in every quarter of the globe like wildfire and gathered further impetus with the setting up of the State of Israel in May 1948. Zionism is like a tree with many roots. One of the roots is the age-long yearning of the Jews in the Dispersion to return to their Holy Land and there to serve their God. Another is a nationalistic movement with colonialistic undertones. But there is also a genuine attempt at emancipation – Pinsker, one of the founding fathers, called it auto-emancipation. It combines the neo-romantic optimism so typical of the last century with the pessimism of the twentieth. Six million Jews done to death seems reason enough why Jews have lost confidence in the goodwill of the world and desire to have, and to defend against all and sundry, a place on earth they can call their own. They have certainly built up the country with a speed that at times was – of necessity – hectic and not always co-ordinated, and they did it in the sweat of their faces and at considerable personal cost. They used the spade and the tractor rather than military means, something which distinguished them honourably from the usual colonists. The tragedy was that the early settlers never took in the reality of there being an indigenous population. As Amos Elon, one of the most popular writers in Israel, says in his book, *Founders and Sons*, the founders just did not perceive the Arabs.

The father of modern spiritual Zionism was Asher Ginzberg, who adopted the pseudonym Ahad Ha-Am (*i.e.* 'One of the People'). He came of a chassidic family and saw in Zionism the very essence of Judaism. He never ceased to demand a spiritual revival as the prerequisite of the return to the Holy Land, and to insist upon the Jews' becoming heroes of the Spirit, and not of worldly power. His ideas were taken up by Bialik, a poet of unusual spiritual depth whose language resembles that of Jeremiah, and who, together with Ben-Yehuda, ranks as the founder of the new Hebrew, *Ivrit*. Later on, Martin Buber declared that Erets Yisrael was not merely a vision in the Jewish mind but a principle never to be given up; to him it meant the synthesis of spirit and reality.

Quite different ideas were prominent in the establishment of political Zionism. It was born of the unspeakable misery and social distress of the Jews in Eastern Europe who, in the second half of the last century, were made the scapegoat of all discontent and political unrest in Russia, Rumania and Turkey. Every year hundreds of Jewish men, women and children lost their lives in the pogroms connived at, if not inspired, by the authorities of those countries. It was in view of that wretched state that Theodor Herzl demanded a land of refuge for his people; but he never linked his argument with religious sentiments. His objective was a political and economic solution to what seemed to him a political and economic problem. Only when his plans for such a land of refuge in other parts of the world had come to naught, did he fix his gaze upon Palestine, and the First Zionist Congress in Basle in 1897 made no reference to any spiritual tendencies, but based its claim to Palestine on political arguments.

Helped by the sad events in Europe and the rapid spread of nationalistic ideas, the political group won the upper hand and eventually achieved the establishment of a sovereign country. The fact was bluntly stated by Professor David Flusser, who, at a Colloquium held in Jerusalem in 1970, said: 'The reasons for the return to the Land of the Fathers were not of a religious nature.' And R. J. Loewe explained: 'Jewry in antiquity turned itself, *faute de mieux*, from a nation into a religious group; it is now in the happy situation of being able to reverse the process and can therefore throw off all religious masquerades.'[5]

This is a far cry from the original ideal. But the peoples of Europe who could not, or would not, safeguard the lives and limbs of the Jews in their midst, are in no position to criticize or judge a development that was caused by their anti-Judaism, going back to the Constantine era, and by their anti-Semitism, a particularly obnoxious product of the nineteenth century that reached its abominable climax in Hitler's holocaust.

Jews are the first to deplore the change. R. J. Loewe writes:

'What Israel is offering the world is merely an excellent example of how Western techniques can be galvanized into greater efficiency by following four factors: (1) national self-consciousness; (2) a self-confidence reinforced by the knowledge that it has its back to the wall, and (like Britain in 1940) has stood alone; (3) a disavowal (unlike Britain in 1940) of a substantial slice of history – diaspora Jewish life – as having lacked all positive and essentially Jewish significance; and (4) a conviction that reawakened nationalism can hark back, behind this interlude, to the supposed virtues of ancient Israel.'[6]

The fact is that, after nineteen centuries, a state with the biblical name *Israel* does again exist and, in its Declaration of Independence, has stated plainly that it will be based on the principles conceived by the Hebrew prophets. This fact has set in motion theological discussions among Christians and Muslims, who had looked upon themselves as rightful heirs to the prophetical promises and never envisaged Israel's resuscitation until the end of time, although, as Professor Flusser declared, 'All this does not mean that a new disaster cannot come, either because of Israel's sins or because of political mistakes or the wickedness of the nations.'[7]

The existence of a new Israel has also set some theologians the

[5] In Longworth (ed.), *Confrontations with Judaism*, pp. 39f.

[6] *Ibid.* p. 46.

[7] *Jerusalem Post*, 27 November 1970.

thorny problem as to where to place this phenomenon that runs counter to the expectations of the Church Fathers and their followers down the ages. Other Christians, however, see the return to Zion as a fulfilment of prophecy and view the state as a visible evidence for the arrival of the end of the age. Meanwhile, the Israelis have victoriously fought off the military efforts made by the surrounding Arab world to destroy them. But that hostility between Jews and Arabs constitutes for the whole world a threat of unimaginable proportions.

There is no lack of critical pronouncements on the situation that exists in Israel after her various wars. Perhaps the greatest shock was caused by a speech Abba Eban, Israel's Foreign Minister at the time, delivered at Haifa University in 1973. He said that Israel

'was in danger of losing sight of her larger moral purposes, and that her vision was becoming distorted. There was no question about her courage or resourcefulness but about her human quality. If Israel upheld the legacy of prophecy, the vision of justice, righteousness and truth, she owed something to their observance, even if this meant a sacrifice. If not, she is manoeuvring herself into a position for which there is no way out, morally or, in the long run, politically either.'

Reference was also made to the 'inflationary boom, bringing in bigger pay packets and crowding the stores with ever-increasing amounts of luxury goods, and Professor Talmon's harsh judgment on the surrender of the spiritual ideal to the notion that might is right.'[8]

Arguments on whether Israel or the Diaspora is more important, have for several years taken up a lot of space in Jewish publications. Jews in such countries as the United States, Britain and France are annoyed when told by Israelis that only in the Land of the Fathers can a Jew lead a full religious life. Their reply is always hinting at the prophets who taught that their God was universal Lord and King who could be served anywhere, as he had overcome national boundaries. Dr James Parkes, lifelong protagonist of the Zionist cause, writes:

'The somewhat contemptuous attitude adopted by Israeli youngsters to Jews who lived in the Dispersion ought to be checked. It is perfectly reasonable that during the last fifty years the main interest of the Jews in dispersion has been the building up of an independent Jewish centre, but it is now time that the centre began to consider how and in what manner it has an inescapable responsibility towards the Dispersion, and thereby for feeding Jewish experience into the non-Jewish world.'[9]

Of the 120 seats in the Israeli Parliament, only fifteen went to the various religious parties in the election held on 31 December 1973. That corresponds to the frequently canvassed opinion that less than fifteen per cent of the Israelis are in favour of Orthodox Judaism, the only type of religion sanctioned by the religious establishment. All other forms of Judaism are definitely discouraged from setting up their synagogues and gathering for worship. The Orthodox are, through so-called home missions, seeking to win new adherents but have not met with any measurable success, the principal reason being their entanglement in politics. The religious heads that are in power have, as R. J. Loewe puts it, 'sold out to secularism by showing a willingness to enter the arena of politics and to compromise with it'. In Israel, religious Zionism has always had to face a genuine quandary: if it recognized in nationalism an indispensable tool, a price had to be paid. 'That price is to find oneself trapped into compounding the felonies of nationalism, by condoning, as valid for politics, ethical standards that would be regarded as deserving of censure in a private person. To play any game is to acknowledge the validity of its rules.'[1] No wonder that some of Israel's best friends are anything but happy with the existing situation. There is a whole gamut of criticism from all over the world.

Rabbi Jakob J. Petuchowksi, Professor for Rabbinics at the Hebrew Union College, Cincinnati, and a guest lecturer at Tel Aviv University, has pointed out in his book, *Zion Reconsidered*, how important it is to realize that prophetic Judaism challenges all who want to reduce it to 'the level of an oriental tribal religion'. He sees in certain aspects of present-day Zionism a retrogression to territorial idols. Similarly, Dr James Parkes, in his book already mentioned, raised a warning voice: 'Either Jewry consists of a Homeland and a Dispersion, both equally alive, or its religion sinks into a Levantine tribalism, while abroad there is no future for Jews except complete assimilation and absorption.' A truly frightening picture for Jews, especially as assimilation and absorption have always been terms connoting the abandonment of the religion and, ultimately, the acceptance, either out of convenience or by conviction, of the Nazarene.

Jesus of Nazareth

What, then, is the Jewish attitude to Jesus Christ? Is he still regarded as a sorcerer and impostor, as in some Talmudic writings? Not at all.

[9] J. Parkes, *Whose Land? A History of the Peoples of Palestine* (Penguin, Baltimore, 1970), p. 320.
[1] In Longworth (ed.), *Confrontations with Judaism.*

The last seventy years have seen a remarkable change, in so far as the study of the Nazarene has become a legitimate branch of Jewish research, with a Chair of Comparative Religion, with special reference to the New Testament and the early church, in the Hebrew University, Jerusalem, occupied by Professor David Flusser. Nothing like it would have been tolerated in the past. Many non-Jews have been led to believe, at least by implication, that a turning-point has been reached in the Jewish mode of thinking and that it is only a question of time before Judaism will accept the Nazarene as Messiah. This opinion is altogether wrong, because it fails to penetrate to the real cause of the change in the Jewish attitude. The figure of Jesus became attractive to Judaism only to the extent that the higher criticism in the liberal Christian theology tended to subordinate traditional orthodox beliefs to modern thought. It is no coincidence that Jewish interest in Jesus occurred at a time when Christian doctrine was toned down and modified. An interpretation of Jesus which stripped him of his deity, explained away his miracles and dissected his words, provided a basis of study quite acceptable to Judaism. It was the time when it became fashionable to question the reliability of the Gospel records, to feel uncertain about the resurrection appearances, and to dismiss everything supernatural as pious myth.

All this will help us to understand the more recent interest in Jesus, and also to appreciate why the acceptability of the Nazarene cannot go beyond a certain point which is observed by all Jewish writers, no matter how enthusiastic they are in their treatment of him. There can be little doubt that he has captured the imagination of many who spent years in studying his life and take great care to be as impartial as possible. Nor can the fact be denied that a few individuals, having fallen in love with the object of their literary interest, found themselves unable to withdraw from him, and discovered, often to their own astonishment, that they had overstepped the bounds of Judaism. But those were exceptions.

It may suffice to quote from some of the more authoritative utterances that have come from prominent Jews in recent years. There was, first of all, Martin Buber, who said in his *Drei Reden über das Judentum*, 'We must overcome the superstitious terror with which we have regarded the Nazareth movement, a movement which we must place where it properly belongs – in the spiritual history of Israel.' He added later, however, 'Whoever regards Jesus as an historical personality, be he ever so high, may belong to us; but he who acknowledges Jesus to be the Messiah already come, cannot belong to us.' There was Albert Einstein who said he was 'enthralled by the luminous figure of the Nazarene', and Rabbi Solomon B. Freehof, who in his book, *Stormers of Heaven*, frankly stated, 'The personality of Jesus was such that his sonship to God was magnificently evident. The divine spirit seemed manifest in his words and deeds. He impressed himself upon the world, perhaps more so than other prophets or saints, as a child of the living God.' Then followed Sholem Asch, the distinguished Yiddish writer, who devoted a whole book of some seven hundred pages to Jesus under the title, *The Nazarene*.

Three more recent voices from different sections of Judaism may also be quoted. Ben Zion Bokser, conservative Rabbi and Professor at the Jewish Theological Seminary in New York, wrote: 'Jesus extolled poverty, he spoke for the simple life, he attacked involvement in mundane concerns and asked for a concentration on the life of the spirit, on faith in God, and the pursuits of mercy and love. . . . He was a son of his people, who shared their dreams, who was loyal to their way of life, who died a martyr's death because of a commitment to his vision of their highest destiny', – but then Bokser adds: 'The image of Jesus as depicted in Christian writings . . . is rather a work of idealization and myth-building, reflecting the faith, primarily, of those who were under the influence of the non-Jewish, Hellenistic, world.'[2] The Professor of Bible and Hellenistic Literature at the Hebrew Union College, the academical school of Reform Judaism in Cincinnati, Samuel Sandmel, published a book under the title *We Jews and Jesus*, 'written for those thoughtful Jewish people who seek to arrive at a calm and balanced understanding of where Jews can reasonably stand with respect to Jesus'. During Lent in 1971, the Senior Minister of the Liberal Synagogue in London, Rabbi John D. Rayner, talked on BBC Radio 4 about his view of Jesus, and, among other things, said:

> 'Jesus was a preacher, concerned with the non-legal side of Judaism which is called Aggadah, that is, religious thought, moral exhortation, and homiletical interpretation of Scripture. . . . But he did not teach only in the manner of an Aggadist, but also in the manner of a prophet; not only as an interpreter of Scripture, but also as a spokesman of God, independently of Scripture. . . . Finally, I think that Jesus believed himself to be the Messiah. This does not make him un-Jewish; on the contrary, only a Jew would have made such a claim. Nor does it make him divine, for the Jewish concept of the Messiah was that of a human being.'

But then followed what, among Jews, has always been the ultimate argument for denying the Messiahship of Jesus: 'There have been many Messiahs, but the Kingdom of God has not come. The world has remained unredeemed. Ignorance and folly have continued. Selfishness and brutality have not ceased.'

When it comes to the question of the resurrection we find that all Jewish writers and preachers are unanimous in denying it, although Klausner, in his *Jesus of Nazareth*, makes the concession that it must

[2] B. Z. Bokser, *Judaism and the Christian Predicament* (Knopf, New York, 1967), pp. 203 and 207.

have been a 'vision' which became the basis of Christianity. 'It is impossible to suppose that there was any conscious deception: the nineteen hundred years' faith of millions is not founded on deception.'[3] Judaism cannot go beyond the death of the Nazarene. But it is significant to note how far an eminent Jew can go when the question of the Lord's return is discussed, as is the case in Professor Schoeps' book *Paulus*. 'The Church of Jesus Christ has preserved no picture of her Lord and Saviour. If Jesus returned tomorrow, no Christian would recognize him by sight. But it might well be that he who comes at the end of the days, and constitutes both the Synagogue's and the Church's expectation, bears the same countenance.'[4] This complements from the theological point of view those reasons for the rejection of Jesus from the national point of view discussed on pages 69f.

What of the future?

Of the seventeen million Jews who lived in 1933, hardly eleven million survived the holocaust. Their numbers have since increased to 14·370 million, of whom some six million live in the USA and 2·7 million each in Israel and the USSR. Thus the focal points of Judaism have shifted from Europe to America and to the State of Israel. Many distinct features of Judaism are fast disappearing on account of an ever-increasing loss of faith. Very often the observance of the biblical rite of circumcision is the only remaining token of allegiance, although we have seen that it is not through any rite or declaration of faith that a Jew is a Jew, but because he is born of a Jewish mother. Is this physical character of Judaism sufficient guarantee for its permanence, or is there something undefinable in Judaism, something that defeats all our efforts to examine and to describe, simply because it touches the very mystery of God?

The Editor of the *Jewish Chronicle*, William Frankel, addressing the World Conference of Jewish Journalists in Jerusalem, had hard words to say of the present situation.

'We think of ourselves as a religious people, but the Jewish way of life is more a subject for sermons than for living. We are proud of high, ethical and moral standards, but my own paper published reports on the increasing number of unmarried Jewish mothers in Britain and of the disturbingly high proportion of Jews amongst the known drug addicts. The trouble with Jewish life in our communities is that, being fed on these myths and choosing to believe them, we settle placidly into an acceptance of unreality . . . Our

---

[3] Klausner, *Jesus of Nazareth*, p. 359.
[4] H. J. Schoeps, *Paul* (ET, Westminster, Philadelphia, 1961), p. 274. *Encyclopaedia Judaica* says of Schoeps: "bringing Judaism very close to Christianity, but stopping short of baptism." (Vol. 14, Col. 991.)

leaders, lay and rabbinic, are all answering the questions which nobody is asking. The main question in the diaspora is why we should remain Jews today. The problem is a religious problem. If Judaism means nothing to our children, they will not remain Jews. And Judaism will not mean anything to them if it is shackled to concepts and attitudes which are either irrelevant or positively repelling or call for the suspension of their reason. Today our religious leaders are unwilling to lose an iota of outmoded dogma, but are quite willing to lose a majority of the Jewish people. Israel, regretfully, is in no position today to give us a lead in this matter.'[5]

Judaism is in search of its identity and no spiritual leader has so far emerged in Israel. In Britain, Rabbi Louis Jacobs seems the only independent thinker, with a number of books, especially *A Jewish Theology*, to his credit. But in America Judaism has, in Abraham Joshua Heschel, produced an original genius who influenced generations of Jewish and non-Jewish students. And in Israel, Jewish students can hear Professor David Flusser expound the life and times of the Nazarene. It is fitting, therefore, that this treatment of Judaism should be concluded with two quotations from their works.

'Biblical history', writes Heschel, 'bears witness to the constant corruption of man; . . . if the nature of man were all we had, then surely there would be no hope for us left. But we also have the word of God, the commandment, the mitsvah. . . . Messianism implies that any course of living, even the supreme effort, must fail in redeeming the world. In other words, history is not sufficient to itself. . . . At the end of the days, evil will be conquered all at once; in historic times evils must be conquered one by one.'[6]

To that dictum of Heschel's, the final sentence of Professor Flusser's article on Jesus in the new *Encyclopaedia Judaica* should be added. 'If, as Christians believe, the martyr was at the same time the Messiah, then his death has a cosmic importance.'[7]

Bibliography

In addition to the books mentioned in the text and footnotes the following will be found useful as works of reference.

Leo Baeck, *This People Israel* (Holt, Rinehart and Winston, New York, 1965).

[5] *Jewish Chronicle,* 16 February 1968, p. 7.
[6] Heschel, in *The Concept of Man,* pp. 155, 157.
[7] *Encyclopaedia Judaica,* Vol. 10, Col. 14.

Gregory Baum, *Is the New Testament Anti-Semitic?* (Paulist-Newman Press, Glen Rock, New Jersey, 1965).

Norman Bentwich, *Israel Resurgent* (Praeger, New York, 1960).

Norman Bentwich, *The Jews in our Time* (Penguin, Baltimore, 1960).

Selig Brodetsky, *Memoirs: from Ghetto to Israel* (Weidenfeld and Nicolson, London, 1960).

Bernard M. Casper, *An Introduction to the Jewish Bible Commentary* (Yoseloff, New York, 1960).

A. Roy Eckardt, *Elder and Younger Brothers: The Encounter of Jews and Christians* (Schocken, New York, 1973).

Sidney Greenberg (ed.), *A Modern Treasury of Jewish Thoughts* (Yoseloff, New York, 1960).

Louis Jacobs, *We have Reason to Believe* (Vallentine Mitchell, London, 1962).

Louis Jacobs, *Principles of the Jewish Faith* (Basic Books, New York, 1964).

Jakob Jocz, *The Jewish People and Jesus Christ* (Allenson, Naperville, Ill., 1954).

Jacob Neusner, *Understanding Rabbinic Judaism: From Talmudic to Modern Times* (Ktav, New York, 1974).

James Parkes, *A History of the Jewish People* (Penguin, Baltimore, 1964).

Cecil Roth, *The Jewish Contribution to Civilization* (Sepher-Hermon Press, New York, 1956).

Fritz A. Rothschild, *Between God and Man: an Interpretation of Judaism from the Writings of A. J. Heschel* (Harper and Row, New York, 1959).

Peter Schneider, *Dialogue of Christians and Jews* (Seabury, New York, 1967).

Geza Vermes, *Jesus the Jew* (Macmillan, New York, 1974).

Herman Wouk, *This is My God* (Doubleday, New York, 1959).

CHAPTER THREE

Islam
Norman Anderson*

The religion of Islam[1] is one of the outstanding phenomena of history. Within a century of the death of its founder, the Muslim Empire stretched from Southern France through Spain, North Africa, the Levant and Central Asia to the confines of China; and, although Islam has since been virtually expelled from Western Europe and has lost much of its political power elsewhere, it has from time to time made notable advances in Eastern Europe, in Africa, in India, and in South-East Asia. Today it extends from the Atlantic to the Philippines, the Caucasus to Cape Town, and numbers some 500 million adherents drawn from races as different as the European from the Hausa-Fulani and the Aryan Indian from the Philippine tribesman; yet we can still speak of the 'world of Islam'. As Dr S. M. Zwemer justly remarks:

> 'A vertebrate and virile creed counteracts the centrifugal tendencies of nationality, race, climate and environment. The Arab is blood-brother to the Negro convert in Africa. The souls of Indian Muslims and Chinese Ahungs throb with indignation when they read of real or fancied wrongs committed against the Riffs of Morocco or the Arabs of Palestine. The question of Zionism is

* After studying law at Cambridge, Norman Anderson went to Egypt as a missionary in 1932. A period of intensive Arabic study was followed by student work, in the course of which he attended lectures in Arabic literature and Islamic law at the University of Cairo. On returning to England, after five years in the army, he gave a course of lectures in Cambridge on Islam, and then accepted a series of teaching posts in Islamic law. This has taken him to most parts of the Muslim world to study, do research, attend conferences and give lectures. He has also written a number of books and articles on the law and practice of Islam.

[1] "Islam," the correct name for the religion of Muhammad, is the infinitive of the Arabic verb "to submit" (*i.e.* to the will of God, as Muslims understand it); while "Muslim," the correct term for one who follows that religion, is the present participle of the same verb.

front-page news in the Muslim Press of India as well as in Egypt; it arouses the Muslims of Saʻudi Arabia, but also those of South Africa and Morocco. This unity and solidarity of the Muslim world through its religious creed, the pilgrimage to Mecca, the power of the press and the continued existence and power of the Sufi dervish orders cannot be denied.'[2]

None the less, it is exceedingly difficult to summarize in one short chapter the history, faith and practice of Islam, since that religion has been, and is, very differently interpreted by a wide variety of sects and schools of thought which would all claim the name of Muslim. In the main, therefore, it will be necessary to confine our attention to what may be termed the central current of orthodox Muslim thought, with only brief and inadequate allusions to other and rival interpretations. If one excepts, however, the more extreme sects of the Shiʻa – and, of course, those communities such as the Druzes and the 'Alawites which can no longer properly claim the name of Muslim[3] – it is to the person, life and revelations of Muhammad that both the faith and the practice of all varieties of Muslims are usually traced. And while the greater part of the alleged sayings and doings of the Prophet must be regarded as fictions which mirror the history of the theology, politics and jurisprudence of early Islam, yet there is a real sense in which R. A. Nicholson is correct when he says: 'More than any other man who has ever lived, Muhammad shaped the destinies of his people, and though they left him far behind as they moved along the path of civilization, they still looked back to him for guidance and authority at each step.'[4]

The origin of Islam

1. Muhammad's early life
Born about AD 570 at Mecca,[5] Muhammad was the posthumous son of an almost unknown father, and his mother died when he was only six. He was brought up first by his grandfather and then by his uncle Abu Talib, worthy members[6] of the family of Hashim and the tribe of Quraysh. Little is known with any certainty of his early life.

[2] S. M. Zwemer, *A Factual Survey of the Muslim World* (Loizeaux Brothers, New York, 1946), p. 5.

[3] See below, p. 106.

[4] R. A. Nicholson, *Literary History of the Arabs* (Cambridge Univ. Press, New York, 1969).

[5] Some scholars think considerably later, *e.g. c.* A.D. 580.

[6] According to orthodox theory they were outstanding members of the tribe, but this has been seriously questioned by Western scholars (*cf.* Sura 43:30, *etc.*). *Note:* The references to the Qur'an in this chapter adopt the verse numberings used, *e.g.*, in Rodwell's translation, from which the translations are usually, but not invariably, taken.

The Traditions tell us that his mother gave him to a Bedouin woman to suckle and that he passed his earliest years among nomad tents; that when twelve years old he went with his uncle to Syria, where he met a Christian monk named Bahira; and that he was later employed by a rich widow named Khadija, who put him in charge of her caravans and finally rewarded his fidelity with her hand in marriage. All that can be regarded as certain, however, is that he grew up an orphan[7] and attained economic security only when, at the age of twenty-five, he married Khadija, then (traditionally) a widow of forty. The marriage seems to have been remarkably successful, for Muhammad took no second wife until Khadija's death some twenty-five years later. A number of children were born to them, but only one daughter, Fatima, survived.

Whatever view may be taken about the Traditions concerning his boyhood, it is abundantly clear that the adult Muhammad soon showed signs of a markedly religious disposition. He would retire to caves for seclusion and meditation; he frequently practised fasting; and he was prone to dreams. Profoundly dissatisfied with the polytheism and crude superstitions of his native Mecca, he appears to have become passionately convinced of the existence and transcendence of one true God. How much of this conviction he owed to Christianity or Judaism it seems impossible to determine. Monophysite Christianity[8] was at that time widely spread in the Arab kingdom of Ghassan; the Byzantine church was represented by hermits dotted about the Hijaz with whom he may well have come into contact; the Nestorians were established in al-Hira and in Persia; and the Jews were strongly represented in al-Madina (Medina), the Yemen and elsewhere. There can be no manner of doubt, moreover, that at some period of his life he absorbed much teaching from Talmudic sources and had contact with some form of Christianity; and it seems overwhelmingly probable that his early adoption of monotheism can be traced to one or both of these influences.[9]

2. His revelations

It was at the age of about forty that the first revelation of the Qur'an (the 'Reading' or 'Recitation') is said to have come to him. It is recorded that a voice three times bade him 'Read (or recite) in the name of thy Lord . . .'.[1] Thereafter no more revelations came for

[7] Cf. Sura 93:6ff.

[8] So called because it affirmed that there was only one nature in the Person of Christ.

[9] Mecca, too, was a considerable market for foreign merchants, while the number of Ethiopic loan-words in the Qur'an is also significant. There were, however, Arab monotheists (named Hanifs) at the time, who were neither Jews nor Christians.

[1] Sura 96:1-5. According to one Tradition Muhammad replied, "I am no reader."

a considerable time; then suddenly, when passing through a period of deep spiritual depression, doubt and uncertainty, he is said to have seen a vision of the angel Gabriel which sent him home trembling to Khadija for comfort and covering, only to hear the Voice saying, 'O thou enwrapped in thy mantle, arise and warn. . . .'[2]

There can be little doubt that these passages mark his assumption of the prophetic office, although many Western scholars consider that certain poetical passages in the Qur'an which breathe the questioning spirit of the seeker rather than the authoritative pronouncement of the Prophet were composed at an even earlier date.[3] It seems, however, that Muhammad himself was at first doubtful of the source of these revelations, fearing that he was possessed by one of the *jinn*, or genii, as was commonly believed to be the case with Arab poets and soothsayers. But Khadija and others reassured him, and he soon began to propound divine revelations with increasing frequency. To the orthodox Muslim every verse in the Qur'an is the *ipsissima verba* of God, communicated to the Prophet by the archangel Gabriel (whom Muhammad seems to have identified with the Holy Spirit).

The earliest Suras[4] of the Qur'an reveal a marked simplicity of concept. They urge the moral response of man created by Allah, foretell the day of judgment, and graphically depict the tortures of the damned and the delights of what appears at first sight to be a very sensual paradise. Increasingly, however, the unity and transcendence of the one true God become the overriding theme. But the response was poor. His wife Khadija, his cousin 'Ali, his adopted son Zayd and a few more believed in his mission, but the leaders of the Quraysh tribe, influenced largely by their economic interest in the pagan rites and pilgrimage of the Ka'ba (a Meccan shrine containing a black meteorite) and by their opposition to his personal pretensions, ridiculed his claims. His preachings and revelations thereupon changed somewhat in tone. More and more he began to recount the histories of previous (mostly biblical) prophets, and to emphasize how they, too, had been mocked and ignored; sooner or later, however, judgment always fell on their traducers.

3. The Hijra

But the response in Mecca was still small, and in AD 622 Muhammad took the decisive step of withdrawing with his followers (some 200 in

Another Tradition, however, makes him reply, "What am I to recite (or read)?" *Cf.* Isaiah 40:6 ("A voice says, 'Cry!' And I said, 'What shall I Cry?' ").

[2] Sura 74:1. This is sometimes regarded as the first revelation of all.

[3] Officially, of course, these too are regarded as part of the divine revelation vouchsafed to him as a Prophet.

[4] Although by no means chronologically arranged (almost the opposite), a large measure of agreement has been reached regarding the date of the different Suras or their component parts.

all) to al-Madina, to which he had been invited by a party of its inhabitants who had met him during the pilgrimage, had accepted his claims and had prepared their fellow-townsmen for his advent. This withdrawal (or Hijra) proved the turning-point in Muhammad's career and has been appropriately chosen as the beginning of the Muslim era.[5] In Mecca he had been the rejected Prophet, pointing his countrymen to the one true God and warning them of judgment to come. In al-Madina he soon became statesman, legislator and judge – the executive as well as the mouthpiece of the new theocracy.[6]

Into the detailed history of the next few years we have no space to enter, but the key to its understanding seems to lie in his attitude to the Jews. There can be little doubt that Muhammad at first believed that he had only to proclaim his message to gain Jewish support – for was not his message the one, true religion preached by Abraham and all the patriarchs and prophets, ever-corrupted only to be proclaimed anew?[7] It was for this reason that his earlier references to the People of the Book (Jews and Christians) were almost uniformly favourable, and that he at first adopted several Jewish practices. At al-Madina he was soon to find, however, that the Jews would not accept his claims. More, they ridiculed his often inaccurate accounts of Old Testament incidents.[8] This was something he could not endure; for he had recounted these incidents as the direct revelation of God (introduced by such words as: 'This is one of the secret histories which We reveal unto thee. Thou wast not present when . . .'[9]) and had denied that he had learnt them from any human source. When it became apparent, therefore, that certain Suras of the Qur'an did not agree with those Old Testament records of the same incidents which he had previously confirmed as authentic, he was driven to allege that the Jews had corrupted, or at least misquoted, their own scriptures.[1] From this time, therefore, date his strictures on the Jews, his banishment or massacre of Jewish tribes, and the decisive turn from things Jewish to Arabia and Mecca discernible in his teaching.[2]

[5] For the rest of this chapter it seems best to give dates A.H. rather than A.D. They can roughly be converted into A.D. by adding 622 and deducting 3 for each century (to represent the difference between lunar and solar years).

[6] This is reflected in the new emphasis in his revelations on obedience to the Prophet (cf. Sura 3:29, 126; 4:17, 18, etc.) and on how he should be treated (cf. Sura 24:63, 64; 33:53; 49:2-5; 58:13, 14, etc.).

[7] Cf. Sura 10:94; 28:52, 53, etc.; 42:11.

[8] One example of this inaccuracy is, perhaps, the depicting of Haman as a minister of Pharaoh (Sura 40:38). But other examples of apparent confusion could be quoted.

[9] Sura 12:103. Cf. also Sura 38:69, 70; 69:43-46.

[1] Cf. Sura 2:70, 73, 169; 3:72; 4:48; 5:16, 45; 6:91, etc. It is not clear whether Muhammad believed that the Jews had actually tampered with their MSS or only falsified their reading or statement of the text.

[2] His religion, he now affirmed, was that of Abraham, who was neither Jew nor Christian (Sura 2:129; 3:60, 89).

Henceforth it was to the Ka'ba rather than Jerusalem that the Muslim community must turn in prayer,[3] and the pagan rites of the pilgrimage were to be purified and incorporated into Islam.[4]

This, again, made it necessary for him to impose his will on Mecca and led to his struggle with the Quraysh – although it also paved the way for the latter's ultimate acceptance of Islam. For our present purpose the details are largely irrelevant. Suffice it to say that, after a somewhat chequered career, Muhammad entered Mecca in triumph in 9 AH, smashed the idols which surrounded the Ka'ba, and had established Islam, nominally at least, throughout the greater part of the Arabian peninsula before his death at al-Madina in 11 AH. It remains, however, to form some estimate of his character and of the source of his revelations; and to this we must now turn.

4. Muhammad's character

The idea – once prevalent in Europe – that Muhammad was an impostor from first to last has, happily, been abandoned, and of his initial sincerity, at least; there seems no doubt. Most scholars explain his earlier revelations in terms of wishful thinking: they depict the misery and frustrations of his early life; his deep conviction that the Arabs, like the Jews or Christians, needed a Messenger and a Book; his longing to be favoured with some revelation that would mark him as their Prophet; and his eventual conviction that words, thoughts and stories which various external or internal stimuli summoned from his subconscious mind constituted instalments of this revelation.[5] It is true that he has sometimes been regarded either as an epileptic, a subject of hysteria,[6] a 'pathological case',[7] or as heir to an 'Ebionitic-Manichaean' doctrine of revelation (which may be thought to have safeguarded his sincerity if not altogether his moral character).[8] Others have occasionally taken a highly critical view and have suggested that there is reason to believe that his symptoms of revelation were sometimes artificially produced.[9] Alternatively, of course, the phenomena may be explained as symptoms of intermittent spirit-possession, as claimed by modern spiritist mediums. The sharp, staccato style of the earlier Suras of

---

[3] Sura 2:136-145.   [4] *Cf.* Sura 22:27ff., *etc.*

[5] *E.g.* C. S. Hurgronje, *Muhammadanism* (Putnam, New York, 1937).

[6] *Cf.* R. Bell, *Introduction to Qur'an* (Aldine, Chicago, 1970), p. 30, where Weil and Sprenger are cited in support of these two views.

[7] D. B. Macdonald, *Aspects of Islam* (Macmillan, New York, 1911), p. 72.

[8] See Tor Andrae, *Mohammed: the Man and his Faith* (Harper and Row, New York, 1960), pp. 260, 264-269.

[9] D. S. Margoliouth, *Mohammed* (Blackie, Glasgow, 1939), pp. 85ff. Also an article on Muhammad by the same author in J. Hastings (ed.), *Encyclopedia of Religion and Ethics* (Scribners, New York, 1908ff.). For another explanation see Fr. Buhl's article on Muhammad in the *Encyclopedia of Islam* (Humanities, New York, 1960-1969), p. 645.

the Qur'an can be explained on any of these hypotheses. But when we turn to the long, rambling accounts of Jewish patriarchs and prophets which occupy so much space in the later Meccan and earlier Madinese Suras, we are confronted by the fact that Muhammad sought (at this stage, at least) to satisfy the natural demand for some miraculous evidence of his Prophetic claims,[1] by ascribing exclusively to divine revelation his knowledge of stories which correspond in such detail with the Talmud that of their essentially Jewish origin there can be little doubt.[2] Thus R. Osborn felt compelled to conclude:

'To work (these stories) up into the form of rhymed Suras . . . must have required time, thought and labour. It is not possible that a man who had done this could have forgotten all about it, and believed that these legends had been brought to him ready prepared by an angelic visitor.'[3]

That it must have taken time is admitted by R. Bell, who substitutes 'suggestion' for the angelic messenger as the normal method of inspiration;[4] but this, as A. Jeffery points out, scarcely justifies Muhammad's exclusive ascription to revelation of material he must have obtained from human sources.[5]

The same problem confronts us once more when we turn to the later Madinese Suras, which contain detailed regulations on all sorts of subjects which govern the lives of Muslims to this day. In these Suras, too, Muhammad adopted the same form of rhymed prose, and represented the words as the direct utterance of God. There is considerable justification, therefore, for the conclusion of D. B. Macdonald:

'You cannot possibly imagine, in the case of long periods dealing with the law of inheritance or with the usages of marriage or with the quarrels of his followers, or emphasizing the position and dig-

---

[1] This demand was later met by the assertion that the very style of the Qur'an was inimitable (Sura 17:90) and by alleged angelic aid at the battles of Badr (Sura 3:11, 120, 121; 8:17) and elsewhere (Sura 9:25, 26; 33:9, 10, *etc.*). Later, Tradition added a plethora of apocryphal miracles of every kind, many of which find a place in the most "canonical" collections.

[2] His opponents alleged that "tales of the ancients" were dictated to him morning and evening (Sura 25:5, 6; *cf.* 16:105; 44:13). It is, however, clear that he was quite unable to read the Hebrew Old Testament (which is probably the true explanation of the adjective *umni* — sometimes rendered "illiterate" — applied to him in Sura 7:156) and completely misunderstood the very nature of the latter, which he conceived as a book "sent down" to 'Isa (Jesus; *cf.* Sura 5:50; 57:27, *etc.*) and to be "observed" like the Law (*cf.* Sura 5:70, 72).

[3] R. Osborn, *Islam under the Arabs*, p. 21.

[4] Bell, *Introduction to the Qur'an*, p. 35.

[5] In, *e.g.*, Sura 12:103; see *The Muslim World*, October 1954, p. 256.

nity of the Prophet himself – you cannot possibly imagine how all these things rose to him from his subconscious, that he did not know very well what he was saying and had not his own distinct objects in the way in which he expressed himself.'[6]

And this conclusion may be thought to find support from the fact that personal (and other) problems were sometimes solved by a divine revelation of the most convenient kind: it was thus that he was granted the right, unlike other believers, to have more than four wives[7] and dispensed from the normal obligation to divide his time equally between them;[8] that he escaped criticism when, in defiance of Arab custom, he married the divorced wife of his adopted son;[9] that he was absolved from his oath to have nothing more to do with his concubine Mary and extricated from the trouble caused thereby among his several wives;[1] and that his wives were bidden to veil themselves,[2] were threatened with a double punishment for unchastity,[3] and were forbidden to remarry after his death.[4]

Other scholars are so profoundly convinced of Muhammad's essential sincerity that they explain all these enigmas on hypotheses which avoid imputing to him any conscious imposture. I should myself regard it as at least possible that, in later life, he had become so convinced that he was the recipient of divine revelations, and so sure that he was the Prophet of God, that he genuinely mistook the pressure of circumstances and of his own inclinations for the divine voice that he believed he had so often heard. But this is primarily a problem for the psychologist, to which history can provide no solution.[5]

For the rest, his character seems, like that of many another, to have been a strange mixture. He was a poet rather than a theologian; a master improvisator rather than a systematic thinker. That he was in the main simple in his tastes and kindly in his disposition there can be no doubt; he was generous, resolute, genial and astute; a shrewd judge and a born leader of men. Occasionally, however, he could be cruel and vindictive; he could stoop to assassination; and he seems to have had a sensual streak. It is true that the size of his *harim* pales to insignificance beside that of Solomon and compares not unfavourably with that of David; that his virtues outshone those of his contemporaries, while his failings can scarcely have provoked comment in his day and generation; and that he introduced a number of genuine reforms. If he had been taken by his followers at his own valuation, adverse comment on his character would have been largely out of place. For the Qur'an, while it asserts his prophetic

[6] Macdonald, *Aspects of Islam*, p. 80.   [7] Sura 33:49.
[8] Sura 33:51.   [9] Sura 33:36-38.   [1] Sura 66:1-5.
[2] Sura 33:53 (*cf.* 32).   [3] Sura 33:30.   [4] Sura 33:53.
[5] But see A. Jeffery in *The Muslim World*, October 1954, p. 256; and R. Bell, *op. cit.*, pp. 31-36.

dignity in no uncertain terms, contains some express allusions to his mortality[6] and imperfection,[7] which seem quite incompatible with his semi-deification in some of those Traditions of his words and actions which soon assumed an importance second only in theory to the Qur'an itself. In words which are either put into his own mouth or regarded as addressed to him by God he is depicted as pre-existent ('I was Prophet when Adam was still between clay and water'); as the purpose of all creation ('Had it not been for thee I had not created the world'); and as the Perfect Man, the impeccable model on which all should mould their lives.[8] Such traditions are, of course, creations of a later date, invented by the Muslim community to put their Prophet on a par with the Christians' Christ. It is his misfortune rather than his fault, therefore, that it is with Christ rather than with David or Solomon that he is habitually compared – for in such company he cannot stand.

5. The Traditions

It is, moreover, one of the paradoxes of Islam that a religion whose founder expostulated against the veneration given to Christ, and who unequivocally asserted that he himself was a mere man, should have ended by advocating a slavish imitation of that founder's personal habits such as finds no parallel in Christianity or elsewhere. D. G. Hogarth justly remarks:

'Serious or trivial, his daily behaviour has instituted a Canon which millions observe to this day with conscious mimicry. No one regarded by any section of the human race as Perfect Man has been imitated so minutely.'[9]

The well-known Traditionalist, Ahmad ibn Hanbal (d. 241 AH), is said never to have eaten water-melons because, although he knew the Prophet ate them, he could never ascertain whether he ate them with or without the rind, or whether he broke, bit or cut them.

In such circumstances it is no wonder that the collecting of Traditions as to what the Prophet had said or done soon became a profession, and that men travelled all over the Muslim world to hear them from those to whom his scattered Companions had allegedly confided them. They were regarded as the uninspired record[1] of inspired

---

[6] Cf. Sura 3:138; 39:31, etc.

[7] Cf. Sura 18:110; 40:57; 41:5; 47:21; 48:2; 80:1-10, etc.

[8] Cf. Sura 33:21. The ethical influence of this doctrine has been lamentable.

[9] D. G. Hogarth, A History of Arabia (OUP, London, 1922), p. 52.

[1] Contrast the Qur'an, of which the most extreme form of verbal inspiration is asserted. It was written from eternity on the Preserved Tablet (Sura 85:22), whence it was sent down to the lowest heaven on the Night of Power (Laylat al-Qadr; Sura 97:1), to be revealed to the Prophet piecemeal as need arose

words and actions, and were handed down from mouth to mouth by a long chain of narrators whose names were always recorded in the first part of the Tradition (the *isnad*) as a guarantee of the veracity of the subsequent subject-matter (the *matn*). Very soon, however, fabricated Traditions began to flood the market, one man alone confessing before his death that he had invented some 4,000; and every vagary of political, philosophical or theological thought sought support in some alleged statement of the Prophet. At a later date the Traditions were collected and arranged by the great Traditionalists, some of whom made strenuous efforts to separate the true from the spurious. Unfortunately, however, they confined their criticism to scrutinizing the trustworthiness of the names in the *isnad* rather than the plausibility of the actual Tradition. Different collections are today accepted as authoritative by the different sects into which Islam has divided,[2] but in all cases such Traditions have taken their place beside the Qur'an as the primary source of Muslim theology, law and practice.[3] In addition, cheap collections of stories of the Prophet, some of very questionable propriety, have until recently, at least, still provided the popular religious literature of thousands.

6. Muhammad's view of Christianity

Of the tenets of Christianity Muhammad seems to have had a very superficial, and in part wholly erroneous, knowledge. In his early life he was as favourably disposed to Christians as to Jews: and even in his later life they seem to have come under less severe strictures than the latter.[4] 'Isa, the Qur'anic name for Jesus, was the Messiah, was born of a virgin and is called God's 'word' and 'a spirit from God'.[5] He was a great miracle-worker and one of the greatest of the prophets.[6] But the Qur'an depicts him as expressly disclaiming deity and seems

---

(Sura 17:107; 25:34). Others, however, interpret Sura 97:1 as meaning that the first revelation was vouchsafed to the Prophet on the Night of Power.

[2] The two most famous collections among the "orthodox" are those of al-Bukhari (d. 257 A.H.) and Muslim (d. 261 A.H.). The former, especially, is accorded a reverence almost equal to that of the Qur'an.

[3] A Tradition depicts Muhammad himself as having said, "What I have commanded to believers outside the Qur'an is equal in quality to the Qur'an itself, or even greater." This is obviously spurious, but illuminating.

[4] The deterioration in his attitude to Christianity at al-Madina may be explained as a reflection of his attitude to the Jews, as caused by the change in his own fortunes, or as representing his reaction to Monophysite as opposed to Nestorian theology. For Qur'anic references, cf. 2:59; 5:58; 57:27 (favourable); 5:21; 9:29, 31 (unfavourable).

[5] Cf. Sura 4:169, etc.

[6] For details, Muhammad's source was chiefly apocryphal works.

to deny that he ever died on the cross:[7] instead, it says that 'it was made to appear so' (or 'he was counterfeited to them') and that God caught him up to himself. This has always been interpreted by orthodox Muslims as meaning that someone else was crucified, by mistake, in his place.

It is interesting to speculate how Muhammad may have come to hold such views. Whether he came into contact with a heretical Christian sect called the Collyridians who actually worshipped the virgin, or merely misinterpreted the excessive veneration given her by some contemporary Christian groups, we shall probably never know. But there can be little doubt that he believed the Christian Trinity to consist of the Father, the Virgin and their Child. (*Cf.* the Ash'arite statement: 'God is One God, Single, One, Eternal. . . . He has taken to himself no wife nor child', and several verses in the Qur'an.[8]) It is not surprising, then, that he not only denounced the doctrine strongly but also repudiated the whole idea of the Sonship of Christ, understanding it as he did in terms of physical generation. Instead, the Qur'an depicts Christ as a prophet whose followers had deified both him and his mother against his will. Similarly, in his denial of the crucifixion, Muhammad may have been influenced by Gnostic views, by his hatred of the superstitious veneration, largely divorced from true theology or living experience, accorded to the symbol of the cross in seventh-century Arabia, or by his repugnance to believe that God would allow any prophet to come to such an end. He even believed that Christ had foretold the coming of another prophet, Ahmad (a variant of Muhammad); and Muslims frequently maintain that Christians have changed this reference into the predictions of the Paraclete in the later part of St John's Gospel.[9] The Traditions add that Christ is to come again, to marry and have children, to break the symbol of the cross, and to acknowledge Islam. In Muslim eschatology the second coming of Christ and the advent of the Mahdi[1] (the 'Guided One') are inextricably mingled. There is much truth in J.T. Addison's summary:

'If Muhammad's knowledge of a decadent form of Christianity had been thorough, or if the Church which he knew so imperfectly had been stronger and sounder, the relations between the two religions might have been very different. As it was, however, what passed for Christianity in his confused mind was a distorted copy of fragments of a notably defective original.'[2]

[7] Sura 4:156. Other verses, such as 3:48 and 19:34, seem to suggest that he did die.

[8] *Cf.* Sura 5:116 with 4:169 and 5:77-79; also Sura 19:35; 19:91; 112:3.

[9] Some think that Sura 61:6 rests on a confusion between "Paraklytos" and "Periklutos," a possible Greek equivalent for "Ahmad".

[1] An eschatological figure who will restore Islam in its purity and power.

[2] J. T. Addison, *The Christian Approach to the Muslims* (AMS Press, New York, 1942), p. 18.

The development of Islam

The scope of the present chapter allows no space for a summary of
the history of Islam after its founder's death. It is impossible, however,
to understand the present divisions of Islam – the different Shi'i
sects, the four Sunni schools, the Ibadis, *etc.* – without a passing
reference to their origin, and to this we must now turn. It should
always be remembered, however, that in Islam, as elsewhere, the
adoption of sectarian views by ethnical and local groups has often
been a mere expression in theological terms of an intense desire
for freedom from foreign domination and for the preservation of
exclusive traditions.

1. The Caliphate

Muhammad died, according to the best-supported view, without
having designated any successor (Khalifa or Caliph). As the last and
greatest of the Prophets he could not, of course, be replaced. But the
community he had founded was a theocracy with no distinction between church and state; and someone must clearly succeed, not to give
but to enforce the law, to lead in war and to guide in peace. It was
common ground, therefore, that a Caliph must be appointed; and
in the event 'Umar ibn al-Khattab (himself the second Caliph)
succeeded in rushing the election of the aged Abu Bakr, one of the
very first believers. But the question of the Caliphate was to cause
more divisions and bloodshed than any other issue in Islam, and
almost from the first, three rival parties, in embryo at least, can be
discerned. There were the Companions[3] of the Prophet, who believed in the eligibility of any suitable 'Early Believer' of the tribe
of Quraysh; there was the aristocracy of Mecca, who wished to
capture the Caliphate for the family of Umayya; and there were the
'legitimists', who believed that no election was needed, but that
'Ali, the cousin and son-in-law of the Prophet, had been divinely
designated as his successor.

Abu Bakr's short rule of two years was chiefly noted for the
'Wars of Secession' and (traditionally at least) for the first compilation of the Qur'an. On the death of the Prophet many tribes had
refused any longer to pay their dues, but Abu Bakr enforced obedience
by the sword. It was, indeed, the death in battle of many of those who
could recite the Qur'an from memory which is alleged to have convinced the Caliph of the necessity of reducing it to writing. On his
death, Arabia had been consolidated for Islam and the principle of
'fighting in the way of God', denounced by the Prophet at Mecca but
adopted with such signal success at al-Madina, had become the
watchword of the young Muslim state.

[3] Themselves at first subdivided into Meccan Emigrants and Madinese Helpers.

Before his death Abu Bakr designated 'Umar as his successor, and his election passed off without incident. He has been called the 'second founder of Islam', for in his Caliphate Syria, Mesopotamia, Persia and Egypt fell to the Muslim arms and many vital decisions were taken. He died without appointing a successor; and in the event 'Uthman was elected, himself an aged and pious 'Early Believer', but a scion of the aristocratic house of Umayya which had opposed the Prophet almost to the last. It was under his orders that the present recension of the Qur'an was prepared in 30 AH and all variant versions were destroyed. But his family proved his undoing and he died by the assassin's knife.

2. The Kharijis

The first actual schism, however, occurred during the Caliphate of 'Ali, who succeeded 'Uthman as the fourth and last of the 'Rightly-Guided' Caliphs. Two leading Companions, Talha and al-Zubayr, supported by the Prophet's widow 'A'isha, rose in revolt. They were beaten at the Battle of the Camel, where some 10,000 Muslims lost their lives – to the horror of the pious when they remembered that the Qur'an condemned to eternal damnation those who killed a brother Muslim without just cause. Soon, however, 'Ali had a much sterner foe to meet, for Mu'awiya, the Governor of Syria, marched against him on the plea of avenging the assassination of his kinsman 'Uthman, in whose death 'Ali was accused of complicity. At first 'Ali seemed again to be winning the day, but at the critical juncture of the battle Mu'awiya cunningly succeeded in inducing 'Ali to submit the question of the Caliphate to arbitration.

This deeply offended some of 'Ali's own followers, who held that this question should never be debated on such human terms; by his agreement to such a course 'Ali, they felt, had forfeited their allegiance. Still less, however, could they accord allegiance to Mu'awiya: so they seceded (*kharaju*) and held themselves apart from the body of 'apostate' Islam (whence their name of Kharijis). Thenceforward they drifted, split into rival sects, and constituted a perpetual thorn in the side of all authority:[4] to them the remainder of the Muslim community was far worse than the Jews or Christians, for the latter were people of a divine Book, while the former were mere apostates who should properly be killed at sight. They held that the Caliph should be elected on a basis of personal fitness, regardless of race or tribe; that the community should depose him if he went astray; that 'works' as well as 'faith' were necessary for salvation; and that one guilty of an unrepented sin ceased to be a believer.

[4] When beaten they retired, like true Bedouin, into the desert to recuperate. On one view they originated in those Arabs who opposed the predominance of the tribe of Quraysh; on another in the early Qur'an readers. Both theories may be in part correct.

There were, however, many sub-sects. Eventually they divided into two main divisions, the one more, the other less, extreme; and the descendants of the moderate party, the Ibadis, still survive in 'Uman, in East Africa, and among the Berbers[5] of Algeria and Tripolitania, today distinguished by little more than minor points of theology and law from the main body of Sunni (*i.e.* 'traditional' or orthodox) Islam.

3. The Shi'a

The vexed question of the Caliphate soon led, however, to a far more important schism – that by which the whole body of the Shi'a (the 'followers' or 'sect' of 'Ali) broke off from Sunni Islam. To the existence of a legitimist party who regarded 'Ali as the divinely appointed successor of the Prophet we have already referred; and such were not deterred in their devotion when the ill-starred attempt at arbitration accomplished little, when 'Ali continued to dispute the Caliphate with Mu'awiya until he died under a Khariji knife, or even when his elder son al-Hasan renounced his claim to succeed him in exchange for a princely stipend and retired to end his life in dissipation at al-Madina. Instead they maintained that al-Hasan had been poisoned by order of Mu'awiya, accorded him the title of 'Lord of Martyrs', and transferred their allegiance to his younger brother al-Husayn. The latter seems to have been made of somewhat better stuff; but when he rose in opposition to Mu'awiya's son Yazid I, he was killed, with most of his family, at Karbala' – a tragedy still commemorated each year throughout the Shi'i world by the Passion Play of the 10th of Muharram. The horror of this butchery of the house of the Prophet rallied much support, however, to Shi'i doctrines, and increasing numbers came to believe that God would never leave his people to impious rulers but that there must always be some divinely chosen Imam, or Leader; that 'Ali, so chosen, had been entrusted by the Prophet with esoteric teaching as to the real meaning of Islam which he had passed on to his descendants; and that after the death of al-Husayn the office of Imam and infallible teacher had passed, as some held, to Muhammad, son of 'Ali by a wife of the Hanafiya tribe, or, as the majority maintained, to 'Ali Zayn al-'Abidin, son of al-Husayn and great-grandson of the Prophet.

After the four 'Rightly-Guided' Caliphs the Caliphate became hereditary in the house of Umayya (41–132 AH) and Mu'awiya and his successors ruled for the most part as Arab kings of the old pattern, paying but scant allegiance to Islam. In such circumstances Shi'i propaganda prospered exceedingly, especially among the Persian 'clients'[6] (*mawali*), who saw therein a way to escape from Arab arro-

[5] Who probably adopted this "heresy" largely from racial particularism.

[6] On conversion to Islam these Persians were attached to Arab tribes in the subordinate position of the pre-Islamic client (originally either a stranger attached to the tribe or an ex-slave).

gance and a doctrine of the Imamate more compatible with their pre-Islamic attitude to their kings. A number of insurrections were put down, but Shi'i supporters eventually played a considerable part in the downfall of the Umayyad dynasty – only to find the throne seized, not for a descendant of 'Ali or the Prophet, but for those of the Prophet's uncle 'Abbas. Thus the Shi'a continued under the 'Abbasid dynasty (132–656 AH) as a vast and partly secret community, whose machinations came to the surface periodically in bloody rebellions, but who were continually weakened by their tendency to split into innumerable sub-sects. They split chiefly on the line of succession to the Imamate. Some, like the Kaysanis and Hashimis, held that it might pass to any child of 'Ali (*e.g.* Muhammad ibn al-Hanafiya); others, like the Zaydis, held that any descendant of al-Hasan or al-Husayn might duly establish himself; but the more general view, shared by the 'Twelvers'[7] and the Isma'ilis, was that the Imamate passed from father to son in the line of al-Husayn by a special form of transmission of a divine light-substance. But they differed, also, as to the nature of the Imamate. To the Zaydis the Imam was not supernatural but could give authoritative teaching; the 'Twelvers' went further, and believed in the infusion of a divine light-substance in the person of the Imam which made him infallible and impeccable; while the Isma'ilis went further still and, in their more extreme sub-sects, believed in a partial incarnation of the Deity either in one individual or, more commonly, in a succession of Imams.

But this did not exhaust their differences. Another common cause of division was their concept of a 'hidden' Imam. Periodically, in most of the Shi'i sects, men would become so attached to one Imam that they would refuse to believe that he had died; instead, he had only gone into hiding, whence he would one day re-emerge to bring in the Golden Age: others in the same sect, meanwhile, would transfer their allegiance to his successor. Sometimes the true explanation of this phenomenon seems to have been the intrigues of a series of adventurers who used the house of 'Ali as tools and themselves acted in the name of the 'hidden' Imam; at others the prudence of the Holy Family, who frequently refused the danger of leading those insurrections for which their followers seem to have been always ready.

The chief branches of the Shi'a found today are the Zaydis of the Yemen, the 'Twelvers' of Persia, India and Iraq, and the Isma'ilis (or 'Seveners') of India, Syria and East Africa. The Zaydis, who are the most moderate of the Shi'a, take their name from al-Husayn's grandson Zayd, who rose against the Umayyad Caliph Hisham and was killed in 122 AH. The Isma'ilis and the 'Twelvers' trace the Imamate not through Zayd, but his brother, Muhammad al-Baqir: the former to Isma'il,[8] son of Ja'far al-Sadiq, and his son Muhammad;

[7] For the origin of this name, see below. The Arabic is Ithna 'Ashariyya.
[8] The seventh in their line of Imams, whence the term "Seveners".

and the latter through Musa'l-Kazim, brother of Isma'il, to a certain Muhammad ibn al-Hasan,[9] who vanished in about 260 AH but is regarded as still alive, as communicating his teaching to his leading divines (who, unlike the Sunnis, still claim the right of *ijtihad*[1]), and as the Imam-Mahdi of the future. This is the state religion of Iran, where the Shah is regarded officially as his *locum tenens*.

But the strangest story in Muslim history is that of the Isma'ilis, among whom secret (*batini* or 'inner') teaching was carried to fantastic lengths. Emissaries were sent far and wide to make capital out of any anti-Government feeling, out of social and economic unrest, racial antipathies, or any form of scepticism. To the Kharijis their teaching was represented as Khariji, to the Shi'is as Shi'i, and to Persian nationalists as anti-Arab. Their technique seems to have been to excite doubt; to stress the need for an authoritative teacher; and to impose an oath of secrecy and implicit obedience. Initiates were passed, where suitable, through several grades, above the fourth of which, it seems, a mystic philosophy took the place of orthodox Islam. To this movement or conspiracy can ultimately be traced, through varying developments, the Qarmatians, who dominated Iraq at the end of the third century AH, practised a form of communism, and scandalized the Muslim world by carrying off the black meteorite from the Ka'ba at Mecca; the Fatimid dynasty, which ruled Egypt for so long; the Druzes of the Lebanon, who still worship as God al-Hakim, one of the Fatimids of Egypt; the Assassins, who terrorized Syria and Iraq from their fortresses in the times of the Crusades and to whose last Grand Master of Alamut the Agha Khan traces his descent today; the Nusayris or 'Alawites of Northern Syria, who deify 'Ali; and those rather shadowy figures of history, the Ikhwan al-Safa.[2]

Many of these sects are (or were) a law unto themselves, and to their beliefs no further reference can be made. The great majority of the Shi'a, however, fully accept the Qur'an, though they often differ from the Sunnis in its interpretation and even accuse the Caliph 'Uthman of having suppressed a number of verses favourable to 'Ali. They also accept the authority of the Traditions, though they reject the Sunni collections in favour of their own. In matters of faith and practice the differences between the two main divisions of Islam are considerable; but for the remainder of this chapter it will be necessary to confine our attention, in the main, to the Sunnis,

[9] The twelfth in their line of Imams, whence their name.

[1] See below, p. 108.

[2] A group which flourished at Basra in the middle of the fourth century A.H. and endeavoured to construct a universal system of religious philosophy. Their encyclopaedic "Epistles" (fifty in number) exercised a widespread influence.

who not only greatly preponderate in numbers, but can also fairly be regarded as the more natural representatives of the central stream of Muslim thought.

4. The four Sunni schools

It was not only about the Caliphate that controversy raged. The eternal conflict between the disciples of reason and of tradition has also been bitterly waged in Islam, both in law and in theology; and it is partly to this conflict that the development of the four orthodox schools of jurisprudence into which Sunni Islam is now divided owe their origin in the early 'Abbasid period. Such are the Hanafi or Iraq school, whose traditional founder was Abu Hanifa (died 150 AH), and which is followed today throughout most of the old Ottoman Empire and Northern India;[3] the Maliki or Hijaz school, which derives its name from Malik ibn Anas (died 179 AH) and which prevails in North and West Africa, Upper Egypt and the Sudan; the Shafi'i school, founded by al-Shafi'i, the 'father' of Muslim jurisprudence[4] (died 204 AH), which is followed in Lower Egypt, East Africa, Southern Arabia and South-East Asia; and the Hanbali school, which is named after the great Traditionalist Ahmad ibn Hanbal, and whose few modern followers are chiefly limited to the Wahhabis of Central Arabia.

In course of time a bitter conflict developed between the speculative jurists, as their opponents considered the Hanafi school, and the Traditionalists, a term claimed by all other schools – although they varied greatly in the degree to which they deserved it.[5] In reality the conflict had not developed in the time of Abu Hanifa and Malik, and the somewhat greater dependence of the latter on tradition and the former on speculation in constructing their systems can be adequately explained by the fact that Malik lived in the very city and milieu of the Prophet, whereas Abu Hanifa in Iraq had to deal with situations for which there was no prophetic precedent. Even so, however, Malik (in company with all the earlier jurists) felt free to follow his own opinion or appreciation of public welfare when circumstances required. But this was just what the extreme Traditionalists sought to exclude, for they held that human reason could not even deduce general rules from specific commands or prohibitions unless the revealed texts themselves indicated the underlying principle (*'illa*): man must not reason but obey. It was the dominant influence of al-Shafi'i which secured the eventual triumph of a middle course, which recognized the overriding authority of 'authentic' Traditions from the Prophet but fully accepted the need

[3] This is by far the most numerous school.
[4] *Cf.* article on "Usul" by J. Schacht in *Encyclopaedia of Islam.*
[5] Strictest of all were the Zahiris, a school of complete literalists which has since disappeared; next the Hanbalis; then the Shafi'is; then the Malikis.

for extending the divine texts by carefully-defined rules of analogy to cover the ever-changing eventualities of daily life. In reality, of course, customary law, administrative practice and the early jurists' sense of equity, expediency and the 'spirit of the law' were major elements in the early development of the Shari'a (as the divinely authoritative law of Islam is called), however much later jurists sought to conceal this fact behind a façade of unhistorical Traditions or a convenient doctrine which grew up concerning the inerrancy and binding force of the 'agreement' of the Muslim community.[6] Eventually, however, all four schools came to accept the Qur'an, the Sunna or practice of the Prophet (as preserved in the Traditions), the Ijma' or agreement of the Muslim community, and Qiyas or analogical deduction from these three, as the four main sources of the law – although the Hanafis in particular championed the right to depart on occasion from the conclusion to which a rigid application of analogy would lead in favour of a solution which they 'considered for the better'.[7]

All four surviving schools are now accepted as orthodox by Sunni Islam and in theory any Muslim may adhere to whichever he likes,[8] although in practice his choice will largely depend on where he happens to live. Most authorities now consider, however, that he may elect to follow one school in one particular and another in another – which may be a matter of considerable convenience. For centuries, however, this right, if it existed, was seldom exercised, and for the most part a Muslim, having chosen his school, was bound by its tenets in all particulars. In no case, moreover, could he go back to the original sources of the law and re-interpret them: this right, known as *ijtihad*, was regarded as having lapsed for centuries, and its place had been taken by the duty of *taqlid*, or accepting the rulings, down to the utmost minutiae, of a long series of successive jurists. Today, however, Muslim modernists are striving to free themselves from this bondage, and recent legislation in many Muslim countries concerning family law (in which alone the Shari'a is still widely applied) has been based on an eclectic principle of adopting whatever jurist's views seem, in each particular, most suited to modern needs.[9] Sometimes, moreover, reforms have been frankly based on a contemporary exercise of the faculty of *ijtihad*; and at others, what is really a wholly new rule has been clothed with traditional authority by the expedient of combining two different (and sometimes even incompatible) opinions in a single whole. This is technically known as *talfiq*.

[6] "My people will never agree upon an error," the Prophet was ultimately alleged to have said.
[7] *Istihsan. Cf.* the Maliki *istislah, etc.*
[8] "The disagreement of my people is a mercy from God" is the traditional saying of the Prophet quoted in this context.
[9] Space forbids a fuller treatment of this very interesting phenomenon.

5. The Mu'tazila

The same conflict between reason and tradition was waged even more bitterly in the realm of theology. As early as the beginning of the second century of the Muslim era we find a tolerably definite group of thinkers known as the Mu'tazila, who dissented from the traditional views and applied the solvent of reason to the dogmas of the Qur'an. They held that there was an intermediate state between belief and infidelity (and thus between bliss and doom). As the spiritual heirs of the still earlier Qadaris they upheld the freedom of the human will and denied that God predestined man's evil and unbelief; and they taught that God must of necessity act in accordance with justice and always do what was best for his creatures.[1] The orthodox, on the other hand, denied any intermediate state and held that all man's actions were decreed from eternity on the 'Preserved Tablet'; there could be no necessity upon God even to do justice, and whatever he did man must unquestioningly accept. More, they denied the very basis of human speculation, for they taught that man could not perceive or distinguish good and evil by the intellect: good and evil derived their nature solely from God's will and could be known only by his commands and prohibitions. There could be no theology or ethics, therefore, apart from revelation.

Yet another subject of debate concerned the nature of the Godhead. The Qur'an frequently makes use of anthropomorphic expressions: God is visible to some, at least, in the next world; he settles himself firmly on his throne; he stretches out his arm, *etc.* Among the Mu'-tazila all such expressions were spiritualized, and God was conceived as the most impersonal of Spirits: but the orthodox replied that the Qur'anic statements must be accepted as they stood (*bila kayfa*, 'without asking how') and neither explained away nor carried to their logical conclusion.[2]

Again, controversy raged around the question of the relation between the divine attributes (knowing, willing, speaking, *etc.*) and the divine essence – and the kindred dispute as to whether the Qur'an was created or eternal. The Mu'tazila held that the attributes were not *in* the divine essence, and thus in a sense separable, but *were* the divine essence; and the Qur'an was clearly created, for any other conclusion would involve making the Qur'an into a second God. To such arguments the orthodox replied that the attributes were neither identical with the essence nor distinct from it ('Not It, nor other than It' – an attitude which bears certain striking

---

[1] Partly for this reason they called themselves the "people of Unity and Justice". The "Unity" refers to the controversy, mentioned below, concerning the divine attributes.

[2] The view here attributed to the "orthodox" was in fact a *via media* between the Mu'tazila on the one hand and the extreme literalists or "anthropomorphists," of whom there were many, on the other.

resemblances to the Christian doctrine of the Trinity, particularly as developed by John of Damascus and other Greek theologians whose influence on Muslim thought has never received adequate attention). As for the Qur'an, its inscription and recitation might be created but its meanings were eternal, being none other than that divine speech which was one of God's eternal attributes. In this the influence of the Christian doctrine of the Logos is obvious.

But the Mu'tazila were never popular with the masses. For the most part they were regarded as heretics, sometimes persecuted and sometimes protected by constitutional authority. In the event it was an evil day for them when the Caliph al-Ma'mun tried to enforce their views by law and penalize all non-conformity. This decision was reversed by a subsequent Caliph, but the harm was done: the Traditionalist Ahmad ibn Hanbal, who had refused either to recant or even argue but contented himself with repeating Qur'anic texts and 'true' Traditions, won far greater support. As time went on, moreover, the Mu'tazila retired more and more into barren scholasticism, a fate which D. B. Macdonald says has fallen on all continued efforts of the Muslim mind.[3] But this dictum may no longer be true today.

6. The philosophers

Their place as the champions of reason was taken by the philosophers, al-Kindi, al-Farabi, Ibn Sina, Ibn Rushd, and their like. These men seem for the most part to have started from the position of sincere Muslims, but they also whole-heartedly accepted Greek philosophy, with all its contradictory theories, as part of the very form of truth. Their fundamental attitude was simple enough. The Qur'an was truth; Plato and Aristotle had both expounded the truth: the Qur'an and philosophy, therefore, whether Platonic or Aristotelian, must all be reconcilable. So to reconcile them they set out, with unconquerable spirit; and it was largely through these men that the philosophy and learning of ancient Greece was preserved and re-introduced into Europe.

7. The scholastic theologians

But parallel with the later development of Mu'tazili views there also grew up among the orthodox a party who were no longer content to assert that the statements of the Qur'an must be accepted as they stood and that any questioning was *bid'a* (innovation): instead, they came to use *kalam* (argument) in order to meet the *kalam* of the unorthodox. It was thus that the scholastic theology of Islam was born. The system must, of course, have been of gradual growth; but the chief credit has traditionally been given to al-Ash'ari (died

---

[3] *Cf.* D. B. Macdonald, *Development of Muslim Theology, Jurisprudence and Constitutional History* (Scribners, New York, 1903), pp. 158-159.

c. 320 AH). Brought up as a Mu'tazili and maintaining their views till he was about forty years old, he then swung over to the other side – and opposed at once the rationalism of the Mu'tazila and the gross anthropomorphisms of the more extreme Hanbalis. As developed by his followers, the Ash'ari system was the application to theology of an extreme atomic metaphysic.[4] To them, space was made up of a multitude of monads each of which has position, not bulk, and is separated from the next by absolute void; and they conceived of time as being similarly composed of a multitude of unrelated time monads. Any idea of causation they utterly rejected. They were compelled, however, to find some explanation of the harmony and apparent connection between one thing and another discernible in nature: and this they found in the will of God, absolutely free and untrammelled by any laws or necessities, which continually creates and annihilates the atoms and their qualities and thus produces all motion and all change. A man sees a beautiful flower; he decides to pick it; he stretches out his hand, plucks it and smells it. But this chain of causation is apparent only. In reality, God at each moment creates and recreates the atoms of the man's mind, of his hand, of the flower and of his nose in such a way as to create the thought, the apparent motion and the result: there is no mutual connection either of space or time except in the mind of God and by the continual exercise of his creative power. On such a basis human free will is neither more nor less than the presence, in the mind of man, of a choice created there by God; there is no order in the universe, and the distinction between miracles and what are normally regarded as the ordinary operations of nature virtually disappears. The sun does not warm, nor water wet: all that can be said is that God creates in a substance a being warmed (if God so wills) when exposed to the sun, and a being wet when submerged in water.

This system seems to have reached tolerably complete form by the beginning of the fifth century AH. For long it was bitterly opposed by the Hanbalis, while, as a *via media*, it was unpopular with the liberals also. Persecutions broke out, and the Ash'ari doctors were scattered to the winds. The reaction, however, was not long in coming and the influence of al-Ghazzali (died 505 AH) firmly established Ash'ari views as the dominant school of Sunni orthodoxy, although the slightly more liberal school of al-Maturidi still claims its adherents. Essentially, however, the Ash'ari teaching may be regarded as a vast negative, for it uses reason and logic to demonstrate the barrenness of both. Philosophy cannot even establish a chain of causation, so how can it arrive at any valid conclusion about the nature and attributes of God and the moral duties of man? For any knowledge of such matters man is entirely dependent on divine revelation, whether prophetic,

---

[4] *Cf.* Macdonald, *op. cit.,* pp. 202ff., on which this section is largely based.

through tradition, or direct, through the mystic's 'inner light'. The profound hold exercised by the former in Islam we have already noticed; and it is to the latter that we must now turn.

8. The mystics

Mysticism seems to have found some place in Islam from the very first. Muhammad himself, although in most ways one of the least mystical of men, was strongly drawn at times to solitude and fasting; and it was along the line of asceticism, of renunciation of the world and its evils, that mysticism first made itself felt in the religion he founded. There was much to encourage such an attitude in the influence of Christian hermits scattered about Arabia; in the development of that fear of hell fundamental to primitive Islam; and in the withdrawal of the pious, first from the obvious godlessness of some of the Umayyad Caliphs and then from the very limited piety of the Abbasids. From an early date, therefore, it must have been a comparatively common sight to see some wandering ascetic surrounded by his disciples, all dressed in the simple woollen garment from which the mystics or Sufis of Islam ultimately derived their name.

But mysticism soon began to develop along more speculative and philosophical lines. In this development it owed much to the Greek church; a good deal to Persian and, indeed, Indian influences; but most of all to Plotinus and the neo-Platonists.[5] It was only by refuge in mysticism that the Muslim philosopher could reconcile some of the teaching of the Qur'an with the abstractions of Greek philosophy; that the scholastic theologian could find any escape (other than that of blind obedience to Tradition) from the utter negation of Ash'ari metaphysics; and that the ordinary Sunni Muslim could find any poetry or warmth in his religion. When the scholastic theologians had done their work, the orthodox were left with no 'natural laws', no chain of causation, and no possibility of theology or ethics except in the revealed will of God. They must either be content to rely utterly on the prophetic revelation of the Qur'an and the Traditions, or they must supplement them by that 'minor inspiration' which, the Sufis asserted, God continuously vouchsafes to those who truly seek him. And to this the true Sufi steadfastly gave himself. He believed that the human soul had in it some spark of the divine, however imprisoned in the world of sense; that the human heart was the mirror, albeit dimmed and blurred, of the Deity. It was the mystic's duty, then, to wean himself from the world of sense; to cleanse this mirror, and direct it to God alone: he would then receive divine enlightenment.

But to the Muslim it was chiefly in ecstasy that the mystic received his revelations. A whole science developed as to how a state of ecstasy could be induced; and a man's piety was judged not by

[5] Probably reaching Islam largely through Christian channels.

his holiness of life but by the degree and frequency of his ecstatic states, for only in ecstasy did he realize his complete oneness with God. For centuries, however, the mystics were regarded with suspicion by the orthodox. Nor was this strange, for there was much excess. Emphasis on the spirit rather than the letter of the law led many to laxity not only of ritual but of morals. As so often in Islam, there was one law for the enlightened and another for the vulgar. Others were not content to claim divine enlightenment; they claimed the very fusion and union of their beings with God. For them the transcendental God of orthodox Islam was deposed, to be replaced by the Only Reality of the pantheist.[6] Perhaps the most famous of these extremists was al-Hallaj, who was put to death with great cruelty in 309 AH for claiming 'I am the Truth'.[7] It needed the immense influence of al-Ghazzali to secure the acceptance of the mystic way within the fold of orthodox Islam.

Later, there grew up the great Dervish Orders which are such a feature of Islam today. The Sufi principle of blind obedience of pupil to master became increasingly emphasized, and in course of time the group no longer broke up on the master's death but formed a lasting fraternity. Each Order traces its origin back to some famous saint whose miraculous powers are held to descend, in some degree, to his successors, and is made up both of professional dervishes and of non-professional adherents who visit the monasteries with greater or less regularity and take their part in the *dhikr*, or that form of repetition of the name of God adopted by the particular Order to induce a state of ecstasy. Membership of such fraternities was (until recently, at least) exceedingly common in Muslim countries, even, to some extent, among the professional classes.

The vast majority of the common people in all Muslim lands, moreover, believe implicitly not only in the miraculous powers of living holy men (*marabuts*, heads of Sufi orders, *etc.*), from whose prayers, touch, breath and saliva virtue (or *baraka*) is derived, but also in those of dead saints whose tombs they visit and whose intercession they implore. Under cover of this cult of saints much pre-Islamic animism has been retained in Islam.[8] Stones and trees which were worshipped in pagan days are now commonly connected with some prophet or saint, but the ancient ritual is largely preserved: thus pieces of the clothing of the sick or barren are still attached to the tree in the belief that some of the 'soul-stuff' resident therein will thereby be transferred to the suppliant. Similarly, relics of holy men and charms of all sorts are in constant demand, as pro-

---

[6] Even the central dogma of Islam, the divine Unity, was interpreted by the Sufis as denying any reality outside God.

[7] This is the reason traditionally given for his execution, although the real reason may well have been political.

[8] As also, of course, in much popular Christianity.

tection against the evil-eye, against the *jinn*, and especially against
the genie- (or devil-) mate[9] which is believed to dog the footsteps
of every mortal. In popular Islam the pure monotheism of the
creed has been diluted with a wealth of animistic survivals, some
sanctioned by the Prophet and some plainly contrary to his teaching,
which still hold multitudes of simple people in the bondage of fear,
tabus, and financial exploitation. To gain protection, healing,
fertility, *etc.*, the aid is also regularly invoked of a whole hierarchy
of saints, led by the Qutb[1] (or 'Axis', *i.e.* greatest living saint) and his
various grades of lieutenants, who periodically hold a sort of mystic
parliament, untrammelled by space or time.

The faith and practice of Sunni Islam

The faith and practice of Islam are governed by the two great
branches of Muslim learning – theology and jurisprudence – to both
of which some reference has already been made. Muslim theology
(usually called 'Tawhid' from its central doctrine of the Unity of
the Godhead) defines all that a man should believe, while the law
(Shari'a) prescribes everything that he should do. There is no
priesthood and there are no sacraments. Except among the Sufis,
Islam knows exhortation and instruction only from those who consider themselves, or are considered by others, adequately learned in
theology or law.

Unlike any other system in the world today, the Shari'a embraces
every detail of human life, from the prohibition of crime to the use of
the toothpick, and from the organization of the State to the most
sacred intimacies – or unsavoury aberrations – of family life. It is
'the science of all things, human and divine', and divides all actions
into what is obligatory or enjoined, praiseworthy or recommended,
permitted or legally indifferent, disliked or deprecated, or positively
forbidden. The Muslim may certainly consult his lawyer[2] as to
what he may do without incurring any legal penalty; but he may
also consult him as a spiritual adviser as to whether acts of which
other systems of law take no cognizance are praiseworthy or blame-
worthy before God. Until recently the pride and power of the 'Ulama',

[9] The *qarin* or *qarina* (see Sura 41:24; Sura 50:22, 26, *etc.*). This mate is regarded
as malignant, jealous, the cause of physical and moral ill, of hatred between
spouses, barrenness, miscarriage, *etc.* except when frustrated by religion or magic.
[1] His two favorite haunts, it seems, are the Ka'ba at Mecca and one of the city
gates in Cairo, on which shreds of the clothing of petitioners can always be
found. Elsewhere the Ghawth (Succourer) is regarded as the chief, and the
term Qutb used for the next grade in the hierarchy.
[2] In most Muslim countries there is also an official called the "Mufti," whose
function it is to give legal opinion (*fatawi*) to individual applicants, to the
government, or to the judges of the Shari'a courts (the "Qadis").

or doctors of the law, was enormous; but their influence is, in general, much decreased today. The whole science of law is known as *fiqh* and formed for centuries the primary study of the pious Muslim.

1. The articles of faith

In Islam no official redaction of the articles of faith (*'aqa'id*) has ever existed, though much has been written on the subject. For our purpose, however, the summary attributed by tradition to the Prophet himself can conveniently be adopted: that a Muslim must believe 'in God, his Angels, his Books, his Messengers, in the Last Day, and . . . in the Decree both of good and evil'.

The importance attached to the doctrine of God can easily be seen from the space allotted to this subject in any Muslim treatise on theology. The fundamental concept is his Unity; and most of the finest passages in the Qur'an are concerned with this subject. Some of them are very fine indeed; and there can be no doubt that Muhammad was passionately concerned that men and women should not lavish the worship due to God alone on a plethora of far less worthy objects. Much the same is true of many of his followers.

In orthodox Islam, however, this concept has been pressed to logical – but unreal – lengths in the doctrines of *mukhalafa* (difference) and *tanzih* (removal, or making transcendent). By the former, God is declared to be so different from his creatures that it becomes virtually impossible to postulate anything of him (he has styled himself the Merciful, for instance, but this quality need have no connection with the human concept of mercy). The latter, on the other hand, so negates any semblance of impermanence and so emphasizes his self-sufficiency as to deny that he can in any way be affected by the actions or attitude of his creatures. As we have seen, moreover, the God of orthodox Islam maintains the whole creation in being, moment by moment, by a continual miracle: even the impression of choice present to the mind of men is his creation. He is the source of both good and evil; his will is supreme, untrammelled by any laws or principles, whatever they may be; whom he will he forgives, and whom he will he punishes.[3] His nature and qualities are chiefly revealed in his ninety-nine 'most beautiful Names', frequently repeated by the pious as they finger their rosaries;[4] some of these names are constantly on all Muslim lips, whether in prayer, salutation, bargaining or swearing, while others are regularly used as charms and talismans.

[3] The Muslim God can best be understood in the desert. Its vastness, majesty, ruthlessness and mystery — and the resultant sense of the utter insignificance of man — call forth man's worship and submission, but scarcely prompt his love or suggest God's.

[4] In popular Islam the rosary is regularly used (1) as an aid to prayer, (2) as a talisman to indicate whether some proposed action is propitious (*istikhara*), and (3) as a magical agency for healing.

A belief in angels is absolutely enjoined on the Muslim: he who denies them is an infidel. Orthodox Islam acknowledges four arch-angels (Jibril or Gabriel, the messenger of revelation – much confused with the Holy Spirit; Mika'il or Michael, the guardian of the Jews; Israfil, the summoner to resurrection; and 'Izra'il, the messenger of death) and an indefinite number of ordinary angels. They are created of light, do not eat or drink or propagate their species, and are characterized by absolute obedience to the will of God. Two recording angels attend on every man: the one on his right records his good deeds, and the one on his left his sins. There are also two angels called Munkar and Nakir, who visit every newly-buried corpse in the grave. Making the corpse sit up, these angels examine it in the faith. If the replies are satisfactory it is allowed to sleep in peace, but if it does not confess the apostle they beat it severely, some say until the day of resurrection. Animals are said to hear its cries, although mortals cannot.

Between angels and men there are also a multitude of creatures called *jinn*. These are created of smokeless flame, eat and drink, propagate their species, and are capable of both belief and unbelief. Muhammad was sent to them as well as to men, and good *jinn* now perform all the religious duties of Muslims.[5] The disbelieving *jinn* – who are often called *'afarit, shayatin*,[6] etc. – were turned out of the first three heavens when Jesus was born, and out of the last four when Muhammad was born. Sometimes, however, they still go eaves-dropping to the lowest heaven, whence they occasionally pass on information to human magicians; but they are chased away by the angels with shooting stars if observed.[7] Reference has already been made to the *qarina* or *shaytan*[8] which is believed to dog every mortal's footsteps and tempt him to evil.

The *jinn* often appear as animals, reptiles, *etc.*, or in human form. Frequently, moreover, a human being will be 'possessed' by one of them – as all poets and soothsayers were held to be; and in such circumstances relief is frequently sought in exorcism, particularly by the incense, dance and sacrifice of the 'Zar' ritual.[9] The devil (Iblis or al-Shaytan) is normally regarded as a fallen angel or *jinn* who disobeyed God's command to the angels to do homage to Adam. He is now the arch-tempter of mankind and the progenitor of the *shaytans*, *'ifrits*, and all evil *jinn*.

Orthodox Islam is divided as to how many prophets there have been: some say 124,000, some 248,000, and some an indefinite

---

[5] See Sura 72:1, 2, 15, 16 and elsewhere, as well as many Traditions.

[6] Singular, *'ifrit, shaytan*.   [7] Sura 72:8, 9, *etc.*

[8] Devil-mate; see p. 114, footnote 9.

[9] This is purely animistic in origin but is now practiced throughout a great part of the Muslim world, particularly among women. Pamphlets have been written against it, however, by the learned.

number. The Qur'an names twenty-eight: most are biblical,[1] while two (Luqman and Dhu'l-Qarnayn) have been generally identified with Aesop and Alexander the Great respectively. Some 313 of these prophets are named apostles, and the six greatest brought new dispensations: such are Adam, Noah, Abraham, Moses, 'Isa (Jesus) and Muhammad.[2]

Among them these prophets brought some 104 divine books. A hundred of these, of minor length, were vouchsafed to Adam, Seth, Enoch and Abraham, but are now lost; while of the four major Scriptures the Law was 'sent down' to Moses, the Psalms to David, the Gospel to Jesus, and the Qur'an[3] to Muhammad. All originally corresponded to a heavenly prototype and all comprised the same central message.[4] To the allegation that the Jews subsequently corrupted their Scriptures we have already referred, and the same charge is brought against Christians by way of explanation of the New Testament references to the deity and cross of Christ, and other doctrines denied by Islam.[5]

The last day (the resurrection and the judgment) figures prominently in Muslim thought. The day and hour is a secret to all, but there are to be twenty-five signs of its approach. All men will then be raised; the books kept by the recording angels will be opened; and God as judge will weigh each man's deeds in the balances. Some will be admitted to paradise, where they will recline on soft couches quaffing cups of wine handed to them by the Huris, or maidens of paradise, of whom each man may marry as many as he pleases.[6] Others will be consigned to the torments of hell. Almost all,[7] it would seem, will have to enter the fire temporarily, but no true Muslim will remain there for ever. Other Traditions picture a bridge as sharp as a sword over the pit, from which infidels' feet will slip so

---

[1] Including Sulayman (Solomon), who is credited with having attained an extraordinary power over the *jinn* and animals. He is thus virtually regarded as the patron saint of "white" magic.

[2] Islam has come to believe in the impeccability (*'isma*) of all prophets — but against the plain teaching of the Qur'an.

[3] Not only bibliolatry but bibliomancy flourishes in popular Islam. The Qur'an must be touched only by the ritually pure; certain chapters are of special power against sickness and demons; and extracts are used for every sort of charm.

[4] *Cf.* Sura 26:195f.; 3:75; 6:92; 35:28; 46:11, *etc.*

[5] *Cf.* Sura 2:141; 3:64. Also *cf.* 5:116, 117.

[6] These are distinguished from such mortal women as shall attain paradise (whose position and marital delights are shrouded in obscurity) by most commentators, although some suggest that virtuous wives become Huris hereafter. For the Huris see Sura 44:54; 55:56, 58, 70-74; 56:34-36. *Cf.* also Sura 2:23; 3:13; 4:60. But it is only fair to add that the sensual delights of paradise are interpreted in metaphorical terms by more spiritually-minded Muslims.

[7] Except martyrs, and some others.

that they fall into the fire, while the feet of Muslims will stand firm.[8]

Finally, a Muslim is required to believe in God's Decrees. As we have already seen, the orthodox belief is that everything – good or evil – proceeds directly from the divine will, being irrevocably recorded on the Preserved Tablet. While the Mu'tazila and others have challenged this view, there is much to support it in the Qur'an – although other passages certainly assume the moral responsibility of mankind. The fatalism to which this cast-iron view of pre-destination logically leads has, in the past, played a large part in the daily lives of millions of Muslims. To this can be partially attributed the lethargy and lack of progress which, until recently, has for centuries characterized Muslim countries.

The Shari'a, as we have seen, covers an exceedingly wide field and no systematic division was ever reached. Sunni Muslims some-times classify it into obligations regarding worship ('*ibadat*), obliga-tions of a civil and personal nature (*mu'amalat*) and punishments ('*uqubat*). Only a very sketchy treatment will be possible here and we shall confine our attention to the main religious observances, to such fundamental social institutions as marriage, divorce and slavery, and to a few representative crimes.

2. The 'Five Pillars'
The religious observances of Islam include the 'Five Pillars' (or foundations) of religion: *i.e.* the recital of the creed, prayer, fasting, almsgiving, and the pilgrimage. The creed (*Kalima*) is a simple one: 'There is no God but God, and Muhammad is the Prophet of God' – but disputes have arisen as to what its proper recital involves. The more exacting require that it be recited aloud at least once; that it be understood with the mind and believed in the heart; that it be recited correctly and professed without hesitation; and that it be held until death. To the majority of Muslims, however, a mere recital of the creed is enough to enrol a new convert in the ranks of Islam; and any more stringent requirement is left to divine omni-science.[9]

Ritual prayer plays a big part in the life of a devout Muslim. He is required to pray five times a day at stated hours, and in this many are most faithful. He may pray alone, in company, or in a mosque; but he must pray in Arabic and must follow a set form of words and a strictly prescribed ritual of stances, genuflexions and prostrations which differs slightly as between the four orthodox schools. Particularly important is the congregational prayer at noon on Fridays, attendance at which is incumbent on all adult male Muslims

[8] Muslim eschatology is a curious hodge-podge of Jewish, Christian and animistic legends and folklore.

[9] The creed – the shortest in the world – is repeated by many Muslims several times a day, in every sort of context.

who live in a sufficiently large community. This service includes a weekly sermon; but the Muslim Friday is not prescribed as a day of rest. Prayer is valueless, however, unless offered in a state of ritual purity,[1] so the law books contain detailed rules concerning the different forms of purification (*wudu'* and *ghusl*), when each is required and how it must be performed.[2] It may also be remarked that in *popular* Islam there is little connection between prayer and ethics: a man who rises from prayer to cheat will be rewarded for the prayer and punished for the cheating, but the one is commonly regarded as having little or no bearing on the other. But this is by no means universally true.

During the month of Ramadan (the ninth month of the Muslim year) all Muslims except the sick, travellers, pregnant women, nursing mothers and young children are required to fast from first dawn until sunset. This involves complete abstinence from all forms of food, drink, smoking or sexual intercourse. As the Muslim year is lunar, the fast sometimes falls at mid-summer, when the long days and the intense heat make complete abstinence, especially from water, a severe ordeal. On the whole, however, it is rigidly observed, especially among the lower classes; and even if the more sophisticated often break their fast in secret, the majority observe it outwardly. The fast is much esteemed as inculcating both self-control and sympathy with the poor and destitute. But it may be observed in passing that the average family spends nearly twice as much in Ramadan on the food they consume by night as in any other month on the food they eat by day. It is probably the consequent curtailment of sleep as much as the rigours of fasting which has such a marked effect on the general output of work during Ramadan.

The emphasis Muhammad put on almsgiving is among the best points in the teaching of Islam, although it has inevitably encouraged the indigent in Muslim lands (for whom, it must be added, little other provision was, in the past, normally made). Himself an orphan,

[1] Muslim prayer — at least in its prescribed form — seems to partake more of the nature of a continual acknowledgement of God's sovereignty than of communion with him. This is shown (*inter alia*) by the insistence on ritual purity and the use of Arabic, an unknown tongue to three-quarters of the Muslim world.

[2] The basic idea, it seems, is not the virtue of physical cleanliness, but the need for cleansing from demon pollution. This has been brought out by Wensinck and Goldziher. The fact that the passing of the hands over one's sandals may often be substituted for washing the feet supports this view. To a similar preoccupation with demons may be traced the use of some object as a *sutra* (that which covers or protects) to mark off the place of prayer ("It protects from the demons"); certain regulations about the position of the fingers and the covering of the back of the head during prayer and about the exact times of prayer; and parts of the ritual followed in the special prayers for rain, *etc.* See S. M. Zwemer, *The Influence of Animism on Islam* (Macmillan, New York, 1920), pp. 43-65.

the Prophet felt keenly for the destitute and needy. The legal alms
enjoined on the Muslim are, however, less than the Jewish tithe, being
limited to one-fortieth of money and merchandise, one-tenth or
one-twentieth of agricultural produce (the rate depending on the
method of irrigation employed), and different rates for cattle, *etc.*
These legal alms are known as *zakat* and are to be distinguished from
sadaqa, or free-will offerings.

We have already referred to the pilgrimage. The actual ceremonies
were taken over from the idolatrous superstitions of pre-Islamic
Arabia[3] and retained by the Prophet, with a new significance, possibly
to conciliate the people of Mecca. At the same time, however, he
destroyed the idols which surrounded the Ka'ba and professed to
restore the Black Stone to the position it held in the days of Abraham.[4]
The performance of the pilgrimage at least once is enjoined on
every adult Muslim, male or female, who can afford it, and its value is
emphasized in such Traditions as 'Every step in the direction of the
Ka'ba blots out a sin', and 'He who dies on the way to Mecca is
enrolled in the list of martyrs'. As a consequence, thousands assemble
in Mecca each year from all over the Muslim world and return to
their homes with a greatly heightened sense not only of the international character of Islam but of its essential solidarity.[5]

It is these Five Pillars, and particularly the profession of the creed
and the performance of prayer and fasting, which chiefly make up
the practice of Islam to the average Muslim. He who acknowledges
the Unity and Transcendence of God, pays him his due in prayer
and fast, and accepts Muhammad as the last and greatest of the
Prophets, may well, indeed, have to taste the fire, but hopes that he
will not, like the infidel, remain in it for ever – through the timely
intercession of the Prophet. The most heinous of sins are polytheism,
apostasy, scepticism and impiety,[6] beside which social sins and all
subtler forms of evil pale into comparative insignificance.

---

[3] Including the sacrifice (Sura 22:33-38), which is also offered at the same
time by Muslims who are not performing the pilgrimage. This is the Feast of
Sacrifice ('Id al-Adha), substituted for the Jewish Day of Atonement, but without the same significance.

[4] It is still, however, kissed and rubbed, as in the pagan ritual. Similarly, the
practice of pilgrims being shaved and cutting their nails at the end of the
pilgrimage rites, and the custom of burying the hair and nail clippings in
sacred soil (see Burton, *Pilgrimage*, Vol. II, p. 205), are obvious survivals of
animism, where hair and nails are regarded as especially charged with "soul-
stuff" and as channels of spiritual communion on the one hand, or deadly
means of enemy attack on the other. Such superstitions still survive in Muslim
(and other) lands quite apart from the pilgrimage ritual.

[5] But often, it has been widely remarked, with little moral uplift.

[6] *E.g.* a man can be forgiven for breaking the divine law, but scarcely for
denying or doubting its validity in the least particular.

3. The Jihad

One more religious duty (other than the Five Pillars) deserves notice: the duty of Jihad or Holy War. It is incumbent in general on all Muslims who are adult, male and free to answer any legally valid summons to war against the infidels; and he who dies in a Jihad is a martyr and assured of paradise. The Jihad, with the fanatical courage it evokes, has been by no means limited to the inception of Islam, and its possible relevance for the future can scarcely be ignored. The matter is greatly complicated, however, by the question as to when such a summons can be regarded as legally valid. From the earliest times Muslims have divided the world into Dar al-Islam, where Islam reigns supreme, and Dar al-Harb (the Abode of War), where the rule of Islam should be extended, if necessary by war. Polytheists were given the option of conversion or death, while the People of the Book (Jews or Christians) were given the additional alternative of submission and tribute.[7] Of recent years the question has arisen, however, as to whether a country which has once been Dar al-Islam but has subsequently fallen under a non-Muslim government is to be regarded as having lapsed into Dar al-Harb. The majority view seems to be that Jihad may be proclaimed only by that lawful Caliph – or, presumably, by the Mahdi[8] whom even Sunni Muslims expect; that it is lawful only in Dar al-Harb; that a once Muslim country does not lapse into Dar al-Harb as soon as it passes into the hands of infidels, but only 'when all or most of the injunctions of Islam disappear therefrom'; and that it is in all cases essential that there should be 'a possibility of victory for the army of Islam'.[9]

4. Family law

Under the general heading of *mu'amalat*, or dealings between man and man, the Shari'a includes provisions corresponding to the modern law of contract and tort (or 'obligations'), in addition to those matters of personal status which are almost the only part of the Shari'a applied by the courts today in the majority of Muslim lands. This law of personal status includes marriage (*nikah*), divorce (*talaq*), paternity, guardianship, maintenance, wills and inheritance.

Marriage is enjoined on every Muslim, and even the ascetic orders commonly marry. The Prophet is reputed to have said, 'Marry women who will love their husbands and be very prolific, for I wish you to be more numerous than any other people', and again, 'when a man marries he perfects half his religion'. A Muslim may have as many as, but not more than, four legal wives at any one time; and he may also cohabit with as many slave concubines as he may possess. 'Marry

[7] And similar treatment was also in practice given to Hindus in India, and others whom Muslims would officially regard as polytheists.
[8] Their concept, however, differs from that of the Shi'is. *Cf.* pp. 101, 104.
[9] *Cf.* T. P. Hughes (ed.), *Dictionary of Islam* (W. H. Allen, London, 1935), "Dar al-Harb".

what seems good to you of women, by twos or threes or fours . . . or what your right hand possesses.'[1] Besides Muslim women, he may marry Jewesses or Christians and these may continue to practise their own religion (although, if they do, the spouses will have no mutual rights of inheritance); but a Muslim girl can be given in marriage only to a co-religionist and there must be no intermarriage of any sort with polytheists. Among the Shi'a temporary marriage (mut'a or enjoyment) is allowed, based partly on the Qur'anic precept: 'Forbidden to you also are married women, except those who are in your hands as slaves. This is the law of God for you. And it is allowed you, besides this, to seek out wives by means of your wealth, in modest conduct, but not in fornication. And give them their reward for what you have enjoyed of them, as God has commanded. But it shall be no crime in you to make agreement over and above the command.'[2] Sunni Muslims deny the Shi'i interpretation of this verse and, although most of them admit that Muhammad at one time countenanced mut'a, maintain that he afterwards forbade it – although it seems in fact to have been first forbidden by the Caliph 'Umar. It is still practised among Shi'is, especially on journeys, when it often approximates to licensed prostitution: mut'a marriage, moreover, may be in excess of the four legal wives to which the Shi'a, too, are otherwise limited. In general, however, the Sunnis and Shi'is concur (except in details) in the rules governing the prohibited degrees of relationship and the dower, maintenance and discipline of wives: for a man who fulfils his own obligations may insist on his wife observing strict purdah and may enforce marital obedience even by personal chastisement.[3] When a man has more than one wife he is enjoined to divide his time equally between them and to treat them with impartial justice (except, the classical commentators add, in those matters of the affections which are beyond his control): if he fears he will not be able to do this he should confine himself to one.[4] This verse is much quoted by modern Muslims to prove that the Prophet virtually enjoined monogamy, since few, they maintain, can behave impartially to a plurality of wives. As a consequence, polygamy has now been forbidden in Tunisia, and restricted in a number of other Muslim countries. Muslims also emphasize that Islam has always allowed married women to keep their property.[5]

A Muslim may divorce his wife at any time and for any reason – although in some Muslim countries considerable efforts have been made in recent years to impose restrictions on such unilateral repudi-

[1] Sura 4:3.

[2] Sura 4:28. It is noteworthy that one early reading included the phrase "for a fixed term".

[3] Sura 4:38.   [4] Sura 4:3.

[5] Any other rule would, of course, be farcical in view of the husband's unfettered freedom of divorce.

ation. When the words of divorce are said only once or twice, the divorce is normally revocable at the option of the husband during a short period known as the '*idda*, until the expiration of which the marriage is regarded in such cases as still extant and the husband is responsible for his wife's lodging and maintenance; but thereafter a new marriage contract is required before the parties can come together again. When the words of repudiation are said three times, the divorce is immediately irrevocable; the parties cannot remarry unless the wife has first been properly married to, and divorced by, another man.

The husband's responsibility for maintaining his divorced wife during the '*idda* is disputed between the schools. Should it transpire, however, that the wife – however divorced – is pregnant, the husband is responsible for her lodging and maintenance until she gives birth to his child. The children of divorced women remain with their mothers until they reach a certain fixed age,[6] and during this period the divorced wife can claim from their father both money for their support and wages for her suckling and care; but after this age the father has an absolute claim on them. It is divorce rather than polygamy – which is decreasingly common – which causes untold suffering to women, and widespread social evil, in Islam today. For it frequently happens that a man will marry a young girl and then, when she has borne him several children and become prematurely aged, divorce her in favour of a younger wife. The divorced wife can then only return to her father or brothers, to be greeted with anything but enthusiasm and to be married off, if the opportunity occurs, to a second husband, however undesirable. It is not surprising, then, that Muslim women, having little sense of marital security, contrive to put something by as a precaution against divorce and normally feel more affection for their blood-relatives than their husbands. The better type of Muslim father not infrequently attempts to deter a prospective son-in-law from frivolous divorce by stipulating a large dowry for his daughter, the greater part of which is payable only on divorce or at the husband's death (to augment the one-eighth of his estate to which alone his widow will in most cases be entitled).

In this connection it must be remembered that the seclusion of women in orthodox Islam means that a large number of men marry women whom they have never seen; that minors (and in some schools virgin daughters of mature age) can be compulsorily married by their fathers; and that in most cases such pressure can be brought to bear on an adult girl – whether virgin, widow or divorcee – as to make that consent to a marriage which the law requires more nominal than real. But much of this has now been changed in some countries.

[6] This age varies considerably as between school and school. The Hanafi rule is seven for a boy and nine for a girl (or, according to a variant view, nine and eleven respectively), while the Shi'is say weaning for a boy and seven for a girl. The other schools are more generous to the mother.

Women, on their part, can in no circumstances divorce their husbands,[7] and it is only in certain schools and particular contingencies
that they can appeal to the courts to annul the marriage. But widespread reforms in this matter, too, have been introduced in one
Muslim country after another.

Islam sanctioned slavery and the slave trade, and the unlimited
right of concubinage which a Muslim enjoyed with his female slaves
has already been mentioned. This extended even to married women
captured in war,[8] and opened the door to terrible abuse during the
early wars of expansion, when almost any woman in a conquered land
could be considered a slave by capture. Stanley Lane-Poole had
some strong words to say on this subject:

'It is not so much in the matter of wives as in that of concubines
that Muhammad made an irretrievable mistake . . . . The female
white slave is kept solely for the master's sensual gratification and
is sold when he is tired of her, and so she passes from master to
master, a very wreck of womanhood. Kind as the Prophet was
himself towards bondswomen, one cannot forget the unutterable
brutalities which he suffered his followers to inflict upon conquered
nations in the taking of slaves. The Muslim soldier was allowed to
do as he pleased with any infidel woman he might meet with on
his victorious march. When one thinks of the thousands of women,
mothers and daughters, who must have suffered untold shame and
dishonour by this licence, one cannot find words to express one's
horror.'[9]

It must be remembered, however, that this was in an age when
the practices of war, all the world over, were distinctly brutal.
In general, it should be said, slaves have been well and kindly treated
in Muslim lands – including, in many cases, the slave concubine,
who was often given no worse treatment than the free wife. Theoretically, of course, the slave had no legal rights: he was a mere chattel, in his
master's absolute power. But this was mitigated in practice by the
influence of both Qur'anic injunctions and prophetic maxims
extolling kindness to slaves and the virtue of setting them free, and
Muhammad himself set a good example in this respect.

5. Other provisions
It can only be mentioned in passing that in matters of diet the flesh

---

[7] Although sometimes husbands expressly delegate to their wives the right to
divorce themselves in certain contingencies.
[8] Muhammad quieted the consciences of those who hesitated to violate women
captives whose husbands were still alive by the divine Revelation already quoted
on p. 122 (Sura 4:28). In other words, captivity annuls marriage.
[9] Preface to *Selections from the Koran*.

of the pig, blood[1] and alcohol are forbidden to the Muslim; that gambling is tabu; and that the law of contract is largely dominated by the prohibition of usury. As a consequence purists disapprove of insurance policies and most forms of investment, if the rates of interest, however modest, are fixed rather than subject to fluctuation. But in this, as in many other respects, the letter of the law has known many evasions almost from the first, and is now largely ignored. Circumcision is officially described as 'recommended' rather than 'commanded':[2] it is, however, regularly practised and is regarded by the average Muslim as one of the essentials of his faith.

The last section of the Shari'a deals with 'punishments' or criminal sanctions. These provide, *inter alia*, for the murderer to be executed by the family of his victim; for one who causes physical injury to another to be submitted to the like; for the thief to have his right hand cut off; and for the adulterer to be stoned and the fornicator beaten.[3] The severity of these penalties is considerably mitigated, however, by such rigorous rules of evidence that the punishment, in most cases, can seldom be imposed. But much lawlessness and injustice result from the fact that it is commonly regarded as legitimate for a man to kill his wife or close female relative for unchastity. In the vast majority of Muslim countries, however, all these (and many other) provisions of the Shari'a have been superseded by a modern civil and criminal code, and Shari'a courts now confine themselves almost exclusively to questions of personal status, gifts, endowments, inheritance and pre-emption,[4] for while it would be regarded as infidelity avowedly to change the Shari'a in any particular, those who pay it lip-service as a divinely authoritative system for the Golden Age often quietly put it on one side in this workaday world in favour of a system more suited to modern requirements. In Arabia, however, the Shari'a is still largely applied.

To many survivals of animistic beliefs and practices in popular and even orthodox Islam references have already been made. The Prophet himself not only firmly believed in the *jinn* and in the power of the evil-eye, but apparently allowed spells to ward off the latter provided only the names of God and of good angels were used. He is also believed to have said that 'the saliva of some of us cures our sick by the permission of God'. The average Muslim today firmly

---

[1] Animals should be slaughtered by cutting the jugular vein, after pronouncing the name of God.

[2] Except by the Shafi'is, who regard it as "commanded" for both boys and girls. Female circumcision — whether in a more or less extreme form — is practiced in most Muslim lands.

[3] The distinction is whether the guilty party has ever enjoyed a valid married life.

[4] *Shuf'a:* a right of the co-owner compulsorily to take over a third party's purchase of another co-owner's share in jointly-held land. It is sometimes extended to a neighbour's right over adjacent property.

believes that man can utilize the power of demons and *jinn* by means of magic, and the practice of 'counter-magic' to protect from evil of all sorts is exceedingly common. Amulets are worn by animals and men, particularly children; magic cups, many of them made in al-Madina, are used both for healing and for more sinister purposes; and ceremonies such as the 'Aqiqa[5] sacrifice for new-born children (so called both from the first cutting of the infant's hair and the sacrifice offered on its behalf) are widespread. Some of these survivals can be traced to pre-Islamic Arabia, while others have been adopted from the conquered lands.

Islam today and tomorrow

1. The enigma

To the detached observer Islam is always something of an enigma. It is not so much its phenomenal expansion in the first century of the Muslim era, which can largely be explained by the decadence and internal divisions of the surrounding kingdoms; by the tough physique and war-like spirit of the Arab armies, intoxicated as they were by the happy alternative of fabulous plunder or paradisical delights; and by the military genius of Khalid ibn al-Walid and others. It is not primarily the splendour of the medieval Caliphate, with its enlightened patronage of learning and its absorption of many alien cultures. The essence of the enigma is the power which the religion of Islam has exercised over its adherents all down the ages and the attraction it has so often exerted over non-Muslims – with the result that it is still, in parts, a missionary religion, and is still winning new converts.

The enigma can, of course, be partially explained. It is easy enough to understand some, at least, of the factors which make Islam such a powerful attraction to 'pagans' – whether in some parts of Africa or elsewhere. They are impressed by the manifest superiority of the Muslim's concept of one true God; for pagans themselves acknowledge, if pressed, the existence of one creator god, although they habitually ignore him in practice and spend their lives trying to propitiate those far more immanent and malignant spirits which so often hold them in a thraldom of fear. Islam, moreover, represents a monotheistic religion which they commonly believe to be indigenous, rather than Western, in origin – and this is a powerful attraction to those who are in revolt against colonialism and all its ways. In point of fact Islam, of course, springs from much the same part of the world as Christianity, but it normally reaches pagans in a far more indigenous dress. Again, they are attracted by its world-wide brotherhood, by the vivid sense of belonging to a

---

[5] In many respects this should probably be regarded as Jewish rather than animistic in origin, but there has been much accretion.

comparatively closely-knit community, and by the fact that as Muslims they will be welcomed by other Muslims when they leave their villages for work in some big town. This sense of community is reinforced by the fact that Muslims frequently pray together, always fast together, and often enjoy the even closer brotherhood of a Dervish Order. By comparison with Christianity, moreover, the dogmas of Islam appear to be simple and comprehensible to the human mind. It is also, I think, fair to say that, whereas many Muslims boast of a moral code which they believe to be less hypocritical (and much more possible of attainment) than what they regard as the impossible demands of a Christianity professed in theory, but abandoned in practice, in the degenerate West, many pagans are attracted by the fact that Islam makes ample provision for the polygamy and easy divorce to which they are accustomed.

To the Copts who embrace Islam year by year in Egypt, on the other hand, the motive is almost always the pressure of economic inducements, the desire to divorce a Christian wife, a determination to marry a Muslim girl or, indeed, the desire to escape from the status of what may justly be described as a somewhat second-grade citizen of a minority community. The Muslim himself, moreover, feels a certain superiority not only to pagans, but even to those Arab representatives of ancient Christian churches who have tended to develop minority characteristics under centuries of Muslim dominance; who do not fully share his cultural heritage, steeped as this is in his religion; whose ritualistic forms of worship seem little short of idolatry compared with the dignified simplicity of that of the mosque; and whose ignorance of the essentials of the Christian gospel is frequently profound. By contrast, the Muslim boasts a doctrine of God which, whatever its ultimate inadequacy, appears comparatively intelligible, a code of ethics whose ample limits are determined by certain express prescriptions, and a conviction that his Prophet has absorbed and retained all that was best in previous revelations.

Yet there is much on the other side. The basic teaching of Islam, however lofty some of its theology and simple its ritual, is at best a cold and formal religion, as the widespread devotion to the Dervish Orders goes to prove. And its central doctrine of the Unity of the Godhead has been carried to a length which – even to human logic, itself manifestly inadequate in this context – raises as many problems as it solves. Again, the finer soul is often repelled by the very laxity of moral standards which attracts others and especially by the degradation of Muslim womanhood. That the religion still grips the greater part of its adherents, including women, and can still arouse their fanatical devotion, remains an enigma. A partial explanation may, perhaps, be found in the remainder of this chapter. For the rest, the reader can only be asked to ponder some of the suggestions made in the final chapter of this book.

2. The crisis

Today, however, Islam is facing one of the greatest crises of its history. This crisis arises from the very nature of Islam when exposed to the conflicting currents of modern life, and can, perhaps, be summarized under three headings.

First, Islam is essentially a *dominant* creed. It is not so much that Islam has sometimes been imposed at the point of the sword[6] as that the whole attitude of Muslims to non-Muslims is conceived as that of victor to vanquished, of ruler to ruled. While polytheists were, according to one view, to be given the alternative of conversion or death, the 'People of the Book' could become *dhimmis* or protected subjects. As such, their persons and property were guaranteed and they might follow their own religion and personal law; but they had to pay tribute, were excluded from full citizenship, and were frequently compelled to show various marks of deference to their Muslim neighbours. In the event their treatment differed widely from age to age and place to place. Sometimes they enjoyed much freedom and even attained high office. At other times they suffered severe persecution. But all this has raised a difficult problem for the modern Muslim who may have to live under a Christian or other non-Muslim government. Such a circumstance seems never to have been contemplated by early Islam and has given rise to a number of difficulties, among them (as we have seen) that of knowing where the line should now be drawn between Dar al-Islam and Dar al-Harb and where a modern Jihad is obligatory or legitimate. There can be little doubt that it is the Muslim's instinctive feeling that the practice of his religion cannot properly be reconciled with living under the sovereignty of a non-Muslim government which, almost as much as the growth of nationalism, has led to the strenuous efforts witnessed during the last few decades in many parts of the Muslim world to achieve either nominal or complete independence: and by the success of most of these efforts Islam may be said in this respect partially to have weathered the storm. Even when independence has been won, however, the Muslim state must still face the problem of its relations with non-Muslim countries in a world where almost perpetual war or isolation is no longer practicable. An up-to-date example of this problem is provided by the Declaration of Human Rights now accepted by all Muslim states, except Sa'udi Arabia and the Yemen, which are members of the United Nations Organization. Yet the clause which affirms a man's right to change his religion if he so wishes runs directly counter both to the Islamic law of apostasy and to the practice of most of the Muslim states concerned.

Secondly, Islam is essentially a *theocratic* creed. In Islamic theory, as we have seen, church and state are one, and the canon law is the

---

[6] The mass conversion of subject peoples was much more commonly the result of sustained social and economic pressure.

law both of the state and the individual, in every aspect of life. Not only so, but Dar al-Islam is regarded as one and indivisible, united under a single Caliph. In 1923, however, the Ottoman Caliphate (itself of doubtful legality, since the Caliph was not of Qurayshi descent) was abolished; and the rivalries of Muslim powers will probably prevent any speedy revival. Meanwhile, modern states, strongly nationalistic in character, have grown up in many parts of the Muslim world, in most of which parliamentary institutions and responsible governments have been set up on the Western pattern – only to be replaced, in many cases, by military dictatorships. The subjects of such states, moreover, are granted (nominally, at least) equal citizenship without distinction of religion[7] and a secular state law has to a great extent been substituted for the Shari'a. Much of this seems incompatible with historic Islam. Yet again, although Islam is usually declared to be the state religion, the state itself is largely secular in character. Where, in the past, popular literature, holidays and entertainments were almost exclusively religious or semi-religious in character, today the press, radio and cinema are mainly secular. In such circumstances the old cohesion and theocratic structure of Islam has been greatly weakened. It must be remembered, however, that Islam represents a complete system of public and private life as well as a religion, in the narrower sense of that term; and that many who are influenced by secularist tendencies still staunchly support the Muslim social order.

Thirdly, orthodox Islam is essentially a *dogmatic* creed. The Muslim should accept the Qur'an as the *ipsissima verba* of God, the Traditions as equally inspired in content though not in form, and the whole vast structure of Muslim law and theology developed by generations of jurists and commentators as binding on his mind and conscience. There have been, of course, progressive movements in Islam, as we have seen. But for centuries orthodox theology has been dominated by Ash'arism.[8] It is no wonder, then, if the modern student, who is thoroughly up to date in Western thought, finds a fundamental conflict between the teachings of the orthodox and the so-called 'assured results of modern science'. In so far as the interpretations and developments of medieval jurists and theologians are concerned, it would no doubt be possible (and the attempt is in fact being made) for modern Muslims to sweep away this superstructure and insist on the right to go back to the Qur'an and the

[7] It should be observed, however, that the "freedom of religion" guaranteed by the Constitution of many modern Muslim states is usually limited in practice to freedom for non-Muslims to worship in their own way. Any attempt to propagate another religion is severely restricted, and no provision whatever is made for a Muslim to change his faith. This is not true of Pakistan, where both preaching and change of faith are allowed, provided only that Islam, the Qur'an or Muhammad is in no way attacked.

[8] *Cf.* pp. 110ff.

Traditions and re-interpret them in terms of modern life. Ultimately, however, the student or reformer is usually faced with a far deeper problem in some explicit dictum of God or his Prophet. This clearly makes the path of reform a slippery one. It must be almost equally difficult for the modern critical mind to accept the whole of the Qur'an as the *ipsissima verba* of God or for the enlightened moral conscience to regard the life of the Prophet as the ideal pattern of human conduct. But it is just as difficult to compromise on either of these issues and remain an honest Muslim. Yet it must be remembered that the strength of any system of thought or belief, and its ability to command men's loyalty, are by no means proportionate to its truth or intrinsic spiritual power, and that Islam has many features which still command the allegiance of most of its adherents.

In the more recent past, moreover, other – and in some respects quite contrary – tendencies have become increasingly apparent. There has been a considerable revival of Islam, particularly in the Arab countries, as a political and religious rallying-point against the 'political, economic and cultural imperialism' of the West. This revival is largely the result of purely political factors: in particular of Arab opposition to the 'fragmentation' policy pursued by Britain and France between the wars and to the menace of Zionism and Israel.[9] As a consequence there has been an increasing tendency to identify nationalism with Islam and national culture with Islamic culture; and this has led to more severe restrictions on foreign missions and to discrimination against non-Muslim minorities. The revival, however, has been religious rather than spiritual; it has been marked by a larger number of officials going on pilgrimage and a greater emphasis on using the Shari'a as a source of law, but has not been accompanied, in general, by any decrease in official corruption or general rise in moral standards.

3. The future

How, then, is the Muslim world reacting to these problems and what does the future hold? To this, only the most sketchy answer can be given. Four different tendencies may be observed.

First, there is a tendency towards *secularism*. The outstanding example of this is provided by Turkey. There, Islam no longer holds the official position it held in the past; the law has been entirely secularized; the Roman alphabet has been introduced; 'Westernism' has been adopted in a wholesale fashion; and monogamy is (officially) enforced by law. True, the mosques are still open and the majority of the population certainly regard themselves as Muslims; but the real religion of many of the élite seems to be Turkish nationalism. Tunisia and Iran are more moderate examples of the same tendency, which seems for the present to be chiefly limited to the non-Arab

[9] Coupled, of course, with a general upsurge of pan-Arabism.

countries where Islam may be regarded as foreign to their native culture. Alternatively, however, the movement may be described as an attempt to separate personal religion from social and national life – and with this many Muslims elsewhere are in sympathy.

Secondly, there is a tendency towards *reaction and xenophobia*. This directly opposite tendency can be seen most clearly in the Wahhabi movement and the early history of the Sanusi Order. Both these movements, in their different ways, represent a puritanical revival in which an attempt was made to get back to primitive Islam. Both alike, moreover, tried to abjure the West and all 'innovation' (*bid'a*) and find salvation in the Qur'an and the Traditions of the Prophet. The intrusions of television, air-travel, oil-wealth and the ever-increasing economic problems and pressures of modern life have, however, made these movements, from the religious point of view, lost causes. Both reaction and xenophobia also show themselves in such organizations as the Muslim Brotherhood in some of the Arab countries, Fadayan Islam in Iran and Jama'at-i-Islami in Pakistan. Not long ago the Brotherhood was exceedingly strong, but the movement has more recently been proscribed in Egypt; and while it seems possible that the Jama'a commands considerable popular support, it is probably much less powerful than it was a few years ago.

More promising from the Muslim point of view is the third tendency, towards *modernism*. This finds its best example in movements such as that led by the late Muhammad 'Abduh in Egypt, which attempts a synthesis of piety with progress, of Western science with the Muslim faith. The key to any such attempt must necessarily lie along the line of the revival of the right of *ijtihad*[1] and the abandonment, or metamorphosis, of the doctrine of 'agreement'.[2] Like the Wahhabis and Sanusis, these modernists would sweep away most of the accretions of the Middle Ages and seek to reinterpret the original sources of Islam. Unlike the reactionaries, however, they would try to reconcile their reinterpretation with the realities of modern life. The attempt is a bold one and beset, as we have seen, with acute problems: but the movement has already exerted a very widespread influence and continues to expand.

The difference between such movements as the Jama'at-i-Islami and what may be termed Islamic modernism may be illustrated by their attitudes to the legal injunctions in the Qur'an. The Jama'at believes that any attack on polygamy is impious; that insurance and fixed rates of interest should be prohibited; that the severe penal sanctions prescribed in the Qur'an for theft, adultery and apostasy, *etc.*, must be reintroduced; and that the control of policy in Pakistan must be reserved for Muslims. The modernists, on the other hand,

[1] See above, p. 108.   [2] See above, pp. 107f.

believe that the Qur'an itself includes such stringent conditions for polygamy that it should certainly be restricted, and may even be forbidden, by statutory enactments; that the prohibition of 'usury' in the Qur'an should be interpreted in terms of the exploitation of a brother Muslim's poverty and need rather than interest on investments in banks or companies; that changes in circumstances justify changes in law (as, for example, in regard to slavery and criminal sanctions); and that modern democracy is thoroughly compatible with Islam.

Fourthly, yet another tendency is represented by such movements as Ahmadiyya. Founded by Mirza Ghulam Ahmad Khan towards the close of the last century, the Ahmadiyya movement has more recently split into two sects, the smaller comparatively orthodox and the larger definitely heterodox. The latter teaches that Christ was in fact crucified but later revived in the tomb, escaped, and made his way to Kashmir where he died at the ago of 120 years; that Mirza Ghulam was both the long-expected Mahdi and the Messiah, and even a reincarnation of Krishna as well; but that instead of world conquest by battle, his mission was peaceable and his holy war to be waged by propaganda. Many Muslims would feel that the extremists' claim that their founder was a prophet in his own right, albeit within the revelation of Islam, amounts to apostasy; but they would accept the more moderate party, which regards their founder as a reformer rather than a prophet, as still within the Islamic fold. Such movements as those of the Babis and Baha'is, however, have clearly ceased to be Muslim. It was in 1844 that Sayyid 'Ali Muhammad of Shiraz proclaimed himself to be the *bāb* or Gateway of divine truth. In essence this is an extreme modern development of certain Shi'i views. But the majority of his followers recognized as his successor Baha' Allah (Mirza Husayn 'Ali Nuri), who issued a modified form of his master's teaching and whose followers are called Baha'is. This claims to be a universal religion, the wholesale adoption of which would bring world-wide peace: it teaches the duty of doing harm to no-one, of loving one another, of bearing injustice without resistance, of being humble, and of devoting oneself to healing the sick. It has no clergy, no ceremonial and countenances no austerities. It will be noticed that the common element in these very different movements is the propagation of what is really a new religion under the pretext of reforming Islam.

What, then, of the future? Prophecy is notoriously dangerous, but the possibilities seem limited to four:
1. The advent of a new Mahdi to lead a sweeping movement of reaction. But while the possibility of the inception of some such movement can never be discounted, the chances of its ultimate success seem negligible.

2. The triumph of materialism, whether in the form of secularism among the richer and better educated classes or of Communism among the undernourished masses. This seems a very real danger, signs of which are already apparent in places. It is often argued, of course, that Islam is a powerful bulwark against atheistic Communism, for Islam is utterly opposed to unbelief. But it is noteworthy that both Islam and Communism represent monolithic ideologies which demand total allegiance; so it would not seem strange for a Muslim who had lost faith in his religion to switch right over to a totally different ideology which may appear to proffer a more credible programme.

3. The development of a new Islam through an extension of such movements as that of Muhammad 'Abduh – an Islam which, while it retains the name and professes to carry on the spirit of the past, differs radically from Islam as this has been known down the centuries.

4. A reappraisal, on a wholly unprecedented scale, of the claims of Christ – never yet adequately presented to the Muslim world.

Since this last subject is frequently misunderstood, a final word must be added concerning past relations between Christianity and Islam and the effect of Christian missions in Muslim lands today. Until the last hundred years, contacts between Christianity and Islam were almost uniformly unfortunate. Allusion has already been made to the distorted impressions of Christian doctrine which clouded the Prophet's mind; to the divisions of Christendom and the decadence of the church which facilitated the Muslim conquests and swelled the number of Muslim converts; and to the ineffective witness of the remnants of ancient churches still surviving in Muslim countries – probably still one of the greatest obstacles to the evangelization of Islam. To these adverse factors must be added that solitary approach of Western Christendom to Islam throughout the Middle Ages, the Crusades – when not only did the followers of the Crucified adopt a method he had expressly condemned, but when they often failed to show to any moral advantage beside their 'Saracen' foes. Apart from a few isolated individuals such as Raymun Lull, the church did nothing to take the authentic gospel of Christ to the Muslim world until the modern era of Christian missions – and even these have been regarded as all too often an ally of colonialism.

Even in this period the results have been meagre, compared with those from any other faith. This is partly due to the extreme poverty of the effort made, for missions have tended to concentrate on more productive fields; partly to the barriers of antagonism which have had to be broken down; and partly to the law of apostasy in Islam (death for a man and death or perpetual imprisonment for a woman) or its more common modern equivalent of loss of family, inheritance and employment, with a possible danger of death by poison. In the event the effect of missionary work has been threefold: a widespread influence on social conditions and moral outlook through the medical and educational services which were virtually non-existent before the missionaries came; a more restricted circle of persons genuinely touched by the gospel, who for one reason or another have stopped short of open confession; and a still smaller number of brave souls who have taken their place as open members of the Christian church.

It is noteworthy, however, that in the last few years there has been a widespread movement in parts of Indonesia, where converts from Islam to Christianity now number tens of thousands. There has also been a not wholly insignificant number of converts in parts of Africa, in Iran, and elsewhere. But we have yet to see what would happen if the gospel of the living Christ were adequately presented to the hundreds of millions of men and women who make up the world of Islam.

Bibliography

1. *The Qur'an*

A. J. Arberry (ed.), *The Koran Interpreted* (Macmillan, New York, 1955).

R. Bell, *Introduction to the Qur'an* (Aldine, Chicago, 1970).

Kenneth Cragg, *The Event of the Koran: Islam in its Scripture* (Allen & Unwin, London, 1972).

Kenneth Cragg, *The Mind of the Koran* (Allen & Unwin, London, 1973).

N. J. Dawood (ed.), *The Koran* (Penguin, Baltimore, 1964).

Arthur Jeffery, *The Qur'an as Scripture* (Moore, New York, 1952).

R. Roberts, *Social Laws of the Qur'an* (Humanities, New York, 1971, repr. of 1925 ed.).

W. Montgomery Watt, *Companion to the Koran* (Humanities, New York, 1967).

2. *General Works*

Aziz Ahmad, *Islamic Modernism in India and Pakistan 1857-1964* (OUP, New York, 1967).

Aziz Ahmad, *Studies in Islamic Culture in the Indian Environment* (OUP, New York, 1964).

Tor Andrae, *Muhammad, the Man and his Faith* (Harper, New York, 1960).

A. J. Arberry, *Aspects of Islamic Civilization* (Univ. of Michigan Press, Ann Arbor, 1967).

A. J. Arberry, *Religion in the Middle East* (Vol. 2 on Islam) (Cambridge Univ. Press, New York, 1969).

A. J. Arberry, *Sufism* (Hillary, New York, 1956).

Kenneth Cragg, *The Call of the Minaret* (OUP, New York, 1964).

Kenneth Cragg, *Counsels in Contemporary Islam* (Aldine, Chicago, 1965).

Kenneth Cragg, *The House of Islam* (Dickenson, Encino, California, 1969).

Encyclopaedia of Islam (Luzac, London, 1919-1938); new ed. in progress (Brill, Leiden, 1954-).

H. A. R. Gibb, *Muhammadanism* (OUP, New York, 1953).

A. Guillaume, *Islam* (Penguin, Baltimore, 1969).

P. K. Hitti, *The Arabs: A Short History* (5th ed., St. Martin's, New York, 1969).

P. M. Holt *et al.* (eds.), *The Cambridge History of Islam*, 2 Vols. (Cambridge Univ. Press, New York, 1971).

Arthur Jeffery (ed.), *Islam: Muhammad and his Religion* (Liberal Arts Press, New York, 1958).

Bernard Lewis, *The Arabs in History* (Hutchinson, New York, 1966).

C. E. Padwick, *Muslim Devotions* (Allenson, Naperville, Ill., 1961).

R. Roolvink, *Historical Atlas of the Muslim Peoples* (Harvard Univ. Press, Cambridge, Mass., 1957).

J. Schacht and C. E. Bosworth (eds.), *The Legacy of Islam* (OUP, London, 1974).

W. Cantwell Smith, *Islam in Modern History* (Princeton Univ. Press, Princeton, 1957).

W. Montgomery Watt, *Muhammad, Prophet and Statesman* (OUP, New York, 1961).

J. A. Williams (ed.), *Islam* (an anthology of Muslim writings) (Prentice-Hall, Englewood Cliffs, New Jersey, 1962).

S. M. Zwemer, *The Influence of Animism on Islam* (Macmillan, New York, 1920).

3. *Christianity and Islam*

J. T. Addison, *The Christian Approach to the Muslim* (Columbia Univ. Press, New York, 1942).

David Brown, *The Christian Scriptures* ("Christianity and Islam" series, SPCK, London, 1968).

David Brown, *The Cross of the Messiah* ("Christianity and Islam" series, SPCK, London, 1969).

David Brown, *Jesus and God in the Christian Scriptures* ("Christianity and Islam" series, SPCK, London, 1968).

Kenneth Cragg, *Alive to God: Muslim and Christian Prayer* (OUP, New York, 1970).

J. Crossley, *Explaining the Gospel to Muslims* (Lutterworth, London, 1960).

E. Bevan Jones, *Christianity Explained to Muslims* (Baptist Mission Press, Calcutta).

CHAPTER FOUR

Hinduism

Bruce J. Nicholls*

Of all the world's great religions, Hinduism is the most difficult to define. It did not have any one founder. 'It grew gradually over a period of nearly five thousand years, absorbing and assimilating all the religious and cultural movements of India.'¹ It has many scriptures which are authoritative but none that is exclusively so. Hinduism is 'more like a tree that has *grown* gradually than like a building that has been *erected* by some great architect at some definite point in time'.²

Hindus call their religion *sanatana dharma* ('eternal religion'). The word *dharma* is sometimes used for the sacred law deposited in scripture, but more often for the religious assumptions of Hinduism. *Dharma* is more than religious belief; it is a total way of life and conduct, a national religious consciousness. As *sanatana*, it is eternal. It has neither beginning nor end, but is coeval with life itself. *Sanatana dharma* is therefore universal truth. It is not revealed by any act of personal God but is seen by those whose pure minds catch its reflection. The ancient seers or *rishis* transmitted this truth to humanity.

All particular religious truths are manifestations of the One Truth. Krishna, in the *Bhagavad-Gita*,³ declares; 'Howsoever men approach me, even so do I accept them; for on all sides, whatever path they may choose is mine.'⁴ The knowledge of this truth is ultimately an inner mystical experience which the Hindu expresses

* Bruce Nicholls is a New Zealander who has been working in India for the last twenty years, with the Bible and Medical Missionary Fellowship. He was a member of the teaching faculty of the Union Biblical Seminary, Yeotmal, Maharashtra, until 1973, and is now Secretary of the Theological Research and Communication Institute, New Delhi, and Executive Secretary of the Theological Assistance Programme of the World Evangelical Fellowship.

¹ K. M. Sen, *Hinduism* (Penguin, Baltimore, 1962), p. 7.

² *Ibid.*, p. 14.

³ For the place of the *Bhagavad-Gita* in the Hindu scriptures, see p. 139.

⁴ *Bhagavad-Gita*, IV. 11.

in the familiar prayer: 'From delusion lead me to truth. From darkness lead me to light. From death lead me to immortality.'[5]

As a way of life Hinduism is fundamentally eclectic and syncretistic. In other words, it selects elements from a variety of religious beliefs and customs and absorbs and adapts them. It looks for the fundamental truths behind all manifestations. There is no sharp distinction between religion and culture as has developed in the West since the Renaissance. Modern Hinduism seeks to absorb the ideals and ethics of Christianity and other religions and at the same time to adapt itself to the secular spirit and to evolutionary science.

Hinduism is not a credal religion as are Islam and Christianity. Hindus are born Hindus, and therefore are predominantly found in the land of India, where Hinduism originated, and in parts of the world to which Indians have migrated in large numbers, including Malaysia, Java, Borneo, Fiji and East Africa. The name 'Hindu' originally had geographical significance, being a corrupt form of 'Sindhu', a region watered by the river Indus. Traditionally Hinduism has not been a missionary faith, though within Hinduism a missionary spirit has by no means been lacking among sectarian movements. Some modern sectarian movements countenance conversion from among those born non-Hindus. In the West the Ramakrishna Mission, the Krishna Consciousness Society and the Divine Light Mission are well known for their missionary zeal. Maharishi Mahesh Yogi, one of the many *gurus* or religious teachers, is winning many disciples through Transcendental Meditation.[6]

Hindu scriptures

In order to understand the basic tenets of Hinduism and to provide a framework for understanding its historical development, it will be helpful at this point to outline briefly the main Hindu scriptures. A more detailed discussion on the historical development of Hinduism will be found below.[7]

The voluminous scriptures, mainly written in Sanskrit over a period of more than 2,000 years, cover a very wide variety of religious beliefs and practices. At different periods in the history of Hinduism, different philosophical schools and religious movements have found in selected scriptures inspiration and authority for their beliefs and social behaviour.

The Hindu scriptures are divided into two classes – *Sruti* and *Smriti*. *Sruti*, or 'what is heard', refers to the eternal truths of religion which the *rishis* or seers saw or heard. They are independent of any god or man to whom they were communicated. They are the primary and final authority of religious truth. Using the analogy of the reflection of an image in a mirror or on the surface of a lake, the intellect of the ancient *rishis* was so pure and calm that it perfectly reflected

---

[5] *Brihadaranyaka Upanishad*, 1.3.28.   [6] See also p. 166.   [7] See pp. 153ff.

the entirety of eternal truth. Their disciples recorded this truth and the record of it is known as the *Vedas*. *Smriti*, or 'what is remembered', possess a secondary authority, deriving their authority from the *Sruti* whose principles they seek to expand. As recollections they contain all the sacred texts other than the *Vedas*. These are generally understood to include the law books, the two great epics, the *Ramayana* and the *Mahabharata*, and the *Puranas* which are largely collections of myths, stories, legends and chronicles of great events. Also included are the *Agamas*, which are theological treatises and manuals of worship, and the *sutras*, or aphorisms, of the six systems of philosophy. There is also a vast treasury of vernacular literature largely of a *bhakti* or devotional type, which continues to inspire the masses of religious Hindus and which different sects accept as *Smriti*.

1. The Vedas

The word *Veda* means knowledge or wisdom and, when applied to scripture, signifies the book of wisdom. The *Vedas*, the earliest Hindu scriptures, are collections of hymns, prayers, rituals and magical formulae. There are four of them – the *Rig-Veda*, the *Sama-Veda*, the *Yajur-Veda* and the *Atharva-Veda*. Each consists of three parts: the *Mantras*, or hymns in praise of the gods; the *Brahmanas*, written in prose as guide-books for the performance of the sacrificial rites for the pleasing of the gods; and the *Upanishads*, which are the concluding portions of the *Vedas* and are speculations in philosophy and mystical discourses on spiritual truths. The most important *Upanishads* are variously numbered as being between ten and thirteen. Coming at the end of the *Vedas* the teaching based on them is called *Vedanta*.

The precise dates of the *Vedas* are uncertain, but they belonged to the period of the Aryan migrations into India, probably some time after 2000 BC. Some elements found in later Hinduism and now known to have belonged to pre-Aryan times are absent from them, suggesting that the *Vedas* belong to the period of up to approximately 600 BC. From these writings we glimpse a picture of the worship of a variety of gods by means of ritual sacrifices. Most of the gods are personifications of the powers of nature, such as the celestial bodies, fire, storm, air, water and rain. It is significant that the theological concepts of propitiation and expiation are most clearly and frequently emphasized in these early *Vedas*.

The *Upanishads* constitute the foundation of later Hinduism. Their teaching centres around the concepts of *Brahman* (that which is ultimately real, or 'Absolute Being') and *atman* (self). They search for the relationship or identity of *Brahman* and *atman* and man's realization or knowledge of his true self. The *Upanishads*, though based on the *Vedas*, reflect a movement away from the sacrifices and ritualism of polytheism to more man-centred philosophies and to the problems of ethical behaviour. Several Western philosophers, notably Schopenhauer, have found solace in the *Upanishads*.

2. The codes of law

Laws for detailed regulating of Hindu society were codified by law-givers from time to time. *Manu* is the oldest giver of law and perhaps the best known. As Hindu society changed, many of the old laws became obsolete and were replaced by new ones. As *Smriti* the law codes carried less authority than the *Vedas*.

3. The Ramayana and the Mahabharata

The two great Hindu epics, the *Ramayana* and the *Mahabharata*, expound the principles of the *Vedas* by interpreting the exploits of the great national heroes. Characters such as Rama and Sita depict the ideals of moral and social behaviour for the individual, the family and the nation. D. S. Sarma writes, 'Even today our domestic, social and national ideals are dominated by characters in the Ramayana and the Mahabharata.'[8] This is clearly seen in the traditional Hindu festivals which are performed each year, as well as in many modern dramas and films. The *Ramayana* relates the story of Rama ,the ideal man, and shows how an individual should behave towards all other men and how a community should live in peace and harmony.

The *Mahabharata* is the story of the conflict between two branches of the same family. Through parables and dialogues the epic seeks to answer the moral, spiritual and metaphysical problems of the times. One such dialogue is the *Bhagavad-Gita* ('Song of the Lord') which consists of a conversation between Arjuna, the warrior-prince, and his charioteer Krishna, who is the disguised incarnation of Vishnu. The *Gita* is the best-known and best-loved scripture of modern Hindus. It calls for disinterested action in doing one's duty according to one's status in society. The dialogue is made an occasion to summarize the main strands of Hindu philosophy. For the first time in the development of Hindu spirituality the love of God for man and of man for God is introduced. R. C. Zaehner comments, 'The *Bhagavad-Gita* is thus the water-shed that separates the pantheistic monism of the *Upanishads* from the fervent theism of the later popular cults. Though not ranking as *sruti* it is nonetheless the focal point around which all later Hinduism was to revolve.'[9]

4. The Puranas

The *Puranas* rank next to the epics in their influence on religious Hindus. They seek to evoke religious devotion among the masses through myths, stories and legends, and events in national history, though they are more concerned with ideal truth than with historical truth. Stories about the several *avatars* or incarnations of Vishnu belong to this category. The most popular *Purana* is the *Bhagavata-Purana* which relates the stories of the ten incarnations of Vishnu

[8] D. S. Sarma, *Essence of Hinduism* (International Publications Service, New York, 1971), p. 13.
[9] R. C. Zaehner, *Hinduism* (OUP, New York, 1966), p. 10.

of whom the last, Kalki, is still to come. The familiar picture in
Hindu homes of Krishna, the most perfect and fully divine incarnation, playing the flute under a tree is derived from the *Bhagavata*.
Legends from the *Puranas* are very popular with children and villagers
and form the plots for films and stage productions. These stories,
in which heroes display virtues such as honesty, chastity and self-
sacrifice, have played a significant part in the formation of the
Hindu moral code.

5. The Agamas
The three main branches of Hinduism, namely, Vaishnavism, Saivism
and Saktism, each have their own theological treatises and manuals
for worship. These are known as *Agamas*. Because of the strength
of sectarian Hinduism these *Agamas* are very important for their
adherents. Although there is great diversity among them, they share
in a common Vedic spirit.

6. The Darsanas
While the *Agamas* appeal to the masses, the *Darsanas* are philosophical
in character and are meant for the scholar. Each of the six main schools
of Hindu philosophy has sought to systematize the Vedic literature
and their own tenets in the form of short aphorisms, or *sutras*. The
Darsanas consist in the collection of the *sutras* attributed to the founder
of each school and in the authoritative commentaries on them that
developed at a later date.

7. Popular literature
The Hindu scriptures were in the main written in Sanskrit, the
language of the scholar. To write a religious or philosophical work
in a popular language was thought to be sacrilegious. But in time
protest movements arose and many hymns and devotional songs were
composed in the regional languages. Tamil, Bengali, Marathi and
Hindi devotional writings beginning in the medieval period (1200–
1700 AD) are among the best known. Thus Hindu scriptures are rich
in diversity and together reflect the complexity of the Hindu view of
life.

Basic concepts in Hinduism

In order to understand the Hindu view of life it is essential to grasp
the fundamental presuppositions which Hindus accept as self-evident
truths and facts of existence.

1. Brahman, God and creation
The search for *Brahman*, Eternal Being or Reality, is the preoccupation of the Hindu mind. To achieve this goal, Hindus are
willing to renounce the world, give up family and all physical

comforts, undertake pilgrimages to sacred rivers and to the Himalayas, and to live alone in dense jungles. Having watched these pilgrims, men and women who risk their lives in the Himalayan snows in order to catch a glimpse of god in an ice cave or to have their sins washed away at the source of the Ganges, one is ashamed at the ease and superficiality of much of western religion.

'Who or what is *Brahman*?' is the fundamental question of Hinduism. Some Hindu philosophical schools, such as the *Vaiseshika* for example, believe in a personal God. Others, notably the *Vedanta*, see *Brahman* as the one, abstract, all-pervading Reality. All reality in the *Upanishads*, including the self (*atman*), is an aspect of *Brahman*. The physical world with its apparent diversity is neither real nor unreal; it is mere illusion (*maya*).

In one of the *Upanishads*, for example, Svetaketu Aruneya is being taught sacred wisdom by his father. His father says to him:

'Place this salt in water and come to me tomorrow morning.'
Svetaketu did as he was commanded, and in the morning his
father said to him: 'Bring me the salt you put into the water
last night.'
Svetaketu looked into the water, but could not find it,
for it had dissolved.
His father then said: 'Taste the water from this side.
How is it?'
'It is salt.'
'Taste it from the middle. How is it?
'It is salt.'
'Taste it from that side. How is it?'
'It is salt.'
'Look for the salt again and come again to me.'
The son did so, saying: 'I cannot see the salt. I only see water.'
His father then said: 'In the same way, O my son, you cannot see
the spirit. But in truth he is there. An invisible and subtle essence
is the Spirit of the whole universe. That is Reality. That is Truth.
THOU ART THAT.'[1]

Most Hindus, including those who believe in a variety of gods and goddesses, accept the notion of an all-pervading God. Sen comments:

'In the Hindu philosophy there is no contradiction between belief
in an all-embracing, all-pervading, omnipresent God and the
puja (worship) of a variety of gods and goddesses in the Hindu
pantheon. In religious ceremonies the images of gods may help
to focus devotion, but in theory they represent nothing more than
imaginative pictures of the infinite aspects of one all-pervading
God.'[2]

God, however defined in Hinduism, is never Creator of the universe

[1] *Chandogya Upanishad*, VI. 11ff.   [2] Sen, *Hinduism*, p. 35.

in the Hebrew and Christian sense. God always creates out of something or out of himself, never out of that which did not exist. Even in the later *Upanishads* and the *Bhagavad-Gita*, where the idea of a personal God is developed, God always tends to be identified with the sum total of creation. Though he may transcend it, he is never entirely separated from it. The general teaching of the *Upanishads* is that the universe emanates from ultimate Reality as sparks emanate from fire or a spider's web flows from the spider itself. The world has neither beginning nor end, but is part of an evolutionary cyclic process, recreating itself from all eternity and dissolving back into the unmanifest condition. These periods of evolution are called 'the days and nights of *Brahman*'. Each day and each night of *Brahman* lasts 1,000 years of the gods and each year of the gods corresponds with 12,000 years of men. Each year of the gods is divided into four periods of varying length. We now live in the fourth period, the Kali age. During each cycle morals decline, only to emerge again from the womb of *Brahman* perfect.

In the early creation hymns of the *Rig-Veda*, creation is a transition from chaos to order which may or may not involve the Creator God. In some hymns creation is the result of the union of the primeval male and female or the birth of the Golden Seed. Again, in one of the creation hymns creation is the sacrificial act in which *purusha* (man), here thought of as primal Being, sacrifices himself in order to produce the phenomenal world from a part of his being. This primeval sacrifice becomes the proto-type of sacrifices representing the initiation and renewal of the creative act. In the *Bhagavad-Gita* God generates the world as the seed or egg fertilizing himself.[3] Why God continues creating is never explained except as his play or sport (*lila*). The concepts contrast with the Jewish and Christian view of creation in which creation is uniquely distinct from God and has a moral purpose. Presuppositions on God and creation are theological watersheds which influence all other theological concepts and their consequent religious practices.

2. Karma, samsara, and moksha

Karma is 'action' or 'doing' and is a moral interpretation of the natural law of causation which states that any action is the effect of a cause and is in its turn the cause of an effect. The law of *karma* is the extension of this physical law to the realm of the spirit and to life, past, present and future. It is a principle of moral reaction applied to both good and evil actions. As a man sows, so shall he reap. Bad actions reap suffering and bondage to human existence. Good actions lead to freedom from this bondage. Just as the law of causation is unalterable in nature, so the law of *karma* is fixed in the spiritual realm. T. M. P. Mahadevan argues:

---

[3] *Bhagavad-Gita*, VII. 10; IX. 18; X. 39; XIV. 3.

'The *karmic* law applies the principle of cause and conservation of energy to the moral world. There is conservation of moral values, just as there is conservation of physical energy. Nothing is lost which has been earned by work; and nothing comes in which is not deserved. Every action has a double effect; it produces its appropriate reward, and it also affects character.'[4]

Inextricably bound up with *karma* is the assumption of *samsara*, rebirth or transmigration of the soul. The soul, as eternal and, according to the *Upanishads*, in some sense identical with *Brahman*, is distinct from the empirical self which transmigrates from body to body, carrying its load of *karma* with it. The wheel of rebirth is a natural principle of the universe, involving man and animals.

According to *karmic* law a man may be reborn as a god, as a member of a higher or lower caste or as an animal, according to his every thought, word and act. Each man, therefore, carries with him his past; in fact he is his own past. Similarly the mental and moral tendencies of this life will work themselves out in the next. All creatures are involved in this cyclic time-process of *samsara*, the state of each creature in any particular life being dependent on the good or evil actions of preceding lives.

Modern exponents of the law of *karma* seek to emphasize both the element of freedom and of predetermination in human action. D. S. Sarma compares the soul to a farmer to whom a plot of land has been given. Its size, the nature of its soil and weather conditions are predetermined; but the farmer is at liberty either to till the ground and raise crops or to neglect it and allow it to run to waste.[5] This duality is further illustrated in the words of Dr S. Radhakrishnan:

'The cards in the game of life are given to us. We do not select them. They are traced to our past *karma*, but we can call as we please, lead what suit we will, and as we play, we gain or lose. And there is freedom.'[6]

While modern Hindus reject the charge of fatalism, they all acknowledge that inequalities of birth and of mental and physical endowment operate according to the laws of *karma* and rebirth. Physical and moral suffering are explained on this basis and in a similar way the distinctions in the caste system are justified.

Karma operates as an inexorable law of retributive justice. It is an internal law of nature, independent of the decrees of God or the gods. *Karma* determines the acts appropriate to each caste. What may be right for one may be wrong for another, and thus the concepts of

---

[4] T. M. P. Mahadevan, *Outlines of Hinduism* (Chetana, Bombay, 1960), p. 59.
[5] Sarma, *Essence of Hinduism*, p. 55.
[6] S. Radhakrishnan, *The Hindu View of Life* (Macmillan, New York, 1939), p. 75.

good and evil are determined by the structures of human society rather than by the moral attributes of a personal God.

The problem of the relationship of the impersonal principle of *karma* to the will of a personal God has long occupied the minds of Hindu theologians. The idea has been developed that the will of God and *karma* are synonymous; that just as his will is unchanging and perfectly just, so his guidance or control of *karma* assures its absolutely just operation. In this way the idea of a rewarding-punishing God is maintained without descending into the vivid heaven-hell mythology of popular Hinduism, so characteristic of much of village worship. In theistic Hinduism the concept of divine grace mitigates the effects of the *karmic* law, though even here the will of God is in accordance with the *karmic* process.

The aim of all Hindus is to escape from the wheel of *samsara* and from *karma* itself. *Moksha*, or *mukti*, is variously translated as escape, release, liberation or emancipation. Salvation in these categories is a fundamental presupposition of all Hindu thinking. Unless the chain of cause and effect is broken, the bondage of the soul to the process of birth, death and rebirth continues. The Hindu longs for release from life that never ends. *Moksha* is release from both righteousness and unrighteousness. It is deliverance from the body-soul bondage and from the universe of time and space, for both are governed by the law of *karma*. The Hindu assumption is that this release is ultimately possible for all.

3. Soul, sin and salvation

All religions are concerned with eternity and with existence beyond physical death. Hinduism is concerned with the eternal Being of the soul (*atman* or *purusha*) rather than with the soul's relationship to God or to other souls.

The soul is eternal and therefore shares the very essence of reality. It is not limited to mankind but is the true essence of all living things, plants, animals and man. The soul is imprisoned within the impurities of finite existence, but in itself it is detached from the personal experiences of the physical, empirical self. The soul does not act, and so is not the agent of sin. For this reason, Swami Vivekananda was consistent when he said, 'It is a sin to call a man a sinner.'

The body, or the empirical self of mind, consciousness and physical body, is, on the other hand, temporal and perishable. It is neither real nor unreal, but exists only in the world 'created' by *maya* (illusion). Personality belongs to the empirical self and is therefore also illusory. Hinduism interprets personhood as a level of reality lower than eternal Being or ultimate Reality, and therefore ideas of incarnation and reincarnation belong to the temporal and are ultimately a curse. The Hindu hope is the realization of the immortality of the soul, either in its individuality or in its absorption into *Brahman*. The body is the prison house of the soul and therefore any idea of an eternal union of body and soul is an embarrassment and anathema. There is no place whatever for the idea of the resurrection of the body in the Hindu scheme of things. Thus in all forms of Hindu religion there is a type of dualism between the two worlds – one of eternal soul and the other of never-ending change and *maya*, the world of cyclic time, space and transient personality.[7]

Sin for the Hindu is, therefore, not the personal moral guilt that it is for the Christian and the Jew. It belongs to the realm of the metaphysical, being defined in terms of eternal principles rather than in relation to a personal and moral God. It is variously defined as *avidya*, or ignorance of truth, *maya*, attributing reality to empirical personhood, and *mala*, the feeling of individuality.

Good and evil are related to the degree of detachment or attachment of the soul to the individual self. When the soul reaches its true self, morality is transcended. In the *Bhagavad-Gita* the idea of *niskama karma*, or disinterested action, is developed. Action is no longer wrong but a virtue if it is performed without attachment to its consequences or fruit.[8]

On the other hand, the consequences of sin as an offence against God leading to a cry for forgiveness is frequently found in the earlier scriptures. In the *Rig-Veda*, the poet cries to Varuna, the guardian of cosmic order, law and truth, 'O bright and stainless Varuna, through want of strength I erred and went astray: have mercy, forgive me, good Lord.'[9] This emphasis is virtually lost in the *Upanishads* but reappears in the *Gita* and in the later *bhakti* poets. Yet even here sin belongs to the empirical self. The true self neither is born nor dies, and therefore Krishna in the *Gita* is able to persuade Arjuna to do his caste duty of killing his relatives in war, for the indwelling soul neither kills nor is killed.[1] In God's presence salvation in Hinduism, as we have already seen, is primarily the separation of the eternal soul from the phenomenal world. It is release, *moksha* or *mukti*, from *samsara*, the wheel of rebirth, and from the bondage of *karma*, or action.

At the same time salvation is thought of in terms of the relationship of the soul to the Absolute Reality or to God. In the dualistic Samkhya school of thought the soul is released and returns to a state of pure consciousness of Self. *Purusha*, or eternal self, is emancipated from *prakriti*, or non-self. When the soul realizes its true distinction it is no longer bounded by the world of nature and the emancipated

---

[7] Jews and Christians view the body and soul as a unity. Man is created in the "image of God" as a rational, moral and free person destined for an eternal I-Thou relationship. The Bible has little or no interest in the soul apart from the body. The Christian hope lies in the resurrection of the body rather than in the immortality of the soul.

[8] *Bhagavad-Gita*, V. 10.   [9] *Rig-Veda*, VII. 89.
[1] *Bhagavad-Gita*, II. 17-22.

soul is eternally freed from rebirth. Salvation is the soul realizing its own immortality.[2]

On the other hand, in the monistic Advaita Vedanta school as systematized by the famous expositor Sankara, the emancipated soul is identified with the ultimate Reality, *Brahman*. The soul enters into mystical union with *Brahman* described as 'dreamless sleep'. The consciousness of the empirical self is completely transcended. The soul, or *atman*, realizes its true knowledge as metaphysically one with *Brahman*. This identification of *atman* with *Brahman* is expressed in the *Mahavakyas* or great sayings of Upanishadic literature: *Aham Brahma asmi* (I am Brahma),[3] *Tat tvam asi* (Thou art that),[4] and *Ekam evatvitiyam* (Being is one without a second).[5] When the enlightened Hindu says 'I am God' he has no thought of blasphemy but is testifying to this monistic view of salvation.

Against these more philosophic views of salvation in which the idea of a personal God plays little part, the majority of Hindus are theistic, worshipping divine incarnations and numerous local deities. For them the highest path of salvation is *bhakti* or devotion to personal God. There are traditionally three *margas* or methods of obtaining spiritual perfection. Each is valid, though some schools of thought and sects consider one way more excellent than the others. None is exclusively held as the only way.

Karma marga is the path of selfless or disinterested action. It is the path of religious duty. *Karma* or action motivated from the desire for its fruits binds the soul to the wheel of existence. Action done without any attachment to its consequences, however, leads to spiritual perfection. We have already noted that the doctrine of *niskama karma*, first found in the *Gita*, is regarded as worship in which the worshipper offers his actions and their results as offerings to the Lord.

The second path to salvation is *bhakti marga*, the path of exclusive devotion to God. For the theist this is the highest path. It is the way of love. *Bhakti* may depend on external aids, such as ritualistic worship, or it may be on the higher level of direct communion with God. Devotion to God may assume many forms reflecting the variety of human relationships. It may be the attitude of servant to master (of which the god Hanuman is the ideal), or it may be the love of a man for his friend. A higher form of devotion is the love of parent for child. The love of wife for her husband is typified in the relationship of Sita and Rama, while the deepest love is that of the lover and the beloved as in the case of Radha and Krishna. A distinction is often made between *bhakti*, or devotion, and *prapatti*, or absolute

---

[2] Jungian psychology is based in part on the Principles of the Samkhya School.

[3] *Brihad Aranyaka Upanishad*, I. 4. 10.

[4] *Chandogya Upanishad*, VI. 8. 7.

[5] *Ibid.*, VI. 2. 1f.

surrender to God. The path of the former requires certain qualifications, such as knowledge, good deeds, and high caste; but the latter is open to all.

The third way to salvation is *jnana marga*, the path of higher knowledge or spiritual insight. It is for the intellectual few. It leads to *moksha* (release) from the bondage of ignorance and to complete union with *Brahman*. In the Advaita Vedanta philosophy of Sankara it is the highest way of salvation, while for others it is preparatory to the supreme path of *bhakti*.

The *Bhagavad-Gita* accepts all three ways as valid paths to spiritual bliss, though in the final chapter *bhakti* is the favoured way. Krishna, God incarnate, says to Arjuna, 'In him (the Lord) alone seek refuge with all thy being, Bharata; by his grace shalt thou win to peace supreme, the eternal resting place . . . . With mind on me devoutly worship me, to me do sacrifice, to me do reverence; to me shalt thou come; true is my promise to thee; thou art dear to me'.[6] Here *bhakti* is the steady concentration of devotion to God. The climax comes in the following verse known as the *charama sloka* (final verse) advocating absolute surrender to God. 'Abandoning every duty, come to me alone for refuge; I will release thee from all sin; sorrow not !'[7]

The place of divine grace in the scheme of salvation deserves special mention. Some have erroneously equated *bhakti* with the Christian concept of grace. *Bhakti* is devotion for its own sake rather than for the glory of God. It has value in itself; it is a method to merit the grace of God. Grace operates within the framework of the law of *karma* and *dharma* (duty). It does not cancel it. In Christianity grace cancels the works of the law; but in Hinduism it hastens the process of deliverance from bondage to *karma* and the wheel of rebirth. The god Siva who is always associated with grace never annuls *dharma*, but guides the soul more quickly through it.

The concept of grace is most clearly seen in those Hindu schools of thought that advocate *prapatti* or absolute surrender to God. We have seen a glimpse of this in the *charama sloka* of the *Gita*. However, the clearest expression of grace is found in the southern school of Vaishnavism, in the worship of Vishnu (sometimes called Hari), as manifest in his two human incarnations as Rama and Krishna and in Krishna's consort Lakshmi. The leader of this school, Pillai Lokachari (1264–1327), took his stand on the *charama sloka* of the Gita, teaching salvation by grace alone. Reliance on grace, he said, is like the mother's milk for an infant; reliance on one's own efforts is like milk bought in the market place. Lokachari, though a devotee of Krishna, rejected *bhakti marga* as being an enemy of grace. Even *prapatti* or surrender to God is not a method of winning God's favour. The grace of God is freely given, thus defying the *karmic* law.

---

[6] *Bhagavad-Gita*, XVIII. 62, 65.   [7] *Ibid.*, XVIII. 66.

While this school comes closer to the Christian concept of grace than any other, it differs from the biblical concept of God as holy and righteous. The Krishna of Lokachari is an indulgent god. The doctrine of the cross, as the necessary ground for the Christian view of grace, has no necessity here or elsewhere in Hinduism. There is no need for a 'once and for all' atonement. Krishna forgives at will.

4. Yoga

The concept of *yoga* is a fundamental method for achieving Hindu spirituality and deserves special attention. The term may be used for the physiological and psychological technique by which all bodily and psychic energy is controlled in order to achieve spiritual perfection, or the term may be used for the metaphysical enquiry associated with the two related classical philosophical schools jointly called Samkhya-Yoga. The word *yoga*, derived from the root *yug*, meaning 'to unite' or 'to yoke', originally meant the joining together of man's total energies in concentration to achieve the spiritual goal. Later *bhakti yogis* used the term for uniting man to God in devotion.

The aim of *yoga* is to produce a radical alteration in the mode of human consciousness through the control of body and mind, so that the *yogin* experiences a state of being which transcends space and time. The practice of *yoga* probably preceded the Aryan invasion of India; figurines of deities sitting in *yoga* positions have been discovered in the early Indus Valley civilization. *Yoga* has come to be universally practised by the religious sects of Hinduism, however much the metaphysical interpretations may vary. In the *Upanishads* and the *Bhagavad-Gita* the *yoga* technique is emphasized but the basic text of classical *yoga* is the *Yoga Sutra* of Patanjali of about the fifth century AD. The system of *yoga* centres on the stopping of the mind as the stream of conscious reflection of the soul. When the mind is stilled and emptied it returns to its original state and reflection stops. Thus the soul escapes the bondage of *prakriti* (nature) from which mind has come. It is the mind that causes *purusha* (soul) to act, to enjoy and to suffer. Through long and arduous practice of *yoga* the soul is freed from these attachments.

The practice of *yoga* involves eight stages or steps, the first two representing inner preparation. The last three steps mark different stages of concentration and constitute *yoga* proper. The steps are as follows:

a. Restraint. This consists of five rules; non-injury, truth, non-stealing, celibacy, disregarding of possessions.

b. Observances. These include purity, contentment, austerity, study and devotion to God. These ethical principles are the 'Ten Commandments' of *yoga* and are necessary preparation for *yoga*.

c. Posture. The body assumes an erect but relaxed position conducive to the control of the mind.

d. The regulation of breath by which slow and controlled breathing aids concentration.

e. The withdrawing of the senses from their respective objects, bringing the mind under control.

f. Concentration, in fixing the mind on a particular spot or object. In classical *yoga* the object is of little importance, though for *bhakti* worshippers, God (*Iswara*) becomes the object of concentration.

g. Meditation, or the continuous and undisturbed concentration on the object.

h. Samadhi or trance, where all mental activity stops and the mind is completely stilled. There are two levels of *samadhi,* the lower in which objective consciousness remains as the mind is completely absorbed in the contemplation of the particular object, and the higher in which objective consciousness disappears and the soul either experiences its won immortality or is absorbed into the Absolute. Ramakrishna Paramahamsa is perhaps the greatest experimenter in *samadhi* in modern times.

The psychic technique of *yoga* has been pressed into the service of many religious sects in India. Primitive Buddhism and Jainism made use of it. Within orthodox Hinduism it came to be closely associated with the dualistic Samkhya philosophy in which soul (*purusha*) and nature (*prakriti*) are eternal verities. Salvation, or emancipation, is the self-knowledge of the soul as distinct from the empirical world. This is achieved through *yoga.*

In the *yoga* philosophy proper, however, a personal God is introduced into the system, not as Creator but as the perfect soul unaffected by *prakriti* (nature). Here salvation comes to mean to become like God in his timeless perfection. The emancipated soul realizes its own immortality. This *samadhi* (trance) experience of pure self-consciousness is the ultimate mystical experience of Hindu spirituality.

Yoga also came to be used by those who adhered to the monistic Advaita Vedanta school associated with the name of Sankara, and by neo-Vedantina such as the Ramakrishna Mission. Modern interpretations of *yoga,* such as those of S. Radhakrishnan and Aurobindo Ghosh, have sought to make it a technique for enhancing spiritual vitality rather than withdrawing from the phenomenal world. The technique of Transcendental Meditation developed by Maharishi Mahesh Yogi, consisting of meditation on a secret *mantra* for a few minutes every day, has been described by his critics as 'instant Nirvana'. Though popular in the West it is largely rejected by orthodox Hinduism.[8]

5. Caste

One of the strongest distinguishing characteristics of traditional

[8] See also p. 166.

Hinduism has been strict adherence to caste. The caste is a closed social group based on heredity, and possessing its own organization and rigid practices in marriage and dining, with strict punishments for those infringing caste rules. Its members normally practise the same or related professional trades.

The origin of caste is shrouded in uncertainty; some scholars think it is pre-Aryan. It seems to have grown with the multi-racial and multi-cultural nature of Indian society. The division of labour along professional lines which subsequently became hereditary must have been an important factor. With each conquest the ruling classes would assimilate the conquered into their classes or reduce them to serfs.

There are four main caste divisions with numerous sub-castes. In theory, the *Brahmins* are the priests and religious teachers, the *Kshatryas* are the kings and warriors, the *Vaisyas* are the traders and merchants, and the *Sudras* are the cultivators and servants. Except in the case of the priests, this division is only approximate in India today. In the procurement of jobs, however, and in social customs, especially in marriage, caste continues to play an important part in Hindu society. Outside the four castes are the untouchables or outcastes, whom Gandhi called *Harijans*, or 'People of God' (Hari). Untouchability is a blot on Hindu society and several reform movements have attempted to eliminate it. Most leaders of *bhakti* movements have opposed caste divisions. The *Alvar* poets of South India from about the sixth to eighth centuries are examples of resistance to the system. Mahatma Gandhi, who was prepared to defend the division of Hindus into four castes, said, 'I consider untouchability to be a heinous crime against humanity.' Today scheduled castes and tribes, as they are known, receive special educational and other benefits. The earlier mass movements into the Christian church were largely from the lower castes and outcastes.

Another concept emphasizing social ideals is the four *asramas* (stages of life) forming the ideal for man's progress and control of spirit over matter. The four stages of student, married householder, forest dweller and *sannyasi*, or one who finally renounces the world, have in the past played an important part in Hindu society.

Customs and festivals

The multi-racial and cultural nature of Hinduism is reflected in the complex and diverse pattern of Hindu social customs and festivals. They vary from one community to another and one place to another. Some religious rituals are performed daily in the home, usually before images of gods or abstract symbols of deity. Some Hindus worship daily in the temple, others less frequently. No fixed day of the week is set apart for religious duties. Festival days are usually reckoned according to the lunar calendar. Astrological calculations determine the auspicious days for undertaking any course of action, in particular for arranging marriages.

Many of the annual festivals are connected with the worship of particular gods and goddesses such as Lakshmi, the goddess of wealth and beauty, Sarasvati, the goddess of learning, Ganesa, the god of wisdom and success, Kali or Durga, the mother goddess. Some festivals celebrate mythical events in the lives of divine incarnations; for example, Dashera celebrates the triumph of Rama. Other festivals are connected with the domestic life of the family or the seasons of the year. Some ceremonies are connected with stages of life such as naming a child, weaning it, initiation into the privileges of caste, marriage and funerals.

Pilgrimages play an important part in the religious life of Hindus. Holy places are numberless. Rivers such as the Ganges and the Godavari are sacred. Holy cities such as Banaras, Puri, Hardwar, are associated with Hindu mythology and attract large numbers of pilgrims. Pilgrim centres high in the everlasting snows of the Himalayas draw large numbers seeking merit and a vision of their god.

In village India, local gods and goddesses are worshipped and propitiated with gifts or food or in certain cases by the sacrificial blood of animals. Animistic spirit-worship plays an important part in the religious life of village people. The spirits of the departed have to be provided for and honoured and demon spirits kept out of the village. Diseases, epidemics and disasters are often attributed to goddesses, who must be appeased. The genius of Hinduism is its capacity to assimilate the religious beliefs and practices of all who come under its influence. Temple and family priests, *gurus* and religious pundits, wandering *sadhus*, numerous festivals and an increasing number of local temples and monasteries guarantee the continuance of the Hindu faith.

Hindu philosophy

In Hinduism philosophy is an integral part of religion. The main philosophical schools were fully developed by the third century AD, though their beginnings go back as far as the ninth century BC as doctrine began to be formulated on the fundamental issues raised in the *Vedas* and *Upanishads*. The six main systems of philosophy are usually grouped into three pairs: first, the *Nyaya* and *Vaiseshika*; second, the *Samkhya* and the *Yoga*; and third, the *Purva-Mimamsa* and *Vedanta*. The systematizer of each school stated the principles in the form of short aphorisms or *sutras*. Later, numerous and extensive commentaries were written on these brief *sutras*.

1. Nyaya and Vaiseshika

Nyaya is a system of logical realism, accepting the reality of the external world on the basis of logical reasoning. An idea must conform to its object. It recognizes four sources of knowledge: perception, inference, analogy and testimony. The analysis of the process of reasoning resembles the syllogistic analysis of Aristotle. The basic text was written by Gautama probably in the fourth century BC. It early accepted the metaphysical scheme of the *Vaiseshika* and its logic and epistemology came to be accepted by the other schools. The *Vaiseshika* school developed an atomistic cosmology reducing the plurality of the physical world to four kinds of atoms, earth, water, fire and air, together with the non-material concepts of space, time, ether, mind and soul. God created the world out of these nine elements.

2. Samkhya and yoga

Samkhya is one of the oldest systems of Indian thought. Its origin is attributed to Kapila, probably of the seventh century BC. It is basically dualistic with the two realities of *purusha* (soul or pure consciousness) and *prakriti* (the primal cause of nature) eternally distinct. *Purushas* are separate entities, infinite in number, without qualities and eternal. *Prakriti* is the basis of all material and physical nature and is unconscious. It comprises the three qualities of *sattva* (goodness or purity), *rajas* (energy or passion) and *tamas* (dullness or darkness). Evolution takes place when the balance of these three qualities is disturbed. The world, inherent in *prakriti*, is made manifest through this evolution. When the *purusha* wrongly identifies itself with the material world, it is held in the bondage of ignorance. *Moksha*, or liberation, comes when the soul knows itself to be independent of *prakriti*. This idea of salvation as the isolation of the soul is distinct from the pantheistic trend which characterizes the *Upanishads* where individual souls are not distinct, but are part of the divine Soul, *Brahman*.

The *yoga* philosophy accepts the metaphysics of *Samkhya* but in addition formulates a method of mind control by which the isolation of the soul from matter can be achieved. *Yoga* is a technique to still and empty the mind so that it assumes its original and pure non-conscious state. The eight well-defined steps in this process have already been described. In the *yoga* philosophy, devotion to God is one of the objects of concentration. God is the supreme *purusha* unaffected by *prakriti*.

3. Purva-Mimamsa and Vedanta

These philosophies attempt to systematize the *Vedas*. The former seeks to establish the authority of the early *Vedas* and is concerned with the nature of *dharma* or right action, especially in the performance of sacrifices. It is more practical than speculative. The latter, which means 'the end of the *Vedas*', seeks to give a systematic interpretation of doctrines drawn from the *Upanishads*, the *Bhagavad-Gita* and the *Brahma Sutra* of Badarayana. *Vedanta* developed along two lines, one strictly non-dual (*advaita*) and the other of varying degrees from modi-fied non-duality to dualism. The most famous exponent of the former is Sankara and of the latter Ramanuja.

Sankara (788–820 AD) identified *atman* (soul) with *Brahman* (Absolute). He did not describe the phenomenal world as pure illusion, however, as is sometimes maintained. Using the analogy of mistaking a coiled rope for a snake, he argued that the world (compared to the snake) is neither real nor unreal. It is not real, for the snake is not there. On the other hand, it is not entirely unreal, for the rope is there. *Brahman* may be compared with the rope. The world's appearance is based on the existence of *Brahman*. This relationship is called *maya* (illusion), and should be thought of as the mysterious power by which the Absolute appears to us as the pheno-menal world. The cause of this confusion is *avidya* (ignorance). The individual soul is a manifestation of *Brahman* which is without attri-butes and beyond all phenomena. Ignorance of the soul's real oneness with *Brahman* is overcome by *jnana marga*, or the way of knowledge, which is intuitive and mystical.

Ramanuja (1017–1137 AD) reacted against this undifferentiated monism of Sankara. He argued for the plurality of reality. God, the soul, the world, are distinct but not separate. The soul and the world are dependent on God in the same way as the body is dependent on the soul. Personal God (*Isvara*) is the manifestation of *Brahman* with attributes. Ramanuja's theism is known as *visistadvaita* or qualified *advaita*. All is a relational unity within *Brahman*. Ramanuja empha-sized the place of *bhakti* or devotion to God as personal and as love.

Madhva (1199–1278 AD) described himself as a dualist (*dvaita*), emphasizing the separate existence of the eternal entities of God, soul, and also the world.

The origin and development of Hinduism

Hinduism, as we have seen, is the present product of many races and cultures. Its origin is obscure and its development exceedingly complex. It was previously thought that Hinduism began with the Aryan invasion into India in the second half of the second millennium BC, but it is now realized that many Hindu concepts and practices originated in pre-Aryan civilizations. Excavations of the sites of Mohenjo-daro and Harappa in the Indus Valley, now Pakistan, have greatly increased our knowledge of the pre-Aryan culture as it existed in the northern part of India. By 2500 BC this largely urban culture had developed a highly advanced civilization, comparable with the then contemporary Mesopotamia.

When the fair-skinned Indo-European race, who called themselves Aryan, entered India from the north-west in a series of migrations, they gradually suppressed the dark-skinned Dravidians. Many tribal groups such as the Gonds were able to retain their self-identity by retreating to the forests and hill country. Today they continue to occupy the less accessible parts of India. By the beginning of the first millennium BC there was a notable fusing of Aryan and non-Aryan religious ideas and practices. The religion of the conquered people was re-emerging, transforming the religion of the conqueror into a new synthesis. A clear example of this is phallus worship, which the early invaders described as belonging to the enemies of the Aryans. The discovery of seals representing an ithyphallic god at Harappa suggests that phallus worship was part of the Indus Valley civilization. In later Hinduism the phallus reappears as the principal symbol of the god Siva. Figurines probably representing the mother goddess have also been found. These are conspicuously absent from early Aryan religion, but in later literature the mother goddess appears in the form of Durga or Kali, the consort of Siva. Other figures suggest a knowledge of *yoga*, which, again, reappeared in later Hinduism.

The development of Hinduism can be broadly divided into five periods.

1. The Vedic period (2000–600 BC)

It appears from the *Vedas* that the Aryans brought with them a religion which consisted in worshipping and propitiating a number of gods who personified the forces of nature, but with the merging of culture the myths of Aryan religion increasingly reflected the developing social structures. As nature-worship, the Vedic pantheon can be divided into three classes of gods: those of the heavens, those of the atmosphere and those of the earth. From an ethnological point of view the divine pantheon is analogous to the three great classes of society – priests, warriors and peasants. A fourth class, servants and slaves, was added, representing in the main the pre-Aryan peoples.

Of many Vedic gods we may note the following: Varuna, the god of creation and ruler of the moral universe; Indra, the god of storm whose character of warrior-king is emphasized; Agni, the god of fire who as priest mediates between the gods and men; Soma, the god of the intoxicating sacred juice essential to sacrifice and symbol of creative power, perhaps pointing to the mystic union of the soul with the All; Rudra, the god of destruction and healing who later received the title of Pasupati, the 'lord of cattle', and who prefigures Siva, the great god of classical Hinduism. Mention should also be made of Vishnu, a minor god in the *Rig-Veda* whose functions are cosmic and who becomes the great god of later Hinduism.

With the gradual synthesis of Aryan and non-Aryan religion, Vedic religion developed in two directions, one ritualistic and the other philosophical. The worship of the Vedic gods gave place to an elaborate sacrificial ritual whose efficacy depended on its correct performance by the professional priests. This no doubt reflected the growing influence of the learned and pious priestly class called *Brah-*

mins. In the *Brahmanas*, composed at this time, the priest was exalted above the gods, for he alone knew the sacred *mantras* which had power over the will of the gods. These were the prayer manuals used by the priests in their practice of public worship. This emphasis on the external forms of sacrificial ritual replaced the simplicity of the earlier polytheism. The emphasis on the correct recitation of the *mantras* or sacred formulae opened the door to magic. The *Atharva-Veda* is a collection of these magical formulae.

The philosophical development in the Vedic period was in part a reaction against the preoccupation with rites and sacrifices. Forest schools began to flourish whose hermits sought for the internal and symbolic meaning of the sacrifices, with little or no interest in their external performances. Towards the end of the *Rig-Veda* period the seers were less interested in the plurality of gods and were concerned to go behind them and grasp the power of which they were the manifestation. Their aim was to discover the unifying principle of the universe. The personalities of the various gods became little more than names for the One Being. The function of the gods became more important than their personal existence. Thus the creative function came to be ascribed to Visvakarman, the maker of all things, or Prajapati, the lord of creatures, or Brahmanaspati, the lord of Brahmans.

This trend is seen in the merging of Vedic polytheism with the pantheistic monism of the *Upanishads*. The beginning of it is seen in the creation hymns of the *Rig-Veda*. Another important philosophical development was the emerging of the concept of cosmic natural and moral order (*Rita*) which was later developed into the characteristically Hindu concepts of *dharma* and the law of *karma*. Through the gods sacrificing themselves this cosmic harmony was maintained. The principle of sacrifice embraces both the process of creation and that of cosmic redemption.[9]

In the search for the unity and ground of the universe the central teaching of the *Upanishads* is, as we saw above, the recognition of the identity of the essential essence of the human soul (*atman*) with the ground of the universe (*Brahman*). The *Brahman* or Sacred Utterance (neuter-gender) in man is the same as the *Brahman* in God. This is the *Tat tvam asi* (that art thou) of the *Chandogya Upanishad*. In this way, *jnana* (knowledge) took the place of *yajna* (sacrifice) as the way to God. *Karma* is given a meaning wider than ritual, and the process of *samsara* (rebirth) developed as a corollary from it. The non-Vedic ideas of renunciation and asceticism opened the way for the classical understanding of *moksha* (deliverance), *upasana* (meditation) and *ahimsa* (non-violence).

[9] An understanding of the Hindu origins of sacrifice can be an effective bridge for Christians trying to communicate the gospel to the Hindus. The nineteenth-century Indian Christian theologian, K. M. Banerjea, used the idea of Prajapati's self-sacrifice in his dialogue with educated Hindus.

2. The period of reaction and renaissance (600 BC–AD 300)

During the sixth century BC there was a wave of revolt against priestly religion and intellectual speculation throughout the ancient world. Zoroaster (c. 628–551 BC), Buddha (c. 563–483 BC), Mahavira (599–527 BC), the founder of Jainism, and Confucius (551–497 BC) were the great prophets of the period. (They were preceded by Isaiah and the other eighth-century prophets of Israel and followed by Jeremiah and Ezekiel.) The reaction was ethical, centring on a concern for morality, renunciation, good works and respect for all of life. In India the new thinkers offered a rational interpretation of the religious quests, and were generally agnostic or atheistic on meta-physical questions. In popular religion the trend was toward a belief in a personal God.

The period was marked by the emergence of two largely non-theistic movements, Buddhism and Jainism. They arose as reforming sects retaining the ethical ideas of Brahmanism but repudiating the authority of the *Vedas* and rejecting priestly religion and sacrifices. Buddha's practical teaching on the Four Truths and the Eightfold Path[1] eschewed any discussion on metaphysical questions. Buddhism early developed its own distinctive doctrines of the soul and the world and *Nirvana*, the state of perfection in which the flame of desire is extinguished. The Buddhist emphasis on monastic life and religion without worship separated it from orthodox Hinduism.

Jainism, which was older and more conservative than Buddhism and of which Mahavira was, strictly speaking, a reformer rather than founder, stayed within the boundary of Hinduism. It repudiated Vedic authority and belief in a personal God, and rejected the caste system. It observed a strict ethic of *ahimsa* (non-killing). Other vows include an undertaking not to speak untruth, not to steal, continence, and renunciation of material pleasures. Jainism is well known for the severe austerities of its ascetics.

The period of reaction is also marked by a renaissance of Hinduism, ushering in the so-called 'Epic Age' during which the *Ramayana* and *Mahabharata* began to take their present form.[2] This Hindu renais-sance was a reaction to the growing influence of Buddhism during this period. During the period attempts were made to codify existing laws for the moral well-being of individual and community life. Reference has already been made to the laws of Manu.

The literature of the period reflects the growing synthesis of Aryan and non-Aryan cultures. Gods and goddesses worshipped by the ordinary people were accepted in the Hindu pantheon and eventually personified as the Supreme. The theistic movements of the *bhakti* cults had their origin in the non-Vedic cultures.

Saivism, or the cult of the god Siva, reflects the amalgamation of the worship of this non-Vedic god with the Vedic god Rudra. Siva

---

[1] For a description of these, see p. 172.   [2] See above, p. 139.

is also found as Yogesvara (the Lord of *Yoga*) and as Nataraja (the Lord of the cosmic dance of creation and destruction). Siva is the reconciliation of all opposites: creation and destruction, good and evil, male and female, rest and activity. He has no incarnations. The cult of Kali, a folk goddess, emerges as the mother force of the universe, the symbol of female energy.

The other great theistic movement whose beginnings are found in this period centres on the god Vishnu, who seems to have assimilated several other deities into his person. The three gods, Brahma, Vishnu and Siva, form a *trimurti*, or triad of three roles of the Supreme. Brahma is the creator, Vishnu the preserver and Siva the destroyer. The worship of Brahma is the least popular and few temples are dedicated to him. The emergence of theistic worship led to great increases in the number of temples, the worship of idols and the popularity of processions and pilgrimages. The temple and image worship became more important than the altar and sacrifice.

Perhaps the most important development during this period was that of the concept of *avatara* (descent) or incarnation, reflecting the strong theistic desire to make imminent the transcendence of God. The concept is absent in the *Vedas* but becomes central in the great epics of the *Ramayana* and *Mahabharata*. Rama and Krishna, the two most popular *avataras* of Vishnu as God temporarily manifest in human forms, are loved by the masses.

The most popular and perhaps the greatest expression of this era of Hindu renaissance is the *Bhagavad-Gita*. The *Gita* synthesizes the Upanishadic doctrine of *Brahman*, the Absolute, with the theistic devotion of God incarnate and reinterprets and applies these concepts to practical life. It attempts to integrate all the teachings of the great schools of thought and the accumulated wisdom of Hindu spirituality and morality. The *Gita* attempts to give a new emphasis to orthodox Hinduism by extending the traditional concept of *yoga* to the whole of spiritual life, and by interpreting *yajna* (sacrifice) as ethical rather than ritualistic, and *karma* as selfless action. The whole field of personal and social ethics comes under discussion. The careful balance of salvation through *jnana* (knowledge), *bhakti* (devotion) and *karma* (action) has ensured its popularity with all schools of thought.

During this period almost all the main concepts and practices of orthodox Hinduism were developed. As teachers systematized and rationalized these many concepts, philosophical systems began to be organized. A great teacher would compile the texts of the school to which he belonged and interpret them in the form of *sutras* or short aphorisms. The six philosophical systems were developed during this period.

3. The Puranic period (AD 300–1200)

The Hindu renaissance of the epic age continued on through the

Puranic age, popularizing Hinduism through the myths, stories and legends of the *Puranas* and through the philosophical *sutras* of Hindu philosophy. In India this period witnessed the slow disappearance and absorption of Buddhism into Hinduism and the decline of Jainism. The *Puranas* were popular among the masses. They also reflect the growing sectarianism of the period.

The Puranic period marked the flourishing of the *bhakti* movement, centring mainly on the gods Siva and his *sakti* (female power) and Vishnu and his consort Lakshmi. During the eighth century and possibly earlier, there arose in South India a number of *Alvars*, men claiming to have a direct knowledge of god, who were wandering singers devoted to Vishnu. Twelve *Alvars* have gained canonical recognition. Their devotional songs are collected in a volume of 4,000 verses. Recognizing no distinction of caste, rank and sex, their number include a king, a beggar, a woman, and others of low caste. By using Tamil rather than Sanskrit they appealed to the masses. Their poems, with which they are said to have sung the Jains and Buddhists out of India, teach that God is accessible to all through devotion and self-surrender. *Prapatti* or complete surrender is prescribed for those unable to attain the art of *bhakti*. Ramanuja, the greatest exponent of the philosophy of Hindu theism, was deeply influenced by the songs of the *Alvars*.

The *bhakti* movement of Vaishnavism, having been provided with an intellectual basis by Ramanuja, eventually split into the northern and southern schools. The former emphasized Sanskrit and the *bhakti-yoga* of Ramanuja. The latter school preferred the use of Tamil, was more monotheistic and emphasized *prapatti*. Reference has already been made to its founder, Pillai Lokachari.[3] Another great *bhakti* leader, Madhva, believed in a dualism of the Lord and individual souls. He accepted the reality of the physical world and of predestination to salvation.

Saivism, or the exultation of Siva above all other gods, is the other great movement. It also is strong in southern India. Siva as a non-Aryan god was only gradually accepted into Hinduism. Early in the Puranic period the worship of Siva is found in many parts of India. He is often depicted as a blue-throated ascetic with a necklace of skulls and a trident in his hand and riding on the white bull Nandi. Sakti, the female power of Siva, also plays an important part in Saivism. The literature of Saivism includes both the *Puranas* and the theological treatises and manuals of worship known as the *Agamas*. Corresponding to the *Alvars* of Vaishnavism, the *Nayanmars* sang the praises of Siva as Lord and Lover of mankind. Bhakti-Saivism flourished from the sixth to the tenth century AD, in South India. The Tamil hymns of the Saiva saints are more chaste than those of the *Alvars* and generally more religious. In Kashmir,

[3] See above, p. 147.

Saivism reflected the influence of the non-dualistic philosopher Sankara,[4] where the Absolute was Siva. In Mysore, Saivism was called Vira or Lingayat Saivism from the fact that every worshipper wore around his neck the *linga* which is the distinctive mark of Saivite worship.

The sect known as Siva Siddhanta flourished in South India until the end of the Puranic era. It claimed the *Vedas* and the Saivite *Agamas* as its authority. Siva is the Lord who is imminent in everything yet transcends everything. He is related to the universe as the soul is to the body. He creates, preserves, destroys, conceals and liberates souls through his grace, the manifesting of his love. *Karma* and *maya* are divine agencies by which Siva purifies the soul, and thus his grace operates through *karma*, not apart from it. By his grace, Siva guides the soul through innumerable births and deaths. Rejecting the doctrine of *avatar*, Siva Siddhanta teaches that Siva may appear in any form to help the devotee, the chief form being that of *guru* or teacher. In many of its tenets it is closer to Christianity than any other Hindu sect.

Another *bhakti* movement developed around devotion to the principle of *sakti* in the form of the mother goddess called in her terrible aspects Kali, or Durga, and in her benevolent aspects Parvati. The movement was strong in Bengal. The texts of this movement, known as *tantras*, contain a mixture of philosophy, mysticism, magic, ritual and ethics. The purer form of *sakti* worship is known as right-hand worship, while the impure forms involving immoral practices are known as left-hand worship.

4. The medieval period (AD 1200–1750)

The chief characteristic of the medieval period is the spread of the *bhakti* movement throughout India, resulting in a flood of devotional literature in the vernacular languages. The *Bhagavata-Purana* became the main source text for the *bhakti* cults and even today continues to inspire the masses in India. This *Purana* is dedicated to the glorification of Vishnu as the one supreme God of love and grace and exalt the way of *bhakti* above that of *jnana* and *karma*. The *bhakti* movemer of the medieval period centred mainly on Vishnu, Krishna and Rama and their consorts. It reached its zenith in the fifteenth to the seventeenth centuries. Zaehner compares it with the Protestant reformation in Europe because of its emphasis on personal religion, the singing of hymns in the vernacular, and general indifference to priestly worship.[5]

In North India *bhakti* spread in two movements during this period, one centring on the worship of Rama and the other on the worship of Krishna. In the first movement we begin with Ramananda, who lived at the end of the fourteenth century and who belonged to

[4] See above, p. 153.   [5] Zaehner, *Hinduism*, p. 138.

the school of Ramanuja but emigrated north to Banaras. He broke with caste altogether. He wandered from village to village teaching in Hindi that Rama was the Supreme Lord and that salvation was found in devotion to him and repeating his sacred name. Kabir, a Muslim weaver, became one of his disciples and preached a message combining the Sufi traditions of Islam and the *bhakti* traditions of Hinduism. He rejected the doctrine of *avatara* and denounced image-worship and ritualism. He retained the strict monotheism of Islam so that Rama became virtually a synonym for God. He was a pioneer of religious syncretism.

Nanak (1469–1538), the founder of Sikhism, was a contemporary of Kabir. He also sought to harmonize Islam and Hinduism. He organized his disciples, called Sikhs, into a close-knit community with himself as the first *guru* or teacher. The tradition of *guru* ended with the tenth, Govind Singh (1666–1708). Since then the sacred book of the Sikhs, the *Adi-Granth*, has become the sole authority. Salvation as mystical union with the Formless One is primarily through the power of *bhakti*. The Holy Name and the *guru* play a mediating role. Sikhism is the only *bhakti* sect to separate itself from the fold of Hinduism.

While Kabir and Nanak worshipped Rama without belief in incarnation, Tulsi Das (1532–1623) preached throughout the villages of North India a religion of intense devotion to Rama as *avatara*. His intense theism marks one of the high points of Hindu spirituality. He is best remembered for his Hindi version of the *Ramayana*. He emphasized *bhakti* devotion to personal god, reverence for the Holy Name and the sanctity of the *guru*.

The second *bhakti* movement centres on the impassioned devotion of Krishna for Radha, the cowherd girl. The first teacher of the cult appears to have been Nimbarka, who held that the difference and non-difference of God and soul are both true. The Radha-krishna cult was further developed by Vallabha (1479–1531). In Bengal, Chaitanya (1485–1533) turned the Krishna cult into a powerful religious movement. His intense emotional devotion to Krishna accompanied by *kirtan* or communal singing has provided the inspiration for the Hare Krishna cult. In Western India, Namdev (fourteenth century) and Tukuram (seventeenth century) are the best-known *bhakti* poets. Tukuram's sense of unworthiness, his trust and self-surrender to God were the 'bridge' that brought N. V. Tilak, the great Christian Marathi hymn-writer, to faith in Christ.

5. The modern period (AD 1750 onwards)

The Muslim domination of India had little influence on the Hindu religion for, in reaction to it, Hinduism turned in on itself and became fragmented through multiple caste divisions and obsession with ritual. At the beginning of the modern era, the Hindu religion and culture had reached a low ebb.

The British subjugation of India did not have much influence on the religious life of the masses, but for the small educated minority it had the dynamic effect of opening up a world of thought and practice totally different from their traditional past. This impact had two sources: western secular culture, and western Christianity. On the one hand, the rationalism and positivism of the European Enlightenment, and especially the social ideals of the French Revolution, had a profound effect on the new intellectual élite of India. On the other hand, the evangelizing zeal of the early Christian missionaries and their attacks on Hinduism and Hindu society resulted in both a number of influential converts and the beginning of a self-reforming movement within Hinduism.

The pioneers of Christian education, notably William Carey of Serampore, Alexander Duff of Calcutta, John Wilson of Bombay, and William Miller of Madras, believed that the imparting of western education would undermine the 'superstitions' of Hinduism and prepare the way for the spread of Christianity as the true religion. Another factor that aroused Hinduism from its sleep was the monumental work of the western orientalists including W. Jones, C. Wilkins, H. T. Colebrooke, H. H. Wilson, J. Muir, M. Monier-Williams and Max Müller who, through their translation of the sacred scriptures from Sanskrit, made available the storehouse of Hindu wisdom to the new educated class. A number of movements and men deserve particular consideration as we look at the modern Hindu renaissance.

a. The Brahmo Samaj. The first reform movement of the modern era was the Brahmo Samaj, founded in 1830, by Raja Rammohan Roy (1772–1833). In the main it took its inspiration from the secularism and the Christianity of the West. Rammohan Roy was a man of wide learning. He was skilled in the Hindu, Muslim and Christian scriptures, studied Greek and Hebrew and had a detailed knowledge of the Bible. He has been described as the father of modern India, and is best known for his social reforms, especially the abolition of *sati* or the burning of widows. He was a pioneer of the science of comparative religion. His approach to the subject was essentially rationalistic and deistic. He accepted the ethical teaching of the Gospels, particularly the Sermon on the Mount, but rejected the miraculous and theological claims of the New Testament. He emphasized universal religion based on morality and rationality.

His successor, Debendranath Tagore (1817–1905), introduced the important principle that the teachings of Hindu scripture were to be accepted only in so far as they harmonized with reason and the light within. This marks the beginning of Hindu liberalism which has so deeply influenced the direction of modern Hinduism.

Keshab Chandra Sen (1836–84), the founder of one of the sectarian Brahmo Samaj groups, introduced a strong element of emotional subjectivism into the movement. In his search for the universal religion, he sought to absorb both Christian doctrine and ethics into an essentially Hindu religious philosophy of life. He interpreted his own movement as the church of the new dispensation, fulfilling the earlier dispensations of the Old Testament and New Testament. His adoption of baptism and the Lord's Supper, his devotion to an idealized Christ, and his acceptance of a modalistic form of the Trinity, reflect a Hindu-Christian synthesis but without the biblical Christ. Today the Brahmo Samaj is a spent force. By syncretizing the ideals of all it has effectively prevented conversions to Christianity. The Brahmo Samaj was a Bengali movement but its influence spread to western India, where parallel *samajs* were formed.

b. The Arya Samaj. Swami Dayananda Saraswati (1824–83) founded the Arya Samaj in Bombay in 1875 and two years later in Lahore, as a conservative reaction to the liberalizing influences of the day. He preached the infallibility of the four *Vedas*, excluding the *Brahmanas* and the *Upanishads*, and on this basis attacked the religious accretions of image worship, the caste system, incarnations, pilgrimages and child marriage. He campaigned for a monotheistic form of Hindu universalism open to all, regardless of caste or nationality. He did accept several post-Vedic doctrines, however, such as *karma*, *samsara* and the sanctity of the cow.

The Arya Samaj has become an intolerant and aggressively anti-foreign movement. In a special ceremony it invests the untouchables with the sacred thread, making them equal to the caste Hindus, and reconverts Muslims and Christians to the Hindu faith. In North India the movement has successfully restricted the growth of the Christian church.

Mention should be made here of the Theosophical Society, founded by Madame Blavatsky and Colonel Olcott, as an occult movement sympathetic to Hinduism and bitterly opposed to orthodox Christianity. In India, Mrs Annie Besant, an ardent theosophist, out-did Hindu reformers in her zeal to defend everything Hindu. She, more than any foreigner, helped forward the movement of Hindu renaissance.

c. The Ramakrishna Mission. In the modern Hindu renaissance the Ramakrishna Mission especially represents the renewal of the wide-ranging religious spirit of India. Sri Ramakrishna Paramahamsa (1834–86) is perhaps the greatest example of the synthesis of Hindu spirituality throughout the ages. He was a life-long devotee of Kali, the mother goddess, and yet he achieved the high point of the absolute trance experience of *advaita* Vedantism. He also went through all the disciplines of the *tantras*, and entered into the depths of Vaishnavism, as a *bhakta*.

Ramakrishna was not a systematic theologian but a deeply religious soul with an insatiable longing for the ecstatic mystical experience of complete union with God. Most of his life was spent as a priest at the Kali temple at Dakshineswar near Calcutta, living a severely austere life. For him good and evil ceased to have any meaning once he had experienced deliverance through *samadhi* (trance). His passion for God-realization led him to seek the religious experiences of other religions, especially Islam and Christianity. He claimed to have had a mystical vision of Jesus Christ.

Ramakrishna's heir and the founder of the Ramakrishna Mission was also a Bengali, Narendranath Datta, known as Swami Vivekanada (1863–1902). On meeting Ramakrishna, Datta fell completely under his spell and became his most devoted disciple. At the same time, he was deeply influenced by European philosophy and social action. His acclaim at the World Parliament of Religion in Chicago in 1893, where he presented Hinduism as a universal religion, gave to Hinduism in India a new self-confidence.

Although Swami Vivekanada proclaimed that all religions are true and lead to the same goal, he assumed that the monism of *advaita* Vedantism was the ultimate truth underlying all particular truths. He severely attacked the Christian view of sin and salvation and the claims of Christianity to be a uniquely revealed faith, believing that every man has within him the power to achieve his own salvation. The neo-Vedantism of the Ramakrishna Mission continues to have a strong appeal in both East and West and Ramakrishna Centres flourish around the world.

d. Tagore and Gandhi. Two men in the twentieth century, in very different ways, have had a profound influence on the Hindu renaissance: Rabindranath Tagore and Mahatma Gandhi.

Tagore (1861–1941) has been called the 'Leonardo da Vinci of our Renaissance'.[6] He was a poet, dramatist, novelist, actor, composer, educator, philosopher, painter and prophet. He was a mystic and a great lover of nature and beauty. For him the finite and infinite were indissolubly connected. His poetry reveals both the devotional mysticism of the *bhakti* tradition and the nature mysticism that sees the whole world as a song, beauty, and the harmony realized in all things. He had a passionate love for the world of creation. Love for humanity stands at the very centre of his religion. Evil is only relative, to be overcome by perfection. Tagore interpreted the *Upanishads* for the modern world in the light of his experiences. He sought to demonstrate his religious philosophy by establishing a school at Shantiniketan in Bengal in which the pupils, through contact with nature, were led to experience the divine. Salvation is for both the individual and the community.

[6] D. S. Sarma, *Hinduism Through the Ages* (Inter-Culture, Thompson, Conn., 1973), p. 167.

Mahatma Gandhi (1869–1948) was both a practical politician and a deeply religious ascetic. He was a modern saint who made the religion of service his life mission. As leader of the Indian National Congress, he did more than anyone else to achieve political independence for India and at the same time gave to Hinduism a new dignity and self-assurance. He practised what he taught. He found his inspiration in the *sanatana dharma* or eternal law of Hinduism, the authority for which he found more in the heart and conscience than in the scriptures. Gandhi interpreted this *dharma* in terms of the basic ideas of *satya* (truth), *ahimsa* (non-violence) and *brahmacarya* (continence).

Gandhi oscillated between a monistic concept of truth as Ultimate Reality and the theism of the heart. Truth is sometimes the Absolute and sometimes the inner voice of conscience. *Ahimsa* is both harmlessness in thought, word and deed and a positive state of love. It is the soul-force that recognizes the sanctity and unity of all life. The difference between man and animal is one of degree not kind. For Gandhi, Hinduism is the 'search after truth through non-violent means'. *Brahmacarya*, which Gandhi believed indispensable in the search for truth, is total self-control in all things including eating, drinking and sexual relations. In both his political fight for freedom and his religious search for salvation, as expressed in his *ashramas*, or retreat centres for communal living, Gandhi ruled his life by these principles.

His views on non-violence were deeply influenced by the writing of Tolstoy and Ruskin. Although his knowledge of Hindu scriptures was limited, he found in the *Bhagavad-Gita* inspiration for his daily living. He interpreted the ethics of the Sermon on the Mount in terms of his own understanding of the eternal *dharma*. He believed that all religions are true, being reflections of the universal religion. While he expressed great admiration for the ideal Christ, he had no interest in the incarnation, atonement and resurrection of the historical Christ. To him the cross was an eternal event symbolizing self-sacrifice. He resented conversion from one religion to another as being an impediment to peace and harmony. He maintained that true conversion was self-purification and self-realization.

e. Sri Aurobindo and Dr S. Radhakrishnan. These are two of the most influential philosophers of the twentieth century.

Sri Aurobindo (1872–1950) was a Bengali, educated in England, who after a short political career retired to found an *ashram* at Pondicherry, South India. He taught that the divine energy is at work everywhere, manifesting its presence in both a descending and an ascending order. It descends through the three orders of reality – a supreme plane of infinite consciousness, a middle plane of supermind or *gnosis*, and a lower plane of mind, life and matter – and ascends again, integrating each level with the higher level. The process of transformation from matter to life, to consciousness, to supra-consciousness, ends in complete identity with the Absolute, and is advanced through a process of *yoga*. Sri Aurobindo looked for the emergence of an élite of 'super-men' who would initiate salvation for all. The influence of this gnostic philosophy has largely been restricted to intellectuals.

Sarvepalli Radhakrishnan (1888–1975) had a distinguished career as a Professor of Philosophy in India and as Professor of Eastern Religions and Ethics at Oxford University. He served a term as President of India. His neo-Vedantism has profoundly influenced the modern educated class, though his syncretism has been severely criticized by conservative Hindu scholars. He was an apologist of Hindu thinking rather than a faithful interpreter. He vigorously defended Hinduism against the attacks of western philosophy and Christianity. In his own religious philosophy he sought to incorporate the ideas of man's internal freedom determining his own destiny and the principle of evolution by which non-Being has emerged from Being and will finally evolve into Being. He advocated a scientific methodology for establishing a philosophy of religion based on the principle of accepting the truth of religious experience that can be demonstrated to be universal. In his writings he sought to show that this is the mystical experience of union with God, which he found common to all religions. He appealed for a Parliament of Religions based on freedom and tolerance, recognizing the relative truths of each religion. His tolerance was passionately intolerant of all dogmas and exclusive claims to truth. By separating the 'Jesus of history' from the 'Christ of faith', he was able to identify Christian concepts with his Hindu idealism. In his attempt to synthesize East and West and to put a new humanism into Hinduism, Radhakrishnan has been a symbol of the Hinduism of the future.

f. Contemporary gurus. If Vivekananda gave self-confidence to Hinduism, and Professor Radhakrishnan intellectual prestige, the modern *gurus* and godmen have given it a popular appeal by relating it to the individual needs of the modern man.

The secular man of the twentieth century has come to a dead end with naturalistic ideologies and has failed to find any meaning for his life. He has begun to feel the dehumanizing effects of our present-day mechanistic society, and in the search for an alternative has turned to the various types of the mystical experience, through *yoga*, drugs, the occult and sex. The modern Hindu *gurus* have capitalized on this vacuum. The prominent *gurus* can be divided into four broad categories.

First, there are those who offer their followers various psychic experiences. Bal Yogeshwar, popularly known as 'Perfect Master', invites people to surrender their minds and bodies to him unquestioningly and in return he helps them to see the 'Divine Light', and to hear the 'Sound' or the 'Holy Name'. Maharaj Charan Singh of Beas, Punjab, and Jai Gurudev of Mathura offer to help open people's 'third eye' through secret ceremonies which give them ecstatic experiences of various kinds.

In the second category are the *gurus* such as Sri Satya Sai Baba and Sri Nil Kantha Bhagwan, both of South India, who claim to have supernatural powers and have a following attracted by the miracles they claim to perform. Then there are thinkers, such as Acharya Rajneesh of Bombay, who have revived some of the old techniques of attaining super-consciousness through nudity and sex-experiences, and who are drawing a large number of converts from the upper classes.

The most influential, however, are *gurus* such as Maharishi Mahesh Yogi, who have combined the offer of psycho-physiological benefits such as mental peace, rest and energy, with an appealing intellectual system of thought as a total alternative to secular, naturalistic world-views. His technique of Transcendental Meditation involves silent recitation of a *mantra* (often a mono-syllabic word) in one's mind. During a twenty-minute period of meditation, the meditator experiences a deep rest because he stops all physical and mental activity. The Science of Creative Intelligence (God) is his term for the pantheistic theory behind the technique. His followers are seeking to re-write the whole of the academic curriculum from his pantheistic presuppositions. This is appealing to a great number of intellectuals who have been dissatisfied with secular, naturalistic world-views. If this catches on further, Hinduism promises to become a great ideological force in the world.

Bibliography

Books marked * are recommended for beginners.

1. *English translations of sacred books*

W. D. P. Hill, *The Bhagavad-gita* (OUP, New York, 1954).

R. E. Hume (ed.), *The Thirteen Principal Upanishads* (OUP, New York, 1931).

S. Radhakrishnan, *The Bhagavad-gita* (Harper and Row, New York).

S. Radhakrishman, *The Principal Upanishads* (Humanities, New York, 1953).

R. C. Zaehner, *Hindu Scriptures* (Dutton, New York, 1966).

2. *General works*

A. L. Basham, *The Wonder that was India* (Grove, New York, 1959).

*A. C. Bouquet, *Comparative Religion* (Penguin, Baltimore, 1967).

Peter Brent, *The Godmen of India* (Quadrangle, New York, 1973).

*R. D. Clements, *God and the Gurus* (IVP, Downers Grove, Ill., 1974).

*M. K. Gandhi, *An Autobiography* (Heinman Imported Books, New York, 1969).

M. H. Harper, *Gurus, Swamis, and Avataras* (Westminster Press, Philadelphia, 1972).

M. Hiriyanna, *The Essentials of Indian Philosophy* (Verry, Mystic, Conn., 1949).

M. Hiriyanna, *Outlines of Indian Philosophy* (Verry, Mystic, Conn., 1932).

*H. D. Lewis and R. H. L. Slater, *World Religions* (International Publications Service, New York, 1966).

*Nicol Macnicol, *The Living Religions of the Indian People* (YMCA Publishing House, New Delhi, 1964).

T. M. P. Mahadevan, *Outlines of Hinduism* (Chetana, Bombay, 1960).

K. W. Morgan (ed.), *The Religion of the Hindus* (Ronald Press Co., New York, 1953).

V. S. Naravane, *Modern Indian Thought* (Asia Publishing House, New York, 1967).

*Jawaharlal Nehru, *The Discovery of India* (Doubleday, New York, 1960).

Swami Nikhilananda, *Hinduism: Its Meaning for the Liberation of the Spirit* (Fernhill, New York, 1959).

L. S. O'Malley, *Popular Hinduism* (Johnson Reprints, New York, 1971).

Karl H. Potter, *Presuppositions of India's Philosophy* (Prentice-Hall, Englewood Cliffs, New Jersey, 1963).

Swami Prabhavananda and F. Manchester, *The Spiritual Heritage of India* (Doubleday, New York, 1963).

Henry H. Presler, *Primitive Religions in India* (South Asia Books, Columbia, Missouri, 1973).

S. Radhakrishnan, *The Hindu View of Life* (Macmillan, New York, 1939).

S. Radhakrishnan, *The Idealist View of Life* (Barnes and Noble, New York, 1941).

S. Radhakrishnan, *Recovery of Faith* (Greenwood, Westport, Conn., 1968).

*D. S. Sarma, *Essence of Hinduism* (International Publications Service, New York, 1971).

*D. S. Sarma, *Hinduism through the Ages* (Inter-Culture, Thompson, Conn., 1973).

*K. M. Sen, *Hinduism* (Penguin, Baltimore, 1962).

Rabindranath Tagore, *The Religion of Man* (Beacon Press, Boston, 1961).

R. C. Zaehner, *Hinduism* (OUP, New York, 1962).

3. *Christianity in relation to Hinduism (and other faiths)*

A. G. Hogg, *The Christian Message to the Hindu* (SCM Press, London, 1947).

Klaus Klostermaier, *In the Paradise of Krishna: Hindu and Christian Seekers* (Westminster, Philadelphia, 1971).

S. Kulandran, *Grace: Comparative Study of the Doctrine in Christianity and Hinduism* (Fernhill, New York, 1964).

Stephen C. Neill, *Christian Faith and Other Faiths* (OUP, New York, 1970).

Raymond Panikkar, *The Unknown Christ of Hinduism* (Humanities, New York, 1968).

Geoffrey Parrinder, *Comparative Religion* (Allen and Unwin, London, 1962).

S. T. Samartha (ed.), *Dialogue Between Men of Living Faiths* (WCC, Geneva, 1971).

Ninian Smart, *A Dialogue of Religion* (SCM Press, London, 1960).

M. M. Thomas, *The Acknowledged Christ of the Indian Renaissance* (Allenson, Naperville, Ill., 1969).

R. C. Zaehner, *At Sundry Times* (Humanities, New York, 1958).

CHAPTER FIVE

Buddhism

David Bentley-Taylor and Clark B. Offner*

Buddhism is the offspring of Hinduism and of India. While Islam arose about 600 years after Jesus Christ, Buddhism came into existence almost 600 years before Christ. Of these three religions which share a world-wide appeal, Buddhism was by several centuries the first to become international.

The successes of Buddhism have been almost entirely confined to the continent of Asia. While Christianity spread primarily westwards into Europe, Buddhism moved in the opposite direction, and it claims attention today as the predominant religion of the Far East, that immense region which stretches from Manchuria to Java and from Central Asia to the islands of Japan.

We tend to think of an unfamiliar religion as a homogeneous whole, but in reality Buddhism presents a vast variety of doctrine and practice. It knows the rival trends of conservatism and liberalism, of orthodoxy and revolt, the tensions of sects and parties, the corrupting influence of other systems and cultures and the recurrent return to the original fountain of the faith. The differences to be found within Buddhism have been compared with those existing within Christianity between Greek Orthodoxy, Roman Catholicism and Protestantism, including the many movements and groupings which each of these itself contains. The divergencies within Buddhism are more basic than this, however. It would be more accurate to draw the comparison between Buddhism and the entire Semitic religious family, including Judaism, Christianity and Islam with their complex relationships based on certain fundamental truths shared by all, yet with completely different developments in both doctrine and practice.

* David Bentley-Taylor (who has written the first section of this chapter, on Theravada Buddhism) read Theology at Oxford and served as a missionary of the Overseas Missionary Fellowship in China, Malaya and Indonesia. He has written several books about the church in Asia against the background of Eastern religions.

Clark B. Offner (who has written on Mahayana Buddhism) has also contributed the chapter on Shinto (*q.v.*, pp. 191ff.).

It should be made clear at the start that there are current today two types of Buddhism, both of which have evolved from a common root. *Theravada* Buddhism ('the Teaching of the Elders') is the earliest form of Buddhism, its teachings being derived from the body of doctrine approved at an important conference soon after the founder's death. This form of Buddhism is characterized by its conservative, legalistic teaching, involving a narrow, austere path to spiritual enlightenment. It is common to see it referred to as *Hinayana* ('the Little Vehicle'), a disparaging name given by those who feel it is too difficult a way for the mass of mankind. It survives today mainly in Southern Asia, Ceylon, Burma, Thailand, Cambodia and Laos, and hence is also known as 'Southern Buddhism'.

The majority of Buddhists today, however, belong to the *Mahayana* school of Buddhism.[1] This later development is a more liberal branch with a broad, lenient path to enlightenment. It is 'the Great Vehicle', the way made comprehensive enough for all people.

Mahayana thought spread and developed in Central and Northern Asia and is therefore also called 'Northern Buddhism'. Today it is the religion of large numbers in China and Japan, Tibet, Mongolia, Korea, Vietnam and Nepal.

We shall consider these two types of Buddhism separately.

Theravada Buddhism

The canon of scriptures of Theravada Buddhism consists of three groups of writings referred to as 'the Three Baskets' (*Tipitaka*), written in the Pali language and held to contain the words of Buddha (although not committed to writing until he had been dead for several centuries). Containing regulations for monastic orders, sermonic discourses of the Buddha and later doctrinal elaborations, the canon is about eleven times the size of the Christian Bible, and this provides abundant opportunity for a variety of interpretations. In spite of such diversity, however, the basic and characteristic features of this teaching, which was mediated through the master-mind of its founder, can still be clearly delineated. It is to him we must turn in order to understand the potency and long-term influence of 'the Light of Asia'. In tracing the course of his ideas we shall in effect be laying down the fundamental teachings of Buddhism, especially as seen in the Theravada school, leaving the subsequent developments found in Mahayana for later consideration.

1. The early life and illumination of Gautama

The word Buddha is not a name but a title, signifying 'the Enlightened One' or 'the Awakened One'. It is especially given to Siddhartha Gautama, who was born about 563 BC near Kapilavastu on the borders of Nepal, 130 miles to the north of Banaras. It is held that this was the last of 550 (though some say myriads of) reincarnations

[1] See below, pp. 180ff.

during the course of which he suffered, sacrificed, fulfilled every perfection, and drew gradually nearer to his goal of winning enlightenment for himself and all mankind. His aristocratic family belonged to the proud Sakya clan, so that Gautama[2] is sometimes called Sakyamuni, the sage of the Sakyas. He is also known by the name Tathagata, meaning probably 'He who has come (as his predecessors came)', which was used in reference to him both by his followers and by Gautama himself.

It is not easy to feel sure about the details of his career, since no biography was written until hundreds of years later. It appears, however, that his early life was spent in ease and luxury, and his father made every effort to see that the boy experienced only beautiful and pleasant things.

During his teens he married his cousin, Yasodhara, moved into a palace which his father had built for him, and continued to enjoy the comfortable life of the élite. One day, however, in spite of every precaution to protect him from contact with the darker side of life, he saw on his way to the royal park an old man, a sick man, a dead man and a begging monk. Thus the hard realities of the world were brought home to his mind. So deeply affected was he by the problem of human suffering that he felt it imperative to break the chains of home life which might prevent him from ever finding the answer to the questions which tormented him. In spite of all kinds of sensual enticements aimed at breaking his resolve, he stole in during the night to look again at his sleeping wife and baby son, whom he had symbolically named Rahula, 'the Fetter', and then abandoned home and family, wealth and prospects, in order to seek the answer to the riddle of life.

He was twenty-nine years old at the time of his renunciation, or 'going out', but it was not until six years had passed that his quest was rewarded. To begin with he put himself under the instructions of two famous Brahmin hermits, Alara and Uddaka, but he was unable to find satisfaction in their teaching, for they could not tell him how to put an end to rebirth.

As a next step he devoted himself with five companions to a life of extreme asceticism in the jungle, existing, it is said, on a mere grain of rice a day, until his delicate body was reduced almost to a skeleton. This led him to another decisive experience, for he perceived that asceticism and extreme self-mortification were delusions; they did not lead to self-realization, but rather enfeebled both body and mind. Accordingly, he turned away from such excesses and devoted himself to a simple life of intense mental activity.

Eventually, as the culmination of prolonged meditation, he sat beneath a fig-tree at Uruvela (known henceforth as the Bo, or Wisdom, Tree) and there achieved his enlightenment which was the

---

[2] The name may also be spelled Gotama.

second major turning-point and truly crowning experience of his life. The seeker had at last found what he sought and had thereby not only solved his own burning problem, but possessed a message which the whole world must hear.

2. The Four Truths

In so far as the content of Gautama's enlightenment experience can be communicated, it consisted of the following four truths.

The first is suffering. The original Pali word has been variously interpreted. It refers to a complex state of suffering, both mental and physical. This truth simply asserts that suffering is omnipresent and involved in the very nature of life. All forms of existence are subject to it. It is inextricably bound up with individual existence, making life basically a succession of suffering experiences.

The second truth deals with the cause of suffering. This Gautama felt to be desire, desire for possession and selfish enjoyment of every kind, but particularly the desire for separate, individual existence. In essence, suffering is caused by a deep, inner craving, rooted in ignorance, which ultimately cannot be satisfied.

The third truth states that suffering ceases when desire ceases, when this selfish craving, this lust for life, has been renounced and destroyed. The state of genuine peace is found only when human passions have been completely extinguished.

The fourth truth is the path which leads to the cessation of suffering. This eightfold path[3] is a kind of comprehensive course in disciplined self-improvement leading to the extinction of man's insatiable desires and resulting in moral perfection. Gautama took over from Hinduism the doctrine of rebirth, teaching that people pass away and are reborn according to their behaviour in a previous lifetime. He believed that only by complete detachment could a man's thoughts, words and actions be deprived of their power to bind him to the inexorable wheel of birth and death, birth and death, following one another hundreds of times throughout the ages. The path to this perfect detachment is also known as the Middle Way, avoiding the two extremes of self-indulgence and self-mortification, both of which Gautama had tested and found wanting.

3. The Eightfold Path

The eight steps in this path are as follows:

1. *Right views.* This involves acceptance of the four truths and a resolute rejection both of incorrect philosophical positions regarding such things as the self and its destiny, and of unworthy moral attitudes, which result in covetousness, lying, gossip and the like.

2. *Right aspirations.* Freeing his thoughts from such things as lust,

---

[3] For a description of it see the next section.

ill-will and cruelty, a man should have a firm resolve to achieve the highest goals.

3. Right speech. A man must speak plainly and truthfully and abhor lying, tale-bearing, and harsh or vain talk. Words must be gentle, soothing to the ear, penetrating to the heart, useful, rightly timed, and according to the facts.

4. Right conduct. This includes charity and abstention from killing any living being,[4] from stealing, and from unlawful sexual intercourse. In Buddhism, morality and intellectual enlightenment are inseparable, in accordance with the saying, 'While morality forms the basis of the higher life, wisdom completes it.'

5. Right mode of livelihood. A man's life must be free from luxury. No living thing must be harmed. Each must take up work which will give scope to his abilities and make him useful to his fellow-men.

6. Right effort, always pressing on and particularly in four directions. First, there is the effort to avoid the uprising of evil; second, the effort to overcome evil; third, the effort to develop meritorious conditions such as detachment, investigation of the law, concentration and rapture; and last, the effort to maintain the meritorious conditions which have already arisen and to bring them to maturity and perfection. The climax of this achievement is universal love.

7. Right awareness, the four fundamentals of which are the contemplation of the transitoriness and loathsomeness of the body, the contemplation of the feelings of oneself and of others, the contemplation of the mind, and the contemplation of phenomena aiming at the complete mastery of one's mental processes.

8. Right concentration. This amounts to complete one-pointedness of thought, concentrating the mind on a single object, all hindrances having been overcome. Such arduous mind-development is the principal occupation of the more enlightened Buddhist and an integral part of the daily life of the humblest follower of Gautama. It leads on into trances where the devotee is purified from all distractions and evils and is filled with rapture, happiness and equanimity. Finally he passes beyond sensation of either pleasure or pain into a state transcending consciousness, ultimately attaining full enlightenment, which is the highest possible state of perfection.

Such is the Way according to Gautama, a combination of morality, concentration, and that wisdom which consists in the long spiritual processes leading at last to Buddhahood. The place given to morality should not be overlooked; failure there spells total failure, for it is only as the mind is pure and the heart is soft that the divine seed of wisdom grows. Such wisdom means the power of seeing things as

[4] Buddhists draw no distinction between animal life and human life, and even the breaking of an egg, a potential life, is condemned.

they really are and perceiving the right way to peace; it is an ideal state of intellectual and ethical perfection which can be attained by man through purely human means.

Buddhism has been well called the most radical system of self-deliverance ever conceived in the world. It is in fact infinitely more complicated, rigorous and intellectual than the outline just given might lead one to expect, for to walk the eightfold path involves passing through four stages in which ten fetters are successively broken. In the first stage a start towards the goal is made, and three fetters – the delusive belief that the individual self is real, doubt regarding the truth of the teaching, and confidence in the efficacy of religious rites and ceremonies – are shattered. During the second and third stages substantial progress is made and the fetters of sensuality and unkindness are done away with. Five hindrances remain to be overcome during the final stage – the desire for separate life in this world and in realms beyond the grave, spiritual pride, self-righteousness, and ignorance.

It must not for a moment be imagined that a normal lifetime will suffice to complete these stages. Even the first one may be but the culmination of many lives of preparation and the whole process covers great periods of time, for which reincarnation after reincarnation is required, while to undertake fully so drastic a course of self-discipline ultimately necessitates the abandonment of family life in accordance with Gautama's example.

4. Some important definitions

For a right understanding of the Middle Way it is essential to grasp what is meant by *karma*, *impermanence* and *Nirvana*, concepts of frequent occurrence in Buddhism.

a. Karma. This signifies action-reaction and denotes the law of cause and effect. What you sow you reap, and neither man, priest nor deity can suspend the operation of that law or withhold the consequences of a deed. But *karma* has a twin, rebirth, which is necessary for its comprehension. The law of cause and effect is an unbroken chain through the ages. You are and do what you are and do, as a result of what you were and did in a previous incarnation, which in its turn was the inevitable outcome of what you were and did in still earlier incarnations. Similarly your future rebirths will be conditioned precisely by what happens in your present life. '*Karma* is father and mother.' 'Each is heir to his own action, each is the fruit of his own action's womb. Each is kinsman of his own action and each has his own action as overlord and protector.' Furthermore, it is not possible to cancel the influence of evil deeds by performing good deeds. Good will bring its reward; evil will bring its reward; the two operate independently. As soon as an individual's present existence terminates, a new being appears by the sheer force of his *karma*. This new being is not identical but has continuity with the one just passed away, because the *karma* link preserves a certain individuality through all the countless changes that take place.

The doctrine of rebirth attempts to account for differences at birth which Buddhists attribute neither to chance, environment, nor Creator. The law of cause and effect is held to operate in the mental and moral domain no less than in the physical world. By its aid circumstances such as love at first sight are readily explicable; the individuals were associated in a former existence. Indeed there is no calamity met with or inherited, no event of life, whether favourable or otherwise, which this theory cannot readily explain. This belief in *karma* and the inexorable succession of cause and effect, evil and good through successive rebirths, produces a fatalism in the thinking of the Buddhist.

What will be will be and cannot be avoided. Suffering and loss, and then death and calamity are all part of *karma*, thus adding to fatalism a sense of irresponsibility. The period which elapses between one life and another is commonly thought of as longer than a normal life-span. While it is sometimes held that acts of a bestial nature may occasion the birth of a beast after the dissolution of the human form at death, others maintain that it is not possible for this to take place. Theravada Buddhism does not accept the theory of transmigration, for it rejected the idea of a soul existing in a body and thus forming the connecting link between successive incarnations. What lives on after death is simply *karma*, the result of what has happened before, not some inward and invisible part of the individual. The true Buddhist doctrine is therefore rebirth without transmigration.

'The King said: "Where there is no transmigration, Nagasena, can there be rebirth?"

"Yes, there can."

"But how can that be? Give me an illustration."

"Suppose a man, O King, were to light a lamp from another lamp, can it be said that one transmigrates from, or to, the other?"

"Certainly not."

"Just so, great King, is rebirth without transmigration." '[5]

But in spite of this it is probable that many Buddhists in practice hold to the view of transmigration.

b. Impermanence. This brings us to the doctrine of *impermanence* and its influence upon the conception of the self. Buddhism teaches that all that exists passes through the cycle of birth, growth, decay and death. Life is one and indivisible; its ever-changing forms are innu-

[5] Extract from *The Questions of King Milinda,* quoted in C. H. S. Ward, *Buddhism,* Vol. I (Epworth Press, London, 1948), p. 87.

merable and perishable, for though in reality there is no such thing as death, every form must die and give place to a different one. The world of phenomena, the very universe itself, has a purely relative existence, and this impermanence, this lack of absolute objective reality, applies to the individual's 'self'. There is nothing eternal or immortal about man nor any part of him. Separate individual existence is really an illusion, for the self has neither beginning nor ending, is eternally changing, and possesses only a phenomenal existence. So long as the phrase is rightly understood, this doctrine can be represented by saying that Gautama denied the existence of the self as a separate entity. 'There is no permanent ego.'

> 'Misery only doth exist; none miserable.
> No doer is there; naught but the deed is found.
> Nirvana is, but not the man who seeks it.
> The path exists, but not the traveller on it.'[6]

'From time immemorial the ignorant unconverted man has held, cherished, and affected the notion, This is mine; this am I; this is my ego!'[7]

c. Nirvana. We move on to slightly more familiar ground in seeking to explain *Nirvana*, although it is not easy to do so adequately. A collection of definitions may perhaps give an impression of its significance. *Nirvana* is an ethical state, a condition which eliminates any future rebirth, the extinction of all craving, the final release from suffering. It may be defined as deliverance from the trammels of the body, a supreme consciousness of peace and rest, a perfect, passionless happiness. It is a state of mind in which *karma* comes to an end. It is the cessation of becoming, for when a process is not continued it simply ceases. It is remainderlessness. It is the peace of the man for whom there will be no rebirth; separateness is ended, the flame of desire has gone out, the limitations of self hood are extinguished.

However near this may seem to total annihilation, orthodox Buddhism frowns on the suggestion as much as it does on the notion that it means continued existence. With our totally different mental attitude the best we can do is to say that it falls somewhere between the two. The wick is finished and the oil is dry. 'The dew-drop slips into the shining sea.' If this goal seems unattractive, it should be remembered that to the Buddhist the curse from which he longs to escape is life itself, which is inextricably tainted with suffering. Believing that he has been for millenniums upon his journey, he sees the highest bliss in the knowledge that he has at last stopped. Gautama persistently refused to give a plain answer to the enquiries of his disciples whether he would, or would not, enjoy any kind of existence after death. Probably the fullest reply he ever provided is this:

[6] *Visuddhimagga* 16.   [7] *Sanyutta-Nikaya* 12:62.

'There is, disciples, a condition, where there is neither earth nor water, neither air nor light, neither limitless space, nor limitless time, neither any kind of being, neither ideation nor non-ideation, neither this world nor that world. There is neither arising nor passing-away, nor dying, neither cause nor effect, neither change nor standing-still.'[8]

It can hardly have escaped the reader that, in defining original Buddhist doctrine, no mention has been made of God. Nothing could be clearer than that Gautama himself avoided all claims to divinity. He professes to point out the way and give guidance to those who seek to walk in it, but it is for every man to do the walking on his own. Gautama is just the Teacher and the commonly used phrase, 'I take refuge in the Buddha',[9] denotes an undertaking to follow his instructions, not an attitude of faith that he has saved or can save anyone by his own virtue or self-sacrifice. God in the objective, personal sense does not fit into the system. The Middle Way has been described by Professor Kraemar as 'a non-theistic ethical discipline', a system of self-training, anthropocentric, stressing ethics and mind-culture to the exclusion of theology. Buddhism as taught by its founder is in no sense a system of faith and worship. He inculcated neither prayer nor praise; he offered neither redemption, nor forgiveness, nor heaven; he warned of no judgment and no final hell. He refused to speculate on ultimate reality or the First Cause which originated the long chain of cause and effect, for that of which the universe is the outward form is far beyond human understanding. He was silent regarding any future life, putting a minimum of positive content into his conception of *Nirvana*.

Faced with the problem of suffering, he taught the way of deliverance from *karma* and the cycle of existence by the elimination of desire. It is an evolutionary process to be achieved by one's own effort, for Buddhism does not accept the view that man is by nature evil, nor does it seek any external agency for the carrying out of its moral precepts. It addresses itself primarily to the problem of pain and suffering rather than to that of moral evil. The inequality of suffering and its frequently inexplicable character often seem to its adherents to clinch the argument against the existence of a personal God. Thus Buddhism is hardly a religion in the generally-accepted sense of the word as connoting some contact between man and divinity. It is rather a moral philosophy and a Way.

5. The later career of Gautama

After attaining enlightenment, Gautama was tempted to keep his discovery to himself, fearing that men's minds were so benighted that any attempt to convince them would be in vain. Having over-

[8] *Sacred Books of the Buddhists*, Vol. II, p. 54.   [9] See below, p. 179.

come this reluctance he sought out the five men with whom he had formerly experimented in the way of austerity. He found them in the Deer Park at Banaras and preached to them his first sermon with such success that they became the original members of the Order which he established on the basis of his moral and philosophical principles. Rules and regulations for this community of believers were gradually formulated and became a part of the Buddhist canon of scripture. Members of these monastic communities were the early propagators of the Buddha's doctrine.

Following the conversion of the first five disciples, 'there were six holy persons in the world', but within three months their number had grown to sixty, most of them being wealthy young noblemen satiated with luxury and pleasure, as Gautama himself had been. These sixty he then sent out in all directions as missionaries, while he himself shared their success and gained adherents even from among his own family. For upwards of forty years Gautama lived as a mendicant preacher in Bihar, Oudh and Nepal. It was his custom to spend the three wet months of the year in retreat and the nine dry ones itinerating. His usual routine is said to have been as follows:

'Rising very early in the morning it was his daily habit, first of all, to accept water from his body-servant to rinse out his mouth, and afterwards to sit down and meditate until it was time for him to go begging. Then, taking his alms-bowl in hand, he went out into the town or village, with eyes fixed on the ground, and passed silently from door to door, accepting whatever food was put into his bowl.

'If he were invited to take his meal in a house, he usually accepted the invitation and ate whatever was put before him. The meal being over, he washed his hands, discoursed to those present on his doctrine, and then returned to the place where he was staying at the time. After sitting quietly on one side while his disciples finished their meal, he retired to his chamber and allowed his body-servant to bring him water to wash his feet. This being done, he returned again to the assembly of the disciples, and addressed them on some point of doctrine or discipline.

'The discourse ended, he retired again to his "fragrance" chamber and rested through the heat of the day, and then, rising refreshed, he went out to receive visitors, and, after accepting their gifts, he taught them such doctrine as he considered suitable for them. When the visitors had gone away, he would go to bathe at the bath-house or at some bathing-tank or pond, and would afterwards retire to his chamber for further meditation.

'When the evening was come, it was his custom to receive any of his disciples who had come to see him from a distance, giving them counsel and advice, and clearing up any difficulties they might have, so that he sent them away cheered and strengthened. The evening being now far advanced, and feeling cramped with so much sitting, the Buddha would spend some time in just pacing up and down to relieve his legs until it was time for him to retire to his rooms for the night.'[1]

His popularity with both high and low was remarkable, while his self-sacrificing life, his gentle and calm spirit, his love for mankind and the lofty character of much of his moral teaching have been largely responsible for his influence in history. He was eighty when he died at Kusinara, travelling northward towards the Himalayas.

6. The spread of Theravada Buddhism

From the beginning, Buddhism was a religion of monks. Gautama himself established the Sangha, the Buddhist Order. On entering it, new recruits are required to pronounce the formula of the Three Refuges: 'I take refuge in the Buddha: I take refuge in the Doctrine: I take refuge in the Order.' Criminals, soldiers, debtors, slaves, or those afflicted with such diseases as consumption, leprosy and epilepsy are disqualified. Applicants must also be over twenty years of age and have their parents' consent.

Members vow to observe the ten precepts, to the first five of which most practising Buddhists are committed. These forbid murder, theft, sensuality, deceit, and the use of intoxicants. The remaining five exclude food taken after midday and any form of self-adornment, involve sleeping on a mat on the ground, and prohibit dancing, theatricals, and the use of gold or silver. In Buddhist monasticism physical labour has been discouraged and there are few celebrations to divert them from seeking their own salvation, apart from two 'abstinence days' every month and an annual 'ceremony of invitation' when mutual criticisms are invited.

Tonsured, celibate, and clad in long yellow robes, the monks begged from house to house and spent their lives in meditation and study. Monasteries were built in Gautama's lifetime, and with the greatest reluctance he yielded to the request of his foster-mother to admit women to the Order. The Order of Nuns, which has in some countries ceased to exist, was made subject to the Order of Monks. Outside these stand the Buddhist laymen, who often have a truer conception of the real nature of their religion than the mendicants. These keep some of the ten precepts for longer or shorter periods; they do not seek for *Nirvana* now, but aim by good living and alms-giving to improve their chances of attaining it in a subsequent rebirth.

For hundreds of years after Gautama's death the influence of Buddhism continued to spread. Generally speaking, China was reached soon after the time of Christ, Korea in the fourth century AD, Japan in the sixth, and Tibet in the seventh.

An important part in the early expansion of Buddhism was played

[1] Ward, *Buddhism*, I, 44-45.

by the monk-king Asoka, who lived in India in the third century BC. He sought to establish a realm of righteousness in Northern India, but gradual corruption by local superstition and magic led to the decline of the religion by the seventh century AD. The death-blow was delivered by the Muslim invaders of the eleventh century, and since that time there have been few Buddhists in the land that gave it birth.

A more enduring memorial to Asoka's work is contained in the lands of South-East Asia, however. It was due to his influence that Ceylon and Burma entered the Buddhist fold, and it is these two countries along with Thailand, which was not won over until the seventh century AD, which are now the stronghold of Theravada Buddhism.

Among the more famous relics in Ceylon are a reputed cutting from the original Bo Tree, a collar-bone of Gautama, the imprint of his foot from a lonely mountain peak, and one of his teeth, to which immense reverence is paid in the Temple of the Tooth at Kandy.

In May 1954 the sixth Great Council of Theravadin Buddhist countries opened in Rangoon, attended by some 4,000 representatives of Buddhist lands throughout the world. This synod lasted for two years, terminating in celebrations marking the 2,500th anniversary of the Buddha's birth. The council not only succeeded in fixing a mutually recognized text of the Pali canon, but decided to publish a condensed form of it (the *Tipitaka*) in Hindi and English as well, indicating the hope of expanding Buddhist influence among readers of these languages.

Mahayana Buddhism

Although there is no definite historical starting-point for the movement which developed into Mahayana Buddhism, its origins can be traced back to the time when Buddhist thought began to spread, giving rise to a variety of traditions with their individual peculiarities. By the third century BC there were as many as twenty different Buddhist schools in existence, some of which may be seen as the predecessors of Mahayana. A potent factor in the expansion of Buddhism has been the tolerance with which it has incorporated ideas and practices which were really alien to its spirit. While this has given it popular appeal, it has also modified its original character. This compromise is specially clear in Mahayana, in which foreign accretions have been combined with metaphysical amplifications to produce systems of thought which seem far removed from the relative simplicity of Gautama's message.

1. Developments and general characteristics

It is not easy to epitomize fairly doctrines which are claimed to be the most comprehensive known to mankind, and in which it is maintained that every seeker can find what is suited to him. Nevertheless, the following developments may be considered general characteristics of Mahayana Buddhism, in contrast with the more primitive Theravada Buddhism. Although the particular elements noted under the general headings will not apply to all the varieties of Mahayana sects (Zen in particular is often an exception to general statements regarding Mahayana), they will serve to make clear the direction in which development has taken place. It should be noted that Mahayana's marvellous facility for making accommodations with its *milieu* encourages local variations, which makes general description yet more difficult. Within this gigantic syncretism of elevated philosophy and popular superstition may be found contrasting extremes of degrading forms and noble ideals which find their unity in an underlying world-view.

a. Scriptures. 'A Mahayanist is one who reads Mahayana scriptures' is the definition given by one ancient Buddhist scholar. In contrast to the comparatively limited scope of the Pali canon used by Theravada Buddhists, Mahayana scriptures have multiplied to the point where standard editions of the Chinese canon encompass over 5,000 volumes. While the oldest scriptures are based on Sanskrit and contain much that is parallel to the Pali canon, other scriptures which have no Sanskrit prototypes have been written in Nepalese, Tibetan and Chinese. Since there are no clear limits to the Mahayana 'canon', comparatively recent works by later innovators are often given *de facto* canonical status in the sects which adhere to their teachings. As there are such a number and such a variety of scriptures, most Mahayana sects have chosen certain favourite ones to which they refer exclusively. The fact is that some such selection is necessary, for this extreme bulk and breadth of the scriptures make it impossible for believers to be acquainted with, let alone understand and practise, the often contradictory teachings found in them.

b. Metaphysical concepts. In contrast with the original Buddhist evasion of metaphysical pronouncements, Mahayana Buddhism has expanded certain implications of the primitive teaching and speculated upon metaphysical concerns, which has resulted in involved systems of thought. Three elements in particular which represent striking developments, if not shocking innovations, are postulation of an Absolute or Supreme Reality, the development of a pantheistic world-view, and the recognition of an individual 'soul' which survives death and may pass through various post-mortem states (heavens and hells) *en route* to final beatitude.

c. 'Buddhology'. The concept of the Buddha evidently began to undergo alteration soon after Gautama's death; in Mahayana Buddhism, the Buddha has not only been deified but codified and

multiplied as well. The human Gautama, considered an atheist by
many scholars (both Buddhist and non-Buddhist), who refused to
speculate upon the existence of deities, is now himself worshipped as
a deity by many Mahayana Buddhists. To the Mahayanist, however,
'Buddha' may refer to quite different concepts, for the Buddha has
been analysed into 'Three Bodies': a 'Manifested Body' (the historic
human being), a 'Mythical Body' (the ideal, perfect, personal being)
and a 'Law Body' (the ultimate reality). Furthermore, in Mahayana,
Gautama is considered as merely one of countless historical manifestations of the True Buddha, all men, in fact, being potential
Buddhas.

d. Salvation. The Theravada Buddhism doctrine of salvation for the
few who, by their own physical discipline and mental prowess,
advance slowly along the difficult, self-renunciating path toward
self-extinction has also gone through a radical transformation in
Mahayana Buddhism. Salvation in the latter is universal: for all men
and all other sentient beings, the bad and good, layman and
'religious specialist' alike. It need not depend upon individual effort,
but may be an unmerited benefaction, granted or attained suddenly,
even in this present worldly existence. The *karma* which troubles the
Theravadist may be severed and *Nirvana* is given a positive significance.
Reliance upon the 'power of Another' often issues in prayers to the
divine, a practice foreign to primitive Buddhism. It must be noted,
however, that Mahayana makes unashamed use of 'expedient'
concepts for unsophisticated believers who think in more concrete
fashion. Thus Mahayanist philosophers may maintain their abstract
principles while permitting the common man to use much cruder
concepts which the philosopher would finally deny. Therefore
laymen's language in relation to Buddhist doctrine cannot always
be taken at face value.

e. The Bodhisattva. For Theravada Buddhism, the *Arhat* ('Worthy
One' or 'Saint') who has attained self-salvation through his asceticism
is the ideal toward which to strive. In Mahayana, the ideal is rather
the *Bodhisattva*, a term referring to one who has earned his own
salvation but voluntarily renounces it out of compassion for his
fellow-men whom he actively seeks to lead to salvation, even though
it may require countless rebirths to do so. This concept of the
Bodhisattva introduces a number of peculiar Mahayanistic elements
such as altruistic activity, vicarious suffering and transferable merit
which are in clear contrast with Hinayana thought.

f. Worship. Finally, in keeping with the conceptual changes noted
above, there have been certain practical transformations in matters
of ritual and worship. Large, ornate temples have been built to house
the many and varied objects of worship – ranging from a 53-foot

high, 452-ton bronze statue of the 'Great Buddha' in the Todaiji Temple in Nara and the thousand 6-foot statues of Kannon, the Buddhist divinity of mercy, accompanying an 8-foot 'thousand-handed' image of the same divinity in the Sanjusangendo Temple in Kyoto, to the more common sculptural representations in wood, stone and metal found in temples throughout Japan and the Buddhist world. These are attempts to give visible representation to the abstract ideas of greatness or infinity which arise in men's minds. While Mahayana Buddhist ritual may also be very ornate, temple ceremonies for the common believer are limited to a few special commemorative festival occasions throughout the year. For the Japanese Buddhist, regular worship is performed before the Buddhist altar in the home in which are enshrined the posthumous Buddhist names of departed ancestors to whom veneration is given.

2. Major schools of thought

Having noted the general direction of Mahayana development and its many variations, we must now describe the major schools or patterns into which this thought may be analysed. Originating in India, many of the doctrines and practices of Mahayana Buddhism were formulated in China. From there they were transmitted to Japan, where they continued to evolve after they had become obscure or forgotten in the Chinese habitat. Since the various schools of Mahayana reached their fullest development and are most clearly delineated in Japan, where they are given at least nominal adherence by the large majority of the population, the following description will reflect the state of Japanese Buddhism in particular. Each of the general schools noted below has numerous sects and sub-sects which are included within them.

a. *The eclectic (comprehensive) school*. Although the scriptures, doctrines and practices of Mahayana Buddhism are so variegated that the possibility of their being harmonized within one system seems remote, this has been the aim of the eclectic school. Represented by Tendai (Chinese *T'ien-t'ai*) Buddhism in Japan, this line of Buddhism emphasizes the essential unity of all Buddhas, times, places and teachings. The multitudinous Buddhist scriptures are all considered to be authentic teachings of Buddha which have been adapted to the receptive powers of his disciples. This progressive revelation, however, is considered to have reached its culmination in the Lotus Scripture (*Hokekyo*), in which the teaching of the identity of the ultimate, metaphysical Reality and the historic, incarnate Buddha is affirmed.

The unity of existence and non-existence, the temporal and eternal and other opposing polarities is found through a 'Middle Way'. In fact, the entire universe somehow participates in the all-pervading Buddha, evident in the smallest particle and the whole cosmos alike, truth being found in man's realization of his own identity with the universal reality. The eclectic school teaches a thoroughgoing universalism, bringing all contrarities into unity and proclaiming ultimate enlightenment for all sentient beings.

The ways to enlightenment are also comprehensive, including the mystical initiation, silent meditation and simple faith propounded in particular by the other schools. Likewise, the object of faith may be Gautama, Amida, Dainichi (see below), other Buddhas, *Bodhisattvas* or even non-Buddhist deities. The believer is expected to live his life in the light of his recognition of his unity with the universe. 'Entering the room of the Buddha' (signifying a spirit of great compassion for all beings), 'donning the robe of the Buddha' (meaning a spirit of meek forbearance) and 'sitting in the seat of the Buddha' (indicating universal emptiness) is the path to be followed by those *en route* to Buddhahood.

b. The esoteric (mystical) school. While the eclectic school attempts to bring unity and harmony to the immense variety of Buddhist teachings, in regard to the wholesale incorporation of originally non-Buddhist elements into its system, the esoteric school is yet more syncretistic. In Shingon (Chinese *Chen-yen*) Buddhism, the universe itself is identified with the body of Dainichi, the Supreme Buddha. The six constituent elements of earth, water, fire, air, ether and consciousness are given symbolic and mystical significance, and the 'three mysteries' of the Cosmic Buddha's body, mouth and mind are considered manifested in the movements, sounds and thoughts of the universe and its inhabitants. There is no particle of mind or matter in which the Buddha is not present.

The pantheon of this all-inclusive mystical school includes many ancient, Indian divinities which have been identified with local deities of the lands in which Buddhism has been propagated. In Japan, the crucial impetus for the unification of Buddhism and the native Japanese religion (Shinto) was provided by Shingon Buddhism and its original propagator, Kobo Daishi, who explained that the Shinto deities were only manifestations of the same eternal Buddha, and therefore the two religions could co-exist without conflict. Likewise, traditional superstitious and magical practices of these lands have been assimilated into esoteric Buddhism, resulting in aberrations such as the Lamaism of Tibet and Mongolia.

Mystical Buddhism recognizes two approaches to enlightenment: that of exoteric or apparent doctrines, such as those taught by Gautama and Buddhist schools in general, and the esoteric or secret doctrines, which are not found in literature but are communicated orally to the initiated. Other religions and other Buddhist schools of thought may be useful in man's lower stages of spiritual development, but the highest stage of true enlightenment, for which the inferior teachings have prepared the way, is found in the union of man with the universe by means of the mystical techniques transmitted in esoteric Buddhism, which uses the *Dainichikyo* and *Kongochokyo* scriptures as its basis. The mysteries taught in this school include fixed movements (bodily postures and hand gestures), ritual utterances (repetition of Buddha's names, mystic formulae or sacred texts) and methods of concentration by which the believer's actions, words and thoughts are united with the Cosmic Buddha, thereby releasing cosmic forces for personal or social benefit.

Special use is made of mystical symbols and diagrams, the most important of which are the two diagrammatic representations (called *mandaras* in Japanese) of the ideal and dynamic sides of cosmic life, which picture the Cosmic Buddha seated in meditation upon a lotus surrounded by lesser Buddhas and *Bodhisattvas*. The appeal of mystical techniques and elaborate ceremonies, the allure of gaining access to supernatural powers and the enlistment of traditional practices and national divinities into the system have brought much greater popularity to this esoteric school of Buddhism than that enjoyed by the eclectic school.

c. The fiducial (Paradisic or 'Pure Land') school. The school which has proved most popular in Japan, however, and which may be considered most representative of 'Japanese Buddhism', is the fiducial or Paradisic (commonly called 'Pure Land') school, which teaches salvation by faith. While the roots of Jodo ('Pure Land'; Chinese *Ching-t'u*) Buddhism are traced to India, the developments which took place in China and, more particularly, in Japan have carried it so far away from traditional Buddhism that, in some ways at least in its popular expressions, it is in a category of its own.

In contrast with the involved scholasticism, rigorous discipline and complicated ritual prescribed by the schools advocating the 'difficult way' or 'holy path' to enlightenment, this school proclaims the 'easy way' to the Pure Land by a simple recitation of the sacred formula which expresses faith in Amida Buddha. Basing their doctrines on three Amida scriptures in the Chinese Mahayana canon plus further amplification by Japanese reformers, adherents of this school consider that the easy way to Paradise is vouchsafed by the vow of Amida. This 'Buddha of Infinite Life and Light', having reached the threshold of enlightenment on the basis of his own hard-earned merit as a man in aeons past, vowed not to enter Buddhahood except on the condition that the entrance to the Pure Land he established would be assured for all beings simply by virtue of their reliance upon him and his name. So it is that ascetic practices, erudite learning, esoteric rites and prolonged concentration are quite unnecessary. While men in former ages may have earned salvation by such means, they are not practical in the present degenerate age – especially for the common man.

Minimizing the traditional separation of a holy priesthood and secular laity, restrictions relating to celibacy, diet and other elements of monastic discipline have been abrogated. All men without distinction may be assured of eternal happiness on the basis of faith toward Amida and reliance upon his vow which is expressed in the repetition of the Nenbutsu invocation, 'Hail Amida Buddha.' A life of joy and gratitude, characterized by good works, is expected to result from the assurance of Amida's salvation.

While some sects of the Paradisic School make allowance for the veneration of other Buddhas or *Bodhisattvas*, the largest and most fully developed sect (Jodo Shin) worships Amida alone, suggesting a monotheistic conception, at least on the popular level. In fact, this school's teaching regarding man's sinfulness and need for salvation, the horrors of hell and bliss of Paradise, the grace of Amida which assures man's entry into the Pure Land where Amida dwells and the simple faith, apart from any other conditions, which is the effective element in gaining salvation, has prompted reference to it as an Eastern version of the Christian gospel. Obvious parallels with the Christian faith may be seen in the following expression of faith by a pious believer of this school.

'I am weak and sinful, and have no hope in myself; my hope is all in Amida Buddha. I believe him to be the Supreme Being. Because of the wickedness of man, and because of human sorrow, Amida Buddha became incarnate and came to earth to deliver man; and my hope and the world's hope is to be found in his suffering love. He has entered humanity to save it; and he alone can save. He constantly watches over and helps all who trust him. I am not in a hurry to die, but I am ready when the time comes; and I trust that through the gracious love of Amida Buddha I shall enter into the future life which I believe to be a state of conscious existence, and where I shall be free from sorrow. I believe that he hears prayer, and that he has guided me thus far, and my hope is only in his suffering love.'[2]

Despite such confessions of faith in the mythical Amida on the part of laymen, however, basic philosophical foundations of this exceptional school remain those of traditional Buddhism, making the similarities with Christianity more superficial than profound.

d. The concentrative (intuitive) school. In contrast with this easy way o salvation by simple dependence upon the grace or power of another which is so far removed from primitive Buddhism, the 'classical' method of attaining enlightenment through self-reliance and mental discipline is found in Zen (Chinese *Ch'an*) Buddhism. This school traces its history to the experience of enlightenment attained by Gautama under the Bo Tree following intensive mental concentration. Since the truth gained in this way is beyond expression in human

[2] Quoted in A. K. Reischauer, *Studies in Japanese Buddhism* (Macmillan, New York, 1917), p. 246.

language, Zen, in contrast with all other schools, emphasizes its lack of dependence upon written scriptures or literature of any kind. Similarly, Zen, in principle, places no emphasis on veneration of Buddha, whether in spirit or before material representations. Rather, man himself possesses the Buddha nature and it is the momentous, intuitive apprehension of one's identity with the Absolute which constitutes the *summum bonum* or enlightenment of this school.

This intuitive grasp of the true nature of Reality is an ineffable, liberating experience which ordinarily requires lengthy preparation of both mind and body. Receiving and following instructions from a Zen master, disciplined effort aimed at bringing body and mind into the condition conducive to attaining enlightenment, adjusting one's daily routine and surroundings to contribute to that end are important elements in the 'religious' activities of Zen Buddhists. At the heart of the disciplinary process is the attempted mastery of one's intellectual faculties by a method of determined mental concentration. To achieve this aim, the Zen practioner may sit for hours, having given initial attention to the correct positioning of legs, arms, hands, back, head and eyes and to correct breathing, while the mind is sharpened by concentration to the point of freedom from all bondage to thoughts or imaginations of any kind, resulting in a state of 'absolute emptiness'. A short phrase or question which seems logically meaningless may be used to assist in concentration and in breaking through the illusory existence in which man is bound.

By overcoming the illusion of individual existence, gaining the intuitive breakthrough that all is one without distinction, that 'Buddha is all and I am Buddha', man sees through the false image of himself as incomplete and sinful, and awakens to the reality of his inherent purity and wholeness. When this liberating, enlightenment experience permeates one's whole existence, rituals, doctrines, scriptures, images, Buddhas and all other traditional religious accretions lose their significance.

e. The puristic (prophetic) school. Finally, there is a native Japanese school of Mahayana Buddhism that is unique in both spirit and practice. In contrast to the general inclusivistic character of other Mahayana schools which willingly accords place to heterogeneous elements even while maintaining their own emphases, Nichiren Buddhism is exclusivistic and intolerant. Nichiren, its founder, consciously rebelled against the all-encompassing breadth of the Tendai School in which he was educated and insisted that the Lotus Scripture (*Hokekyo*) was the only channel of truth in this age. With patriotic vigour and apocalyptic passion he denounced all other schools and sects with vehemence, asserting that in this end-time earlier and transitory teachings of Buddha, which had been abused and corrupted by the other schools, must be discarded in favour of the quintessence of Buddha's thought found in the Lotus Scripture.

Nichiren's religious ardour was coupled with a patriotic fervour in which the fortunes of the nation were linked to national acquiescence to his proclamations, introducing into this school a continuing interest in political affairs. In the puristic school of Mahayana Buddhism, Nichiren is considered a kind of latter-day prophet or messiah, who was inspired to call men back to the truth of the Eternal Buddha as it is found in the *Lotus Sutra*,[3] and represented by means of a special object of worship and a sacred formula which are the indispensable means of salvation. The only object of worship permitted by the Nichiren purists is a *mandala* scroll, in the centre of which are written in Chinese characters the words of the sacred formula with the names or titles of Indian and Japanese divinities around it, representing all classes of existence in their relationship to the cosmic truth. The sacred formula (*daimoku*), which is chanted enthusiastically by the adherents of this school, is an invocation addressed to the *Lotus Sutra* itself, 'Hail to the Lotus Sutra!' Repetition of this formula and worshipping before the Nichiren *mandala* is considered effectively to unite the soul of man with the Eternal Buddha Spirit. The enthusiasm with which its adherents engage in religious propagation, its tendency to emphasize a politico-religious union and its prophetic vision of the day when the world will be converted to its brand of Buddhism, with its headquarters near Mount Fuji, are other unique features of this puristic school.

In recent years, new religious vitality has become evident in the Nichiren stream of Buddhism in the form of numerous 'New Religions' in Japan. While some of these 'New Religions' have arisen out of Shintoistic backgrounds and most of them are syncretistic in nature, showing evidence of Shinto, Buddhist and Christian influence, a number of them are directly related to Nichiren Buddhism in particular. The major examples of Soka Gakkai, Rissho Kosei-kai and Reiyukai are all of this school, relying upon the *Lotus Sutra*, worshipping before the Nichiren *mandala* and repeating the sacred *daimoku* formula. These laymen's associations each have their own particular characteristics.[4]

Reiyukai was the earliest of these lay Buddhist movements and has become the parent body of many offspring, which have slightly altered or added to the Reiyukai distinctives. These distinctives include small gatherings in homes where personal problems are shared; simplicity of ritual but earnestness of faith in the object of worship (*mandala*) and the efficacy of the hallowed chant (*daimoku*); careful adherence to ceremonial observances toward departed ancestors and involvement in social services.

---

[3] *Sutra* is a Sanskrit word meaning "thread," referring to a Buddhist scripture, traditionally spoken by Buddha.

[4] See also the Section "Sect Shinto and 'New Religions' " in chapter 6 (p. 215).

The largest and most active of Reiyukai progeny is Rissho Kosei-kai. This 'society of laymen who seek the perfection of their character and the attainment of Buddhahood by following the religious teachings of Sakyamuni Buddha' has perfected the small-circle discussion groups to the point where they have become generally recognized as effective instruments for group therapy. Soka Gakkai has achieved notoriety by its over-enthusiastic attempts to gain converts by high-pressure tactics. It has provided a rallying-point for large numbers of dissatisfied, frustrated people who seek an easy answer to life's problems in its promises of immediate material, physical benefits certain to result from faithful adherence to the prescribed religious activities which include daily worship (*sutra*-chanting), conversion efforts, discussion meetings and pilgrimage to the mecca of the faith near Mount Fuji. Expansion of activities into cultural and political fields has made this movement of more than religious interest.

In conclusion, it should be noted that the philosophical monism, pantheism and reverence for life of the traditional Buddhist schools, the mental discipline of Zen and the enthusiastic positivism of Soka Gakkai have proved attractive to some Western minds also. These emphases are accompanied by a conspicuous lack of any deep, theological sense of sin, guilt or separation from Ultimate Reality which would add to its attractiveness for many who have been burdened by negative overemphases of Western religions. Although obviously there are temporary, superficial faddists included among the Buddhist adherents in the West, there are also serious scholars who find in this Eastern wisdom emphases which make a noteworthy contribution to the world of Occidental thought. While there is a basic metaphysical world-view underlying the entire Buddhist conglomerate which the serious Buddhist adherent must affirm, the varied concrete expressions of this philosophy in the teaching and practice of the manifold divisions within the Buddhist spiritual family is so comprehensive, that there are few people who could not find elements to which they might easily give their assent.

Bibliography

Masaharu Anesaki, *History of Japanese Religion* (C. E. Tuttle, Rutland, Vt., 1963).

Edward Conze, *Buddhism: Its Essence and Development* (Harper and Row, New York, 1959).

Charles Eliot, *Hinduism and Buddhism* (Barnes and Noble, New York, 1921).

Charles Eliot, *Japanese Buddhism* (Barnes and Noble, New York, 1935).

Richard A. Gard, *Buddhism* (Prentice-Hall, Englewood Cliffs, New Jersey, 1961).

Christmas Humphreys, *Buddhism* (Penguin, Baltimore, 1962).

Christmas Humphreys, *Exploring Buddhism* (Allen & Unwin, London, 1974).

K. S. Latourette, *Introducing Buddhism* (Friendship Press, New York, 1963).

Kenneth W. Morgan (ed.), *The Path of the Buddha* (Ronald Press, New York, 1956).

Maurice Percheron, *Buddha and Buddhism* (Harper and Row, New York, 1957).

J. B. Pratt, *The Pilgrimage of Buddhism* (Macmillan, New York, 1928).

A. K. Reischauer, *Studies in Japanese Buddhism* (Macmillan, New York, 1917).

F. Harold Smith, *The Buddhist Way of Life: Its Philosophy and History* (Hutchinson University Library, London, 1951).

D. T. Suzuki, *The Essence of Buddhism* (International Publications Service, New York, 1968).

C. H. S. Ward, *Buddhism* (Epworth Press, London, 1948).

CHAPTER SIX

Shinto
Clark B. Offner*

Shinto denotes 'the traditional religious practices which originated in Japan and developed mainly among the Japanese people along with the underlying life attitudes and ideology which support such practices'.[1] Various implications can immediately be derived from this statement of a modern Shinto scholar. First, Shinto does not refer to an organized, clearly-defined body of doctrine nor to a unified, systematized code of behaviour. The origins of Shinto are lost in the hazy mists enshrouding the ancient period of Japanese history, but from the time the Japanese people became conscious of their own cultural character and traditions, the practices, attitudes and ideology that eventually developed into the Shinto of today were already included within them.

Types of Shinto

In contrast with religions which base their teachings and conduct upon revelation given through a founder or upon writings of inspired men, Shinto has neither a founder nor a written canon. Lacking such objective, authoritative standards, it is not surprising that Shinto has never developed a systematic doctrine. Nor is it strange that a great variety of both thought and practice has become associated with and assimilated by Shinto throughout the ages. Even today there are countless local varieties of popular practices that defy any rational attempt to unify them or classify them neatly. While many of the superstitious practices of the Japanese hinterland are currently

* Clark B. Offner holds degrees from the University of Dubuque, New York University, New York Theological Seminary and Northern Baptist Theological Seminary and has taken post-doctoral studies at the University of Chicago. Except for furlough years in the USA, he has resided in Japan since 1951 as minister of the Christian Catholic Church. He is author of *Modern Japanese Religions*.

[1] Naofusa Hirai, "Shukyoshiteki ni Mita Shinto no Tokushitsu" ("The Character of Shinto Viewed from a History of Religion Perspective") in *Deai* (*Encounter*), May 1969, p. 40.

relegated to the fringe of Shinto and not considered a part of its central 'essence', they also are included in the broad, inclusivistic definition of Shinto, being grouped together under the designation of *Folk Shinto*, which is such a diversified, particularized and disorganized category that it cannot be treated in the present brief description.

On the other side of what is considered to be the central core of Shinto tradition are found organized groups which partake of a completely different religious character, some of which have historical founders, canonized scriptures, an organized membership, systematized doctrine and specific ritual. These groups are designated *Sect Shinto* and will be noted in the concluding section of this chapter. The remaining core of traditional religious practices, which centre in rites related to the numerous shrines found in every locality of the country, is referred to as *Shrine Shinto*. It is this particular division of Shinto that is commonly indicated by the general term 'Shinto'.

Some Shinto specialists make other divisions such as *Domestic Shinto*, in reference to the particular rituals performed at homes rather than at the communal shrines, and *Imperial Household Shinto*, for the special rites followed by the Imperial Family at the special shrines within the Imperial Palace. It should be noted that another term, *State Shinto* or *National Shinto*, was used prior to the disestablishment of Shinto in 1945 in reference to the particular situation (including state control, chauvinistic teaching and enforced ritual observances) which existed in the years preceding and during the Pacific War.

The land and people of Shinto

Shrine Shinto, with which this chapter is primarily concerned, is basically the present form of primitive clan ritual and belief that has continued throughout the ages despite the fluctuations which have characterized Japanese social, political and religious life. Its spirit and form cannot be understood apart from some understanding of the land in which it originated and the people among whom it developed.

The mountainous chain of islands rising from the ocean floor off the coast of the Asian mainland, and constituting the land of Japan, exhibits immense variety and striking beauty: rugged coastlines, precipitous, pine-clad cliffs, forested mountains with rocky peaks, rushing rivers and a few fertile plains. Yet the usually calm and lovely face of nature is regularly confronted by an undercurrent of violence: typhoons seasonally sweep across seas and lands, earthquakes rock the islands, mountains are scarred by landslides, throughout the country hot springs bubble with boilings fluids from beneath the peaceful surface, and even the matchless Mount Fuji herself is crowned with a heap of volcanic dust and lava. The temperate climate with its clearly defined seasons throws over this fascinating landscape a variety of moods: beautiful clear skies, hot sunshine, delicate mists skirting the mountain sides, torrential rains, strong winds and a covering of snow.

The ancient people who established themselves in this environment could not help but be affected by it. Japan's early inhabitants quickly developed a deep respect for the generally rhythmic, but periodically discordant, forces of nature. They were grateful for nature's benevolence, awed by her power and smitten with her beauty. Rigid discipline and persevering industry mixed with an aesthetic sensitivity were moulded into the Japanese character, while the natural boundaries of mountains, rivers or seas encouraged the development of distinctive local peculiarities, provincial pride and community spirit on the part of individual clans. The oldest records relating to Japanese society also make clear characteristic respect for recognized, communal formalities and for human authorities (both living and dead).

Until the advent of a cultural invasion from the Chinese mainland which forced the Japanese consciously to reflect upon their own traditions, there was no entity known as 'Shinto'. There were traditions that had developed among the various Japanese clans. Local traditions at times gave way to those of a stronger clan that had gained ascendancy, while other customs continued to be maintained in particular areas even after a divergent standard tradition became accepted over the general region. Reflecting the basic unity of the communal life of the clans, these traditions were not divided into religious and non-religious classifications. It was after the Chinese 'Way' was introduced from the mainland that the Japanese were forced to consider the spiritual character and implications of their own way of life which they had been following from of old.

The meaning of Shinto

To distinguish the Japanese traditions from the Way of the Buddha or the Teaching of Confucius, the term 'Shinto' ('the Way(s) of (the) Kami') was coined to refer to them.[2] Consequently, the word does not refer simply to a religious faith or a religious way of life. Rather, today

'it is an amalgam of attitudes, ideas, and ways of doing things that through two millenniums and more have become an integral part of the *way* of the Japanese people. Thus, Shinto is both a personal faith in the kami and a communal way of life according to the mind of the kami, which emerged in the course of the centuries as various ethnic and cultural influences, both indigenous and foreign, were fused, and the country attained unity under the Imperial Family.'[3]

[2] For the meaning of *kami*, see below, p. 197.
[3] Sokyo Ono, *Shinto: The Kami Way* (C. E. Tuttle, Rutland, Vt., 1962), pp. 3, 4.

The cultural invasion from China introduced not only new ideas, but a complicated form of writing as well. Chinese characters were subsequently adopted by the Japanese to represent their spoken language and the two characters which constitute the word 'Shinto' require further explication. The second character, *to* or *do* (also read as *michi* in Japanese) is the Chinese *Tao* with its rich historical significance from both Taoism and Confucianism,[4] indicating the universal Way of moral and physical order, the Way of thinking, the Rule of living, the Path of reason, truth, virtue, the Way both approved and followed by heaven itself, the Ultimate. While this depth and breadth of meaning cannot be applied *in toto* to the concept included in the 'Kami Way' (Shinto), this is the background from which the word was chosen. Current Shinto thought interprets it as the Way to 'kamihood', the Way of following the mind of the *kami* and living in accordance with the will of the *kami*.

This brings us to the initial character in the compound term: *Shin*, which is also read as *kami* in Japanese and may be either singular or plural. Whether we speak of 'the Kami Way' or 'the Way(s) of (the) Kami', the idea of *kami* is basic to an understanding of Shinto. At the same time, it is a very difficult concept to elucidate with precision. The use of the English word 'god' as a translation of the Japanese *kami* probably results in as much confusion as enlightenment. It seems advisable to make use of the transliteration *kami* in English rather than to substitute an inexact translation for such a crucial concept. Transliterations of similar concepts, albeit with their own peculiar nuances, have already entered the English language from Latin (*numen*) and Polynesian (*mana*).

One gains a significant insight into the spirit and character of Shinto (and the Japanese mind) when it is recognized that there was no serious attempt to give a rational elucidation of the fundamental concept of *kami* during over a millennium and a half of its existence. Only in comparatively recent years have efforts been made to expound upon the concept or to develop a 'kamiology'. Present-day Shinto scholars are united in their affirmation that the concept is vague and imprecise by its very nature. Throughout Japan's long history the *kami* and the *kami* concept have been apprehended by the people intuitively rather than rationally. Consequently, even in our day Shinto is without a clear idea, let alone a definition, of *kami*. Among the numerous suggestions regarding the etymology of the word, there is broad agreement that the idea of 'above' or 'superior' is involved. According to Motoori, the great scholar of the Japanese classics who pioneered the Shinto Revival beginning in the eighteenth century, 'in ancient times, anything that was awe-inspiring was called *kami*'.[5] Such a broad definition is

[4] See further, below, pp. 219ff.
[5] *Motoori Norinaga Zenshu (Complete Works of Motoori Norinaga,* I, Tokyo, 1901, p. 150).

obviously very inclusive. Awe-inspiring natural phenomena and things (living or lifeless) considered to be extraordinary are numerous. Eventually many such things were accorded superior powers whether they actually possessed them or not. The sun, the wind and the thunder, mountains, rivers, trees and rocks, wolves, snakes and foxes, mirrors, beads, and swords, strange men, chief men and wise men, ancestral spirits, guardian spirits and evil spirits, all are included in the *kami* classification. The common Shinto term for the whole *kami* pantheon, *Yao-yorozu-no-kami*, implies both the great variety and infinite number of the *kami*.[6]

While any and all kinds of things, inanimate, living or dead, may and have been 'kamified' in Japanese history, most of them are of little importance and many of them have only a local significance. Although the character, capacity or function of any particular *kami* is usually quite vague, the Folk Shinto of many locales maintains traditions regarding the powers and nature of the particular *kami* of that area. Sect Shinto has generally emphasized or recognized only a limited number of *kami* which have become more precisely delineated. For Shrine Shinto, the more important are those which play the major roles in classical mythological or historical traditions of the nation as a whole.

Shinto mythology

1. The main themes

Japanese mythology is found primarily in two basic works compiled in the eighth century, the *Kojiki* ('Records of Ancient Matters') and the *Nihon Shoki* ('Chronicles of Japan'), supplemented by secondary materials of the same general period. Although influenced by and modelled on Chinese writings, the legendary plots probably reflect certain actual circumstances, customs and patterns of thought of ancient times. Certainly there are Shinto concepts which continue today whose origins may be traced to these mythology narratives. Although there are numerous variations of some mythological episodes, the basic motif, as found in the oldest writing, the *Kojiki*, is as follows.

When heaven and earth began, there was a seemingly spontaneous generation of an original *kami* trio, 'the Lord of Central Heaven' (a modern Shinto scholar prefers 'the Lord who fills heaven, *i.e.* the universe'[7]) and two *kami* related to the generative processes, on the high plain of heaven. Subsequently, numerous other *kami* were generated or procreated. However, none of these *kami* is more than

---

[6] Literally the expression is made up of the characters for 800, 10,000 and *kami*, but *yao* (800) is also commonly used to indicate variety, while *yorozu* (10,000) indicates a large but indefinite number.

[7] Yoshitada Takahara, "Shinto no Seishin" ("The Spirit of Shinto") in *Deai*, May 1969, p. 9.

an intriguing name (which some modern commentators identify with divine qualities) until the appearance of the last of the 'celestial *kami*', the creative couple of Izanagi and Izanami. This male-female team, in response to the desire of the heavenly *kami*, stood on the Floating Bridge of Heaven and stirred up the brine beneath with a spear. When the spear was drawn up, an island appeared from the drops which fell from it, and to this they descended and began a series of creative acts which resulted in the generation (through copulation or spontaneously) of numerous islands and earthly *kami* – including the *kami* of sea and wind, rivers and mountains, trees and plants and food.[8]

Izanami was fatally burnt while giving birth to the *kami* of fire and departed from earth into the realm of the dead (*yomi*). After angrily despatching this final offspring of their union, Izanagi followed her to the nether world in hopes of bringing her back to the land of the living. He was too late, however, and, in disobedience to her expressed appeal, viewed her formerly beautiful body in a state of putrefaction; whereupon he was forced to flee from the Furies of Yomi and was barely able to escape their rage and the wrath of his erstwhile mate. Arriving back in the upper world, he cleansed himself of the pollution that adhered to him. This moment-ous act of purification resulted in the generation of many other *kami* from parts of his garments that he discarded or from the filth that he washed away, culminating finally in the auspicious trio of the sun-goddess, Amaterasu O Mikami ('Great Kami Shining in Heaven'), who was born of the discharge of his left eye, Tsukiyomi, related to the moon and the world of darkness, who appeared from the washing of his right eye, and Takehaya Susano O, in the storm-god tradition, who originated from the cleansing of his nose.

The mythological narrative next moves to a description of the problems developing between the benevolent and ritually correct rule of Amaterasu in heaven and the impetuous, uncontrollable behaviour of Susano O, at first upon earth, but eventually in heaven as well. The destructive, unseemly conduct of the latter, which was contrary both to the *mores* of an agricultural community and to the sense of propriety and purity of a ceremonially conscious society, so offended his elder sister that she withdrew into a cave in heaven, leaving the world in darkness. In consternation, the entire assemblage of *kami* (*Yao-yorozu-no-kami*) united their efforts to bring Amaterasu and her heavenly sunshine back into their lives. A large mirror was

[8] It may be of significance in regard to the relative place of man and woman in Japanese thought that the first creative act of this couple proved a failure be-cause the initiative was taken by Izanami, the female *kami*. When the act was repeated with Izanagi taking the initiative, the result was successful. Ancient Chinese documents indicate that some Japanese clans in the first centuries of the Christian era were under female leadership, but eventually male authority was established.

constructed and hung in a *sakaki* tree outside the cave along with a
string of jewels and strips of cloth. An arousing dance with obscene
gestures by a female *kami* caused the heavens to shake with the
laughter of the *Yao-yorozu-no-kami*, prompting the curious Amaterasu
to open the cave door. She was further coaxed outside by her own
brilliance reflected from the mirror.

Susano O was then banished from heaven to the land of darkness.
Among his subsequent adventures was the slaying of an eight-headed
serpent, in whose tail he found a miraculous sword which he later
presented to Amaterasu, his elder sister. Among his descendants who
ruled over the western area of Japan (Izumo), the most auspicious
was O Kuni Nushi ('Lord of the Great Land'). This *kami* later nobly
submitted to the decree of Amaterasu that her grandson, Ninigi,
was to descend to Japan to rule there and consequently he has been
revered as a model of sincere loyalty and humble obedience. Prior to
Ninigi's descent, there were given to him three sacred treasures: a
mirror, a string of jewels and the sword. Following his arrival on
earth, Ninigi married the beautiful blossom princess, the *kami* of
Mount Fuji. A great-grandson of this union was Jimmu, the first
Emperor of Japan.

2. The kami concept

The above presentation of the main theme of the mythological
accounts will serve a larger purpose than to provide insights into the
Shinto concept of *kami*, but its instruction in this regard will be
considered first. While little of the more fanciful stories of the *kami*,
their nature, names and activities has been included in the above
description, it should be clear that at times the *kami* are identified
with and indistinguishable from natural phenomena, such as islands,
sun and mountains, or powers and processes, such as birth and
growth. Their generation may be spontaneous, without explanation,
they may suddenly appear from natural objects or they may be
born as the result of physical union between parent *kami*. The *kami*
often act in very human ways, but frequently evidence powers that
are beyond human ability.

Whether or not one postulates an evolutionary development from
primitive nature-worship (where natural objects themselves are
worshipped) through polydemonism (wherein supernatural spirits are
believed to indwell the physical objects) to polytheism (where true
personification takes place, making it correct to speak of gods and
goddesses),[9] these various facets of *kami* concepts are seen in the
myths. Some modern Shinto scholars find pantheistic or monotheistic
implications in these ancient stories as well, giving figurative or
philosophical explanations to the names and activities of the various
kami and finding ethical as well as historical truths imbedded in the

[9] See Genchi Kato, *A Study of Shinto: The Religion of the Japanese Nation*
(Barnes and Noble, New York, 1971), pp. 7ff.

narratives. For the ordinary Shinto believer of today, *kami* may refer to spiritual beings existing today, mythological entities of ancient times, natural phenomena (including both inanimate and living things), physical objects of worship or ancestral spirits. Thus the concept remains vague today, but during Shinto worship the idea of ancestral spirits – whether of a particular clan chieftain who became a tutelary deity of a certain area, of a great national figure in Japanese history, of those who died for their country or of ancestors in general – is probably predominant.

This lack of definiteness regarding the *kami*, which most religionists of theocentric traditions would consider to be the essential concept in Shinto thought, suggests that Shinto is in another religious tradition. The lack of a clear distinction between the *kami* and things that are not *kami*, plus the fact that this tradition has been maintained for approximately 2,000 years without clarifying this term, may indicate both that the concept is not so important in Shinto thought as non-Shintoists imagine and that Shinto, due to its inherent nature, does not require clarity here but is content with and even encourages vagueness. As it is a man-centred religion with emphasis upon maintaining communal, ceremonial traditions for the purpose of human (communal) well-being rather than upon conformity of doctrine, abstract conceptualizations are not so important. Through the centuries, Shinto has managed to keep its simplicity because it has not concerned itself with rational explanations but with following ancestral patterns.

3. Mythology and Shinto values

A consideration of Shinto mythology also provides an insight into Shinto morality. 'Goodness' and 'badness', which may be attributed to *kami* as well as to men, is not determined by measurement against a clearly-defined standard or moral code. There is no suggestion of any absolute or fixed character of the qualities themselves. They can be attributed to inanimate objects as well as to rational beings. The 'good' seems to be identified with that which possesses, or relates to, beauty, brightness, excellence, good fortune, nobility, purity, suitability, harmony, conformity, productivity. The mythologies contain numerous stories of *kami* activities that are narrated without a hint of disparagement but which would be labelled immoral according to certain puritan standards foreign to Shinto. If an order of Shinto moral values were to be attempted, certainly purity and harmony or conformity would rank among the highest.

Both of these values are given lucid expression in two of the principal mythological tales. The deeds of the unpredictable Susano O which caused Amaterasu to hide her brightness and finally resulted in his banishment from her heavenly realm of order and purity were both offensive to concepts of purity (befouling her palace with excrement) and destructive to orderly society (breaking down embankments between rice fields). Izanagi also overstepped the bounds of propriety when he stubbornly followed his wife to the land of the dead and gazed upon her decaying form. After fleeing from the nether world, he had to purify himself from the defilements which clung to him after his contact with death.

These accounts reflect a concern that has remained a consistent characteristic of Shinto throughout the centuries. While man is basically good (sharing the *kami* essence along with the rest of nature), he must act in ways that enhance order and harmony in society. He is part of a community – both horizontally, with the present society (family, neighbourhood, nation) of which he is a part, and vertically, with the domestic, provincial and national ancestral traditions in which he finds himself. His behaviour should be in keeping with the *mores* of the community. While man is basically pure, contact with what is impure (blood, sickness, death), the action of evil spirits, or ceremonial laxity, may bring defilement and require ritual purification. Traditionally, Shinto has been more concerned with external, ceremonial purification than an inward cleansing.

The numerous fanciful stories included in the classical myths provide the basis of countless traditions preserved in local shrines throughout Japan. Traditions that are of more than local significance include the liturgical usage of branches of the *sakaki* tree and strips of white cloth or paper; ceremonial dancing by young women; ritual-istic purification; defilement resulting from the contact with death; the establishment of the Grand Shrine of Ise in honour of Amaterasu and the Grand Shrine of Izumo in honour of O Kuni Nushi; the enshrinement of the three sacred symbols at major shrines (the mirror at Ise, the jewels at an Imperial Palace Shrine in Tokyo and the sword at the Atsuta Shrine in Nagoya); conceptions that the Japanese islands and the people have a divine origin, that Japanese Emperors, descendants of the sun-goddess, rule according to divine appointment, and that submission to higher authority is the path of virtue. Historians see in these mythological accounts reflections or fanciful embellishments of actual historical events.

4. Other Shinto scriptures

Along with the *Kojiki* and the *Nihon Shoki*[1] which are the basic source materials for considering the origins of Shinto and its early history are other old documents of the same era such as the *Kujiki* ('Records of Old Matters'), *Kogoshui* ('Gleanings from Ancient Stories'), and a few *Fudoki* ('Records of Local Features') which supplement them. Added to these writings are the poetic expressions of religious and moral sentiment expressed in the *Manyoshu* ('Collection of Myriad Leaves', or 'Collection for a Myriad Ages'), a late eighth-century compilation, and an early tenth-century collection of ceremonial

---

[1] See above, p. 195.

prayers and rituals called the *Engishiki* ('Ceremonies of the Engi Period'). Together, these writings may be considered the scriptures of Shinto in the sense that they are accorded a special place of respect as the most ancient written sources of the traditions and, to an extent, are considered authoritative. But they have not traditionally been considered a canon which the Shintoist is bound to accept, nor have they traditionally been used to formulate Shinto dogma or to place limitations on further development of belief and practice of Shintoists, most of whom have never read them. They are recognized as the products of a certain period of history, reflecting the thought and customs of that day. Their special place is based on their being the oldest written records of the tradition which is still being maintained.

While the traditions of the Japanese people contained or reflected in these classics continue to be honoured by Shintoists today, they are usually 'caught' rather than 'taught'. Verbal communication of ideology, whether for explaining to non-adherents or for instructing adherents, has not generally been engaged in by Shrine Shinto. The Japanese child is brought up to respect the traditional practices and to follow them as a member of the community. Although with the modernization of Japan patterns of thought and practice are changing, in rural areas it still may be considered an act of defiance, both anti-social and anti-Japanese, not to respect the traditional ways. The unhappy consequences of such defiance proves a strong deterrent and the social pressure for conformity remains firm.

Shinto worship

1. Shinto rites

Rites rather than writings are the basis of the religious education and the channel for mediating the divine word to the Shintoist. Shinto rites vary from the routine worship performed in the home and the perfunctory visit to a neighbourhood shrine to the highly ceremonial rituals of the major shrines on special occasions. Whether simple or ostentatious, Shinto rites are ordinarily performed at specified locations in the presence of, and directed towards, *kami*, in places where *kami* or their symbolic representations are enshrined. Thus rituals are usually performed before a home altar, at small, private shrines built and maintained by private individuals or a group, or on larger, public shrine grounds. An exception to this general rule is the ceremonial purification of a land site preceding construction, which is performed to drive out evil *kami* from the area and to console the good *kami*, hopefully resulting in less chance of accidents during construction and greater prosperity for whatever the land is used for.

The home altar (*kamidana*, literally '*kami* shelf') is usually of simple, wooden construction protruding from the wall at an elevated level in the living-room – making it impossible for people to look down upon it. It is basically a shelf with a small, roofed structure in the centre back in which is placed one or more sacred tablets, each bearing the name of a shrine or *kami* that have been purchased at a shrine. On the shelf in front of this structure may be placed a small mirror, sprigs of *sakaki*, two small lanterns and a stand upon which to place offerings. A straw rope with white paper pendants attached cut in the traditional zig-zag fashion may be hung above the shelf. Before this home altar, which is a kind of miniature shrine, religious rites may be performed.

2. Shinto shrines

It is the shrine, however, which is the centre of Shinto worship. The purpose of the shrine is both to furnish an abode for the *kami* and to provide a place for worship of the *kami*. Its location is usually in the natural setting of a wooded area, often chosen because of some special natural object in the vicinity (a tree, rock, or mountain which may themselves be objects of worship, considered either a *kami* or the abode of *kami*) or because of its historical association with the *kami* enshrined there. The surroundings are expected to be conducive to worship. The entrance to the shrine grounds is marked by a distinctive structure called a *torii* (literally, 'bird perch') made up of two upright pillars with two cross-beams under which the worshippers must pass. The *torii* provide a symbolic passageway from the profane world into the sacred precincts, and the act of passing through this gateway is considered a kind of purification.

Near the *torii* or deeper in the shrine grounds there may be images of a couple of ferocious, dog-like creatures to scare off evil spirits. Within the shrine grounds, use is made of straw rope with the characteristic white strips of paper or cloth hanging from them to designate particularly sacred objects or structures. This *shimenawa* may be hanging around a tree or a rock or from the eaves of a building. It seems that, in the more primitive stage of development, there were no structures erected to house the *kami* but only some such mark of designation of a place or natural object as sacred. Along the path to the holy abode will be found an ablution pavilion where water is provided for ceremonial purification before approaching the sacred dwelling-place.

Within the precincts of the larger shrines, there may be a number of *torii* at a distance from one another along the paths to the sanctuary. There may be various buildings including a shrine office, a place to prepare offerings, priests' quarters, a hall for ceremonial dances, a storehouse, *etc.* Generally, the buildings on the shrine grounds are simple, unpainted, wooden structures of a traditional architectural style. Certain shrines, however, show the result of foreign influence in their more ornate embellishment. In front of the sanctuary is a large offering-box, into which money is tossed during the worship ritual, and over which may be a bell which is sounded by jiggling the rope hanging down from it. This sound may serve to drive off evil spirits or to arouse the *kami* to the worship being performed.

The sanctuary itself is usually an unimposing structure into which the worshipper does not enter. Individual worship is performed in the outer oratory in front of the sanctuary, not in the sanctuary itself. In the innermost part of the sanctuary is the sanctorum where the material, symbolic representation of the *kami* is enshrined. This symbol, called the '*kami* body' (*shintai*) or 'spirit substitute' (*mitama-shiro*) is never seen by the worshipper, who is often unaware of the specific object enshrined. Among the more common items used for *kami* bodies or spirit substitutes are mirrors, swords, stones, beads, and inscribed tablets, but the nature of the object of worship is not important. The fact that the ceremony is being performed is what is of significance. There are no images in the shrine which receive worship, but another Shinto symbol called a *gohei* (a short, upright wooden or bamboo rod with paper, cloth or metal cut in the characteristic zig-zag fashion hanging on two sides from the top) is the most sacred visible emblem in the shrine, signifying the presence of the *kami*.

The *kami* being venerated at a particular shrine is often unknown even to the worshippers and many shrines are related to a plurality of *kami* simultaneously. Traditionally, each *kami* is considered to have a particular character or function of its own with a peculiar power in certain limited areas – whether geographical, tribal, occupational, climatic or in regard to particular problems such as barrenness, certain ailments, *etc*. The origin of these *kami* and the traditions related to them are often lost in antiquity and in many cases various traditions are concurrently extant. Obviously some traditions betray the influence of the long period of close association with Buddhism such as those of the Inari shrines which have a special appeal to shopkeepers, manufacturers, farmers and barren women, and the Hachiman shrines which are associated with the military.

In the case of certain special shrines, however, the *kami* being worshipped is very clear. The Inner Shrine of the Grand Shrine of Ise, for example, which in some ways is in a special class by itself as the central shrine of the whole nation, is dedicated to the sun-goddess, Amaterasu O Mikami, from whom the imperial line is said to find its source. The sacred mirror given by the sun-goddess as a symbol of herself to her august grandson when he descended to earth is said to be enshrined there. However, the case in which this holy symbol is contained is never opened, even when it is transferred to its alternate location within the shrine grounds when a new sanctuary is built for it every twenty years. There are shrines in memory of outstanding historical figures such as Ieyasu, the founder of the Tokugawa Shogun-ate, and Emperor Meiji. Their spirits are considered to be the *kami* enshrined in the Toshogu Shrine in Nikko and the Meiji Shrine in

Tokyo respectively. In the famous Yasukuni Shrine in Tokyo are enshrined the spirits of those who died in the military service of their country.

The most common general class of shrines are those enshrining the tutelary *kami* of a certain clan (*uji*). The ancient clans which settled in the various areas of the country developed their particular traditions which were eventually united with or subordinated to that of the Yamato Clan which gained precedence. Some of these varied traditions are reflected in the classical mythologies where they are either amalgamated with the predominant strain or continue as an independent tradition. The chieftain (*kami*) of the clan in life often became the guardian spirit of that clan in death, when he was symbolically enshrined as the *ujigami*. Whereas these *ujigami* were originally the tutelary divinities of groups linked by a common lineage, they later were considered the protecting spirits over a given area – and in some cases became especially related to certain occupations or were attributed special powers for the alleviation of particular kinds of misfortune or for granting particular benefits.

At the present time, every area in Japan has a shrine where the *ujigami* of that community is enshrined. The inhabitants of the area are considered protégés (*ujiko*) of that guardian spirit by virtue of the fact that they reside in the area under his protection. Although there may be other shrines of another special character in the same community, it is the *ujigami* which has the deepest roots in the local soil, to which the 'parishioners' generally feel their deepest obligation. It is ordinarily to the *ujigami* that the supplicant or the grateful soul will retire for individual worship.

3. The elements of Shinto worship

Shinto worship consists of four basic elements: purification, offering, prayer and a sacred meal. While the more religiously inclined may perceive inward, spiritual meaning in the worship rites, generally speaking they are looked upon simply as traditional ceremonial observances with little conscious thought or explanation given regarding any deeper significance. The final element of worship is regularly omitted on less formal occasions.

Purification rites to rid oneself of impurities or defilements which would hinder one's approaching the *kami* (or 'kamihood') are the first step of worship. In the home, before presenting oneself before the *kamidana*, purification takes the form of bathing, rinsing the mouth or simply washing the hands. On an individual visit to the shrine also, after passing under the *torii* (symbolizing purification), the worshipper rinses his mouth and pours water upon his fingers in the ablution pavilion before approaching the sanctuary. A person with any illness, an open wound, flowing blood or in mourning should not participate in Shinto worship, since these things make him ceremonially unclean. As has been noted above, purification ceremonies are also performed upon land sites using a purification wand (*haraigushi*), a wooden stick with paper streamers attached to it. One of the annual Shinto rites of national significance is the Great Purification Ceremony which will be noted again below.[2]

The offering presented to the *kami* at the home altar is usually a small quantity of rice (either cooked or raw), water, salt, fish, rice wine, vegetables or other foodstuffs. This is placed upon the little stand on the shelf in front of the enshrined tablet. At the communal shrine, the normal offering is money tossed into the offering box in front of the sanctuary. Prayers, whether at home sitting on the *tatami* mat floor before the altar, or standing outdoors without hat or overcoat before the sanctuary at the shrine, are not vocalized by the worshippers and are accompanied by a series of bows and two hand-claps. Personal prayers are usually limited to petition, thanksgiving or a kind of reporting to the *kami*. Frequently, there is not even a mental verbalization of prayer thoughts but only a feeling of communion with the *kami*. On occasions of more special requests or more intensive gratitude, the worshipper may desire a more formal ceremony. If the shrine facilities and personnel permit, the worshipper may pay a fee or make a monetary offering for a formal prayer (*norito*) to be offered by a ceremonially-garbed priest before the enshrined *kami* in the presence of the worshipper. This ritual takes place in a building, closer to the actual spot where the *kami* is enshrined. For a higher fee or offering, a dance by ceremonially-garbed maiden dancers (*miko*), which should enhance the effectiveness of the ritual, may be requested. The sacred meal is considered to be a means of having fellowship with the *kami*, with whom the meal is symbolically being shared.

4. Shinto festivals and ceremonies

The times when worship is performed in the truest sense and with the greatest formality are during the festival days or on regular ceremonial occasions. Every Shinto shrine has a regular, usually annual, festival day which, especially for the *ujigami* shrines, is a gala occasion for the whole community. Before these festivals, which usually take place just before or after the planting or harvesting seasons, the shrine is well cleaned and specially decorated for the event. On the festival day, in the presence of the assembled worshippers who have been purified by having the purification wand or a branch of the *sakaki* tree waved in front of or over them, the momentous time arrives when the doors of the small, inner sanctorum are opened to the accompanying strains of traditional Japanese music. The enshrined *kami* (symbol), however, remains hidden from the view of priest and layman alike. While the doors are opened, offerings of food and wine are ceremonially brought in and placed before the

---

[2] See pp. 205f.

kami while sacred music is played. A formal *norito* prayer is read and the worshippers, or their representatives, perform the ritual bowing with hand-claps before the opened holy of holies. Following this, the offerings are removed, again in ceremonial fashion, and the worshippers symbolically partake of the sacred meal by taking a sip of rice wine while the priests and shrine officials withdraw for the real feast.

Sacred dances (*kagura*) are also performed on the festival days in the shrines that have facilities for them. For the general community, the main event of the day is the joyful carrying of a portable shrine through the community in a merry procession. The small palanquin shrine contains either the holy *kami* symbol itself or a substitute and is carried on the shoulders of the young men of the community. The procession is a gay and, at times, rowdy one as both carriers and bystanders have usually been celebrating the festival in their own homes or in those of friends where rice wine has been flowing freely. The portable shrine may be temporarily deposited at a place of some traditional significance for that *kami* or returned forthwith to the permanent shrine after this annual visit to the community over which it grants its protection. The festival time is usually a community-wide celebration with various types of entertainment provided which are also determined by the traditions of the locality.

Besides the regular festival day of a particular shrine on which all faithful parishioners try to visit the shrine, the first hours and days of the New Year are the most popular time for crowds to go to the shrine for worship. Although there are irregular, special rituals performed at the time of an emperor's enthronement and the like, the traditional Shinto ceremonies of major national importance that are regularly performed are those of the Harvest Festival (*Niinamesai*, or *Niiname matsuri*, literally, 'New Taste Festival') and the Grand Purification Ceremony (*Oharai*). Since the disestablishment of Shinto in 1945, these ceremonies have not attracted the public interest of former years, but they continue to be performed as two of the most ancient rituals and may serve to indicate certain basic Shinto characteristics. The *Niinamesai*, at which the Emperor himself performs the priestly functions, is performed annually following the autumnal harvest (now celebrated on 23 November as a national holiday called Labour-Thanksgiving Day). In this ritual the Emperor, as an expression of gratitude for the harvest, presents first-fruits to the *kami* and partakes of them himself. This ceremony is considered the most solemn and mysterious of all Shinto rites, being performed in the darkness of midnight except for a few torches nearby. During this rite, the Emperor is considered to be in direct communication, or even united, with the *kami* whose descendant he is considered to be.

The Great Purification Ceremony is performed twice a year, on the last days of June and December, with the purpose of cleansing people and land from the pollution and impurities incurred during the previous half year. At this time, the shaking of the purification wand and the sprinkling of water, as symbols of purification, are accompanied by a recitation of an ancient ritualistic prayer which records explicitly the kinds of sins committed by the 'heavenly race who populated the peaceful land'. These include breaking down the divisions between rice fields, plugging up irrigation channels, breaking water-troughs, double sowing of seed, flaying live animals, cutting live or dead bodies, being a leper, incest, bestiality, evils or misfortunes caused by creeping things, high *kami* and high birds, killing animals, and witchcraft. The essence of this archaic prayer has been put into modern Japanese and translated into English as follows:

'In accordance with the command of Amaterasu O Mikami dwelling in heaven, the people of the divine land called an assembly, at which they resolved that the August Grandchild of the August Great Ancestress should be asked to bring the rule of peace to the land of Japan, and the government was therefore entrusted to him.

'The August Grandchild, after having subdued and pacified violent and savage Earthly Deities then still rampant in the land entrusted to him, and also reduced to silence even those rocks, trees and herbs which lack the power of speech, descended from Heaven to rule over the nation (the Central Land of Reed-Plains), leaving the Heavenly Rock-Seat and cleaving this way through the fold clouds.

'As the centre of the land which in obedience to the divine will he should govern in peace the August Grandchild chose the province of Yamato, building there a fine palace to dwell in.

'Now, the sins committed purposely or otherwise by the people born in this peacefully governed land will be large in number, whether they arise from the people's agricultural activities or from their fleshly lusts; but at such times, in accordance with the laws of the divine land, you must offer the Deities certain things which are good for the world, as atonement for your sins – making quantities of firewood, or splitting hemp into fine lengths – and you must utter sincere words in repentance.

'And then the Deities dwelling in Heaven will deign to hear your prayer, opening the door and thrusting apart the fold clouds in Heaven, and the Earthly Deities will likewise deign to hear, going up to the summits of the high and low mountains, putting aside the clouds and mists.

'If the prayer is thus heard, the sins and impurities of the whole land, including the Court, will be expiated, just as the wind blows away piled-up clouds; as the breezes sweep off the morning and evening mists; as men sail away in big ships to the great ocean by casting from their mooring; as the trees growing thick yonder are cut down with a sharp axe.

'Then the sins and impurities thus purified and cleansed will be carried away to the sea by the goddess Seori-tsu-Hime who lives in the rapids which rush down from the high and low mountains. When carried away thus, they will be swallowed by the goddess Hayaaki-tsu-Hime dwelling at the point far out at sea where all tides meet; when thus engulfed deep to the bottom of the sea, they will be completely blown off into the Nether-Distant-Land by the god Ibukido-nushi who dwells at the gate leading to the Nether-Distant-Land; when blown off into the Nether-Distant-Land thus, the goddess Hayasasura-Hime who dwells in the Nether-Distant-Land will carry them and cast them away.

'Know therefore that, when cast away thus, all the sins and impurities will be thoroughly purified and cleansed from this day forward so that any and every one of them will altogether disappear from this world.'[3]

The ritualistic practices described in relation to these two most important ceremonies make clear the central significance of the Japanese Emperor as the divine or divinely-appointed ruler of a divinely-generated people. As has been noted before, Shinto is a Japanese tribal religion centred in national traditions which are symbolized in the person of the Emperor with a heavenly-ordained role. These ceremonies also indicate the feeling of an intimate relationship with the *kami* which are all about, from which man is not clearly separated and upon which bountiful harvests and other benefits depend. They show a primary, this-worldly character, being concerned with natural, agricultural and human values. The sins of men which require purification are basically physical or material rather than spiritual, and the means of purification is primarily ceremonial.

Early Shinto history

The ancient beliefs and customs of the Japanese clans which developed into the Shinto of today were characterized by a feeling of awe and a thrill of mystery in the presence of the superior, the strange, the unknown and the inexplicable, combined with a keen sense of tribal cohesion. These primitive traits encouraged the development of an unsophisticated nature-worship, an attraction to the occult and a deep respect for authority, tradition and communal *mores*. Until the advent of Chinese cultural influences – including forms of art and writing, and forms of thought such as Confucianism, Taoism and Buddhism – Japanese (Shinto) ideology remained naïve. There seemed little or no distinction between heavenly and earthly worlds, the world of the living and that of the dead, living beings, inanimate objects and the forces of nature, *kami* and the objects they indwell or which represent them.

[3] Translation into modern Japanese by Yoshitada Takahara, head priest of Yasaka Shrine, President of Kogakukan University; and into English by Yoshijiro Sato.

Religious rites, which were mainly related to agricultural activities and ceremonial purification, were performed by clan chieftains or peculiar individuals who were considered to possess unusual powers. While occult practices and forms continued their development in a largely unorganized fashion resulting in the Folk Shinto of today, the more organized, central clan observances, under the recognized leadership of the tribal chief or a hereditary priestly line, became centred in a specified location where the tutelary *kami* of the clan resided and later was enshrined. The worship pattern described above became the means of expressing a fidelity to ancestral traditions, present leadership and communal harmony, as well as seeking to please the *kami* or to gain its favour. As the various tribes became united under the Yamato clan, the tutelary *kami*, Amaterasu O Mikami, the sun-goddess, and particular traditions of that clan became predominant throughout the land, and the clan's chieftain was recognized as the national leader while regional traditions and worship at local shrines continued with little change.

With the advent of Chinese cultural influences in the fifth and sixth centuries, adjustments became imperative, not only in government and society at large, but in relation to the native religious beliefs and customs as well. The Yamato chieftain became an 'emperor' in the Chinese tradition while maintaining his role as high priest of the native cult. Ethical and philosophical concepts from Confucianism and Taoism, along with elements of primitive Chinese superstition, were incorporated into the Japanese religious system. It was the 'Way of the Buddha', however, that posed the greatest problem for the custodians of the native traditions. It forced them for the first time to make a conscious assessment of their values and basic principles implicit in their traditions and to recognize the existence of a particular life outlook and ceremonial pattern which was designated the 'Way of the Kami' or Shinto. Buddhism, with its more highly-developed doctrines, organizational structure, artistic and ceremonial forms, soon proved superior in many ways to the undeveloped, loosely-organized, more primitive traditions of Shinto and became the religion of the upper classes and, in effect, the state religion. Nevertheless, Shinto thought and customs continued among the common people and were never truly supplanted by Buddhism. Rather a form of co-existence, which developed into a virtual amalgamation during certain periods, evolved.

In the eighth century (Nara period), in which Buddhism was reaching an overpowering dominance, the oral traditions of Shinto were written down, resulting in the appearance of the *Kojiki* and *Nihon Shoki* scriptures. Large Buddhist temples were built after appropriate Shinto ceremonies had been performed and many temples continue today to have Shinto shrines in their precincts as guardian spirits. It was, however, during the classical Heian period of Japanese history (794–1185), that Buddhism and Shinto became most closely associated. Both the Tendai and Shingon Schools of Buddhism[4] developed theories whereby the multitudinous Shinto *kami* were considered manifestations of pre-existent Buddhas or *Bodhisattvas*. Buddhist names were given to Shinto *kami* and Buddhist priests read Buddhist *sutras* at the Shinto shrines. While the Shinto tradition continued despite its subordinate position, it became inextricably mixed with Buddhist elements which have defied subsequent efforts at separation.

The inevitable Shinto reaction against Buddhist pre-eminence during the Kamakura period (1185-1333) centred in the hereditary priests of the Ise Shrine who attempted to reverse the order of primacy and, in the 'Shinto Pentateuch', a series of five works, propounded the doctrine that Buddhas and *Bodhisattvas* were the manifestations of *kami*. Subsequent theorists (Kitabatake, Ichijo, Yoshida) developed a syncretic, philosophical monism postulating a universal *kami*-spirit underlying all reality and including deities of both Buddhism and Shinto. Underlying such re-formulations of Shinto thought were feelings that the Japanese people and their faith possessed a uniqueness which must also be appreciated.

It was, however, during the feudalistic Tokugawa period (1600–1868) that a true Shinto revival occurred. Although Buddhism remained the predominant religion and Shinto practices were officially recognized, Confucianism became the ideological framework of the feudal regime.

A new alignment of a Confucian-Shinto nature brought new vitality to Shinto theory, supplying certain inherent philosophical deficiencies with Confucian concepts. The 'Supreme Ultimate' of Confucianism was identified with one or more original Shinto *kami* and a moral-political respect for the Emperor was emphasized.

Having experienced both the benefits and disadvantages of intimate association with both Buddhism and Confucianism, Shinto scholars in the latter half of the feudal era made an effort to purge Shinto of all foreign accretions, basing their attempt upon philological studies of the Japanese classical writings of the eighth century. A trio of Shinto scholars, Mabuchi (1697–1769), Motoori (1730–1801) and Hirata (1776–1843), despite individual peculiarities of emphasis and methodology, were united in their aim of reviving the pure, unadulterated Shinto of the golden, primaeval period before the advent of foreign, corrupting influences. The unphilosophical simplicity of the primitive traditions was considered the apex of religious thought, the ideal to be returned to. Metaphysics were rejected as a sign of degeneration of a purer, original simplicity and a system of ethics was considered unnecessary for a people descended from the *kami*. For them, following their natural instincts was held to be sufficient. Needless to say, such a movement was imbued with a fervent nationalistic spirit. Not only was the divine

[4] See above, pp. 183f.

prerogative of the Emperor to rule Japan emphasized, but a divine mission of Japan to rule the world was added to it. The seeds sown by these 'purists' did not bear fruit immediately, but the political upheaval which brought an end to the feudal regime and a restoration of imperial rule in 1868 provided the setting in which Shinto nationalism could reach its climax.

Modern Shinto history

When the young Emperor Meiji mounted the throne in 1868, it was the first time in over 500 years that a Japanese Emperor was more than a fictional ruler. In fact, it was close to 1,000 years since actual imperial rule had been sustained for any length of time. The time was ripe for an attempt to restore the ancient traditions to a place of pre-eminence in Japanese society under the regnant heir of the sun-goddess. An immediate effort was made to dissociate Shinto and Buddhism; a special department of Shinto was established separate from the cabinet and having precedence over the Grand Council of State. Until the Meiji Restoration, Shinto shrines were basically communal institutions maintained and supported by the local communities in which they were located. Rituals at the various shrines had become the responsibility of a hereditary priesthood. Under Meiji, Shinto was designated the national religion, most shrines were brought under government control and officiating priests were appointed by the government and were considered government officials.

Along with the establishment of Shinto a differentiation was made between the national faith with its government support and various local strains which had developed around a certain shrine, a particular tradition or a charismatic personality and had produced a degree of doctrinal independence and an organization that was not limited by community boundaries. Such groups had evolved over the closing decades of the feudal age and, in order to distinguish them from the established religion, were designated Shinto sects. Thirteen sects were officially recognized and placed in a category separate from the State Shinto which the government sought to promote as the custodian of national, ancestral traditions upon which the nation was founded and to which all Japanese owe respect and allegiance.

Eventually, in order to maintain the constitutional guarantee of religious freedom, State Shinto was formally removed from the 'religious' classification altogether. The ritual conducted and the worship offered at the State Shinto shrines were considered expressions of patriotic rather than religious feeling. As a national obligation, all Japanese, whatever their faith, were required to participate in rites at the shrines, to show the deepest respect toward the divine personage (a veritable *kami* in the flesh) who ruled under the imperial mandate preserved inviolate throughout the age from Amaterasu O Mikami herself, and to submit to the governmental edicts which were promulgated in his name. Shinto indoctrination was carried on in the schools through courses on Japanese history, moral teaching, citizenship and the like. Ultimately, State Shinto became a tool in the hands of a militarist government that plunged the nation into the disastrous Second World War, culminating in both a military defeat and a profound spiritual disturbance.

Following Japan's unconditional surrender (which was delayed due to Japanese government attempts to guarantee the status of the Emperor), Allied governments presided over the thoroughgoing disestablishment of Shinto, prohibiting 'the sponsorship, support, perpetuation, control and dissemination of Shinto' by government institutions,[5] and the public pronouncement by the Emperor that the ties between Emperor and people 'do not depend upon mere legends and myths. They are not predicted upon the false conception that the Emperor is divine and that the Japanese people are superior to other races and are fated to rule the world.'[6] Both these events had far-reaching effects on Shinto – both practically and theoretically. Nation-wide, close to 110,000 shrines that had been supervised and regulated to a greater or lesser degree by the national government for the past seventy years and had received regular financial assistance from national, prefectural or local government bodies, were suddenly made completely independent with no continuing means of support other than the voluntary contributions of worshippers. Moreover, fundamental doctrines for which countless thousands willingly gave their lives were suddenly declared myths, legends and false conceptions by the very ruler who had been venerated as divine, but who now lowered himself to the level of a mere mortal.

Organizationally, the majority of Shinto shrines were soon joined together into a major, nation-wide shrine association which presently numbers close to 80,000 members and a few regional associations. A few large, nationally popular shrines have remained completely independent. The national Association of Shinto Shrines (*Jinja Honcho*) is governed by a board of councillors made up of representatives of prefectural associations. This board selects an executive secretary and is responsible for major policy decisions. At the Association headquarters there are departments of the secretariat, finance, general administration, teaching, investigation and mutual aid. Locally, the shrines are administered by committees representing the local shrine community (parishioners). Many of the smaller shrines continue to face financial difficulties, are without resident priests and are active only on festival days, although the grounds are always open for those who wish to come for private worship at any time.

---

[5] "Shinto Directive" of 15 December 1945 from the General Headquarters of the Supreme Commander for the Allied Powers to the Imperial Japanese Government.
[6] Broadcast by the Emperor on 1 January 1946.

The priesthood is open to any person (including women in the post-war period) who has been recommended by the local shrine committee for appointment by the president of the Shrine Association and who has received the minimal training required for qualification. Since the priest functions primarily as a performer of ritual, such training is basically of a ceremonial or liturgical nature, relating to Shinto rites and festivals, and may be received from individual priests, Association-sponsored classes or in advanced study at the Kokugakuin University, Kogakukan University or other specialized schools. Each shrine has a head priest (*guji*) and larger shrines may have an assistant head priest (*gon-guji*) or priests of the two lower ranks (*negi* and *gon-negi*). Many priests of the smaller shrines have full-time secular occupations and function as priests only on special ceremonial occasions. While support for the local shrines is legally a matter of voluntary contributions, regular and systematic appeals are made to all inhabitants of a community (regardless of personal beliefs). Since many community leaders continue to consider support for the shrine to be a communal responsibility regardless of one's personal religious inclination, and because of Japan's particular historical heritage and consciousness of communal cohesion, many find it difficult to refuse to make their 'voluntary contributions'. Since the war, certain shrines have endeavoured to attract other sources of income and to perform other services such as wedding rites. Charms for various purposes continue to be sold at the shrines and supplement the income from the offerings during worship.

The Emperor, according to the new Japanese constitution, is now 'the symbol of the state and of the unity of the people'. No longer closeted in mystery behind the Imperial Palace doors, he has travelled about the country, establishing human ties with the people. He continues to function, however, in a personal capacity as the high priest of Shinto, officiating at traditional ceremonies performed according to the ancient patterns at one of the three shrines within the Imperial Palace grounds. Since the end of the American Occupation, there has been constant agitation to moderate or undo the wholesale severance of government and official public life from the ancient Shinto traditions which were considered more than merely religious observances. Public officials in private capacities have made visits to the Grand Shrine of Ise to make reports to the sun-goddess and ancestral *kami*. National Foundation Day has been reinstituted as a national holiday on 11 February, commemorating the mythical date of accession of Japan's first Emperor, Jimmu. Social and political agitation for the nationalization of important shrines of national significance (Ise Shrine and Yasukuni Shrine, in particular) has increased.

Considering the firm roots and respected place of Shinto thought and practice in the history of the Japanese people, it is not surprising that it has endured the national, political and religious upheaval following the Second World War. While its place as a national tradition will doubtless continue, its future significance as a religion seems less assured. Although the statistics given in the annual, government-compiled Religious Yearbook cannot be accepted at face value owing to the questionable and very loose methods of calculating or estimating adherents used by Shinto bodies, these statistics reflect a regular and general decline in the number of Shinto believers, with the 1969 Yearbook listing 68,311,818 adherents for all Shinto bodies of both Shrine and Sect categories, which is about two-thirds of the population, a large percentage of which are related to Buddhist temples as well.

Present characteristics of Shinto

It should be sufficiently clear from the preceding account that little of a systematic, doctrinal character can be articulated in regard to Shrine Shinto. Hopefully, however, its general feeling or atmosphere, including certain doctrinal implications, has been conveyed. It may be well to close this section with some explicit affirmations and a few general critical observations regarding Shrine Shinto doctrine and practice before moving on to a brief treatment of Sect Shinto and newer religious movements. The following statement of three basic principles which are said to express 'the true feelings of the people and the true nature of Shrine Shinto' published by the Association of Shinto Shrines will serve as the starting-point. The principles are:

'1. To express gratitude for divine favour and the benefits of ancestors, and with a bright, pure, sincere mind to devote ourselves to the shrine rites and festivals.
2. To serve society and others and, in the realization of ourselves as divine messengers, to endeavour to improve and consolidate the world.
3. To identify our minds with the Emperor's mind and, in loving and being friendly with one another, to pray for the country's prosperity and for peaceful co-existence and co-prosperity for the people of the world.'[7]

Shinto is by nature a religion limited to a particular people. It is a *Japanese* religion with a central emphasis upon the Japanese Emperor, the Japanese people and their ancestors. There has been no attempt made to spread the faith beyond the Japanese people (with the exception of the efforts of over-zealous militarists to force the inhabitants of lands under Japanese domination to show their

[7] Quoted in Sokyo Ono, *The Kami Way*, p. 82.

deference to Japanese rule and the Japanese Emperor through formal involvement in Shinto ceremonies). There would be an inevitable awkwardness in any attempt to initiate non-Japanese into Shrine Shinto, for it is essentially a simplistic, tribal faith that has endured throughout the ages despite the numerous political and cultural threats to its existence and integrity.

Various reasons for its amazing persistence will point up other characteristic features. It has a deep respect for *tradition* and seeks to perpetuate the traditional patterns. Because of a basic concern for *ritual* rather than doctrine, the onslaughts of other philosophies and ideologies were not so serious as would have been the case with a religion concerned with doctrinal purity. Rather than transmitting a creed based upon inspired writings, Shrine Shinto aims to communicate a tradition by means of rites centred in the shrine. This permits it to be very *adaptable*, another Shinto trait. Throughout its history it has both easily assimilated foreign elements and later just as easily discarded them, somehow maintaining a constancy, notwithstanding.

Content-wise, Shrine Shinto is concerned with man's place in the present world. Shinto writers call this *realism*, emphasizing the present, physical, material world as real, rather than indulging in vague abstractions about another world. It is true that even the fanciful, imaginative, mythological narratives have a very earthy quality. It is man's happiness in the present world rather than future bliss which is of primary concern. Lest this be considered, however, an invitation to complete egocentricity, which it may be, another facet of Shinto should be noted as a restraint to this proclivity. Shinto is not basically a personal faith, but a *communal* tradition. The individual is submerged in the community and should work for communal *harmony* rather than any individual distinction. Not only does the Shintoist seek for harmony with his human community, he sees himself as a part of a wider commonwealth which includes nature.

In the *natural surroundings* of the shrine, the worshipper feels in the presence of the *kami*. The *kami* concept itself is another characteristic of Shinto. There is an easy identification of *kami* with natural phenomena and a related lack of clear distinction between *kami* and man. This has further implications in regard to the Shinto concept of man, which is very *optimistic*. Man is basically good with the possibility of being or becoming (a) *kami*. What defilement or impurity he may have acquired can easily be purified by a simple ceremony. *Brightness*, *purity* and *sincerity* are the ideal characteristics of man. His essentially good nature does not require a legalistic code of ethics, but, as a member of the community, man's actions should be in keeping with communal well-being. There is no idea of an individual 'salvation', but man living a healthy, happy life as a harmonious member of the wider community would be the Shinto equivalent.

From a Christian standpoint, Shrine Shinto is seen to have various limitations. Its racial character prohibits a universal appeal or universal application (although certain scholars have tried to interpret it in such a way as to overcome this restriction). It lacks a firm philosophical foundation and the superficiality of its view of man, nature and *kami* fails to bring lasting, spiritual satisfaction to deeply-troubled souls. With its primary focus upon the past and upon ceremonial forms, it has failed to remain relevant to the modern age or to make constructive contributions to the solution of present-day problems. Its lack of moral or doctrinal standards tends to make it an elusive entity with real possibilities for being used for evil as well as for good. On the other hand, Shinto has proved itself to be a unifying force among the Japanese people. Its spirit of respect for the past and its emphasis upon man's place as a responsible member of an ongoing community is commendable and its sense of the divine immanence with which man can come into immediate contact must also be considered a positive factor.

Sect Shinto and 'New Religions'

During Shinto's long history, there have always been local variations of tradition including both theoretical and practical aspects. Ordinarily such peculiarities or special strains would not be singled out nor given particular attention. They would merely be lumped together in the inclusive Shinto designation which included both Folk Shinto, with its countless varieties, and the Shrine Shinto described above. Certain local traditions, however, gained a popularity that went beyond their locales. They evidenced a special appeal to segments of the population which failed to find satisfaction in the traditional forms. In 1882, the Meiji government, in its effort to establish a particular 'mainstream' of Shinto, unilaterally decreed a formal distinction between the more conventional Shinto shrines, which it subsequently nationalized as Shrine (National, or State) Shinto, and all other non-Buddhist, non-Christian religious associations, which it designated Sect Shinto.

Although most of the thirteen religious groups thus designated were definitely of Shinto lineage and worshipped Shinto *kami* according to their own distinctive ritualistic variations, two of the groups professed their ultimate allegiance to deities which were not found in the Shinto pantheon. Other smaller groups which were not accorded independent status as Shinto sects were forced to align themselves formally with one of the recognized sects in order to continue their particular traditions. During the period when Shinto was the established, government-supported religion, sectarian Shinto was entirely dependent for its support upon the fees paid or the offerings given by its adherents.

The thirteen Shinto sects given official recognition by the Meiji government have usually been classified under five headings. Three of them were considered *Pure Shinto Sects*. They considered themselves in the true line of primitive Shinto, purged of its foreign impurities, based on the classical myths, with emphasis upon loyalty to the Emperor and gratitude to ancestors. The two *Confucian Sects* consciously combined Confucian ethics with Shinto beliefs. Three sects which considered mountains (Mount Fuji or Mount Ontake) as the dwelling-place of *kami* and encouraged pilgrimages to these sacred habitats were referred to as *Mountain Sects*. The two sects with special emphasis upon purification of body and mind through particular rituals were labelled *Purification Sects*. The three remaining sects might well be designated *Revelation or Redemptive Sects*, for they are based on revelatory experiences of individual founders and are characterized by a message of redemption. While all the traditional Shinto sects had, to a greater or lesser degree, peculiar doctrines or practices which distinguished them as separate entities and differentiated them from Shrine Shinto as a whole, those included in this last grouping in particular (Kurozumikyo, Konkokyo, Tenrikyo) would most easily fall into a separate category of *New Religions*.

In post-war Japan considerable notoriety has been given to the phenomena of the 'New Religions'. Throughout Japanese religious history, however, there have been countless occasions when new religious movements, centring upon certain holy places, spirit-possessed individuals with peculiar powers, particularly effective rituals or special doctrines, have arisen. In many instances, such movements never progressed beyond strictly local traditions. Often they expired with the death of a key personality or due to other circumstances – including repressive measures taken by concerned governments, disapproving communities or jealous religious bodies – and were never widely publicized.

When the Meiji government made the formal distinction between Shrine Shinto and Sect Shinto, however, thirteen of the current 'off-centre' religious movements were given official recognition. Many other smaller groups then nominally affiliated themselves with these recognized sects and continued their peculiar practices as a sub-group of the larger sect. Following Japan's defeat in 1945 and the granting of total religious freedom by the occupation authorities, a large number of religious groups, which had been sheltering under the wings of factually unrelated organizations, established themselves as independent religious bodies. They were joined by other groups which had likewise affiliated with Buddhist sects, by others that had been active surreptitiously or that had been dormant, and by still others that were completely novel, post-war developments. This whole conglomerate has been lumped together under the misleading appellation of 'New Religions'.

While many of these religious bodies did have a formal association with Sect Shinto, others were Buddhistic in both doctrine and practice, and most of them were eclectic in nature, making use (often unconsciously) of elements of Folk Shinto, Buddhism, Confucianism, Taoism and Christianity as well as of Shrine Shinto. Some of those that were always considered as Sect Shinto groups now affirm that they never were Shintoistic in essence but were forced into the Shinto mould to maintain their existence. Although the Sect Shinto category is still being used, it is actually an unnecessary designation with only a historical significance now that all Shinto shrines are independent religious bodies without government ties or support and are free to join or to refrain from joining associations of related shrines. It remains true, however, that Shinto Sects continue to have an organizational structure and doctrinal formulations which might separate them from Shrine Shinto. Yet certain 'Shinto Sects' do not consider themselves Shinto at all and have joined the Association of New Religions.

Generally speaking, Japanese 'New Religions' have arisen during times of accelerated social change which generated peculiar problems, anxieties and feelings of insecurity which were not adequately met by traditional religious procedures. Frequently a charismatic personality, having some unusual ability or having had some extraordinary experience, becomes the efficient centre of a new movement which then requires an organizational figure to ensure its continuity. Combining both old traditions and novel innovations, unsophisticated doctrine, easily-performed rituals, promises of present physical, material benefits, opportunities for self-expression, purposeful activity and congenial fellowship, these religious groups have proved very attractive to many confused, frustrated, dissatisfied, seeking souls. Some of the larger and more popular of these groups have attempted overseas evangelism and are seeking to extricate themselves from their provincial Japanese *milieu*. They will inevitably exert an influence upon the character of Shinto as a whole, even as so many other religious elements have left the marks of their associations in the past.

Bibliography

Masaharu Anesaki, *History of Japanese Religion* (C. E. Tuttle, Rutland, Vt., 1963).

W. G. Aston, *Shinto: The Way of the Gods* (Longmans Green, New York, 1905).

Jean Herbert, *Shinto: Fountainhead of Japan* (Stein and Day, New York, 1967).

D. C. Holtom, *Modern Japan and Shinto Nationalism* (Paragon, New York, 1963).

D. C. Holtom, *The National Faith of Japan* (Paragon, New York, 1965).

Genchi Kato, *A Study of Shinto: The Religion of the Japanese Nation* (Barnes and Noble, New York, 1971).

Sokyo Ono, *Shinto: The Kami Way* (C. E. Tuttle, Rutland, Vt., 1962).

Ryusaku Tsunoda *et al.* (eds.), *Sources of Japanese Tradition* (Columbia University Press, New York, 1958).

A. C. Underwood, *Shintoism: The indigenous religion of Japan* (Epworth Press, London, 1934)

Confucianism
Leslie Lyall*

Ethics rather than religion

Had Confucius lived in the twentieth century, he would surely have been the patron saint of the humanists. While he would have enjoyed the religious ritual of the established church, he would not have held any deep convictions about religion itself. Indeed, he would have been something of a religious agnostic, largely un-concerned with the unseen world and sceptical about an after-life. He would, however, have been an enthusiast for anything which built up self-respect in the individual or promised to improve human relationships. Any scheme for moral and social reform would have had his patronage, while personally he would have been held in high esteem for his blameless character. The very last thing he would have contemplated would have been to found a new religion. He was far too much of a conservative for that!

It is common to speak of the 'three religions of China', Taoism and Confucianism being native religions and Buddhism having been introduced from India. In reality, there are not three religions but three schools of thought or three elements in one religious complex. Taoist mysticism is in contrast to Confucianist pragmatism, and where these failed to satisfy the Chinese spirit, Buddhism filled the need. But the Chinese people are not among the most deeply religious people of the world. The masses are superstitious animists rather than Buddhists. They tend to find their deepest spiritual values in ethical systems which regulate conduct without emphasis on gods or the after-life. The Chinese do not associate Confucius with 'religion', but speak of 'the School' or 'the Teaching'. His personality and character have had a decisive influence on Chinese thought and moral ideals, while his literary works have given to Chinese ethics an authoritative and classic form. Although not primarily religious in content, these

* Leslie Lyall spent 23 years as a missionary with the China Inland Mission until the withdrawal from China in 1951. He subsequently became Candidates Secretary of the CIM (now called the Overseas Missionary Fellowship) and later the Editorial Secretary, until his retirement in 1973.

works were regarded until this century with religious veneration. Confucius would have been horrified to learn that, years after his death, attempts were made to deify him, temples were built in his honour and sacrifices offered at his tomb.

But the veneration of Confucius is by no means confined to China. The Confucian classics are as highly regarded in Korea and Japan as in China, and their teaching has had as profound an influence on Korean and Japanese social life as it has had in China. It was only after its contact with China that Japan began to realize the need for an accepted code of morality. First Buddhism and then Confucian teaching exercised a profound influence. But in Japan Confucian ideals underwent a transformation. The cult of unquestioning loyalty to the Emperor took precedence over all other virtues, even filial piety. One sect of the Shinto religion is known as 'Confucian Shinto'. The famous 'Bushido' idea of chivalry owes as much to Confucius as to Zen Buddhism.

Vietnam also has its vigorous Confucian sect which endeavours to preserve and to practise the ethics of the Great Sage. Thus Confucianism continues to have great influence as being at once oriental and compatible with the Western secularist outlook.

Confucius

1. Some biographical details

Kung Fu-tzŭ or Kung the Sage, latinized by the early Jesuit missionaries to Confucius, was born in 551 BC. He was thus a contemporary of Gautama, the founder of Buddhism, and lived just before the time of Socrates and Plato. The Chinese Empire was at this time ruled by the Chou Dynasty which was composed of a number of small and semi-independent feudal states, often engaged in internecine wars. It was a troubled period of oppression, luxury and lust. But against this background it was also a time of intense intellectual activity, the classical age of Chinese literature.

Confucius himself came from an aristocratic but impoverished family in the principality of Lu in what is now the province of Shantung. At fifteen he set his heart on learning. At nineteen he married but was not, apparently, a family man. He divorced his wife and maintained an aloof relationship with his son and daughter. At twenty-two he became a teacher. At thirty he 'stood firm' and had settled opinions, whilst at forty he 'had no doubts'.

Meanwhile, in his thirties he had gone to the Court of Chou to study the ceremonies currently in use. While in the capital he is reported to have met his senior citizen Lao-tzŭ, or Laocius, the founder of the Taoist religion.[1] Laocius, believing in the unity and harmony of the universe, advocated the achievement of 'oneness

[1] Some authorities believe that Laocius was a mythical character. If so, his reported meeting with Confucius must also be regarded as mythical.

with the Tao (Way)' by a return to nature and spontaneous self-expression. He had nothing but scorn for the young upstart who wanted to regulate life by strict rules of conduct. On his return home Confucius, undeterred, gathered pupils around him, of whom the names of thirty-six have been identified.

His reputation became such that the prince of Lu, his native state, appointed him in 500 BC to be chief magistrate of a town and later Minister of Justice when he was fifty years of age. So successful were his moral reforms that the neighbouring princes became jealous of the prosperity of Lu and, to distract the Prince, sent him a gift of dancing girls and fine horses. When the Prince rejected his minister's advice to refuse the gift, Confucius resigned in protest and for thirteen years wandered from state to state, only to be disappointed and saddened everywhere by a refusal to respond to his moral challenge.

Finally he settled down and gave himself to research in ancient history, poetry and ritual. In personal habits he was simple, but precise and fastidious, insisting on the appropriate costume for the particular occasion and the suitable sauce for each dish. His last five years were devoted to writing. A temple still marks the place in Chüfou, Shantung, where he lived and died in 479 BC.

2. His literary works

The famous 'Four Books' of Confucius are *The Analects*, *The Great Learning*, *The Doctrine of the Mean* and *The Works of Mencius*. The first of these is a collection of Confucius' sayings, and so a trustworthy account of his interests and opinions. The 'Five Classics' always associated with the 'Four Books' consist of *The Book of Changes*, *The Books of Poetry* and *The Book of History*, all older writings taken as authoritative by the Confucian school; *The Spring and Autumn Annals*, traditionally said to have been written by Confucius; and *The Book of Rites*, a collection of later Confucian writings on ritual matters, including stories about and sayings of Confucius.

'I am a transmitter,' Confucius agreed, 'a believer in, and admirer of, antiquity.'

3. The Confucian ethic

The teachings of the sage are preserved in *The Analects*, which consist of questions by his disciples and the appropriate answers. This is in no sense a religious work but an expression of the views of a pragmatic moralist with an interest in religion in so far as its observance was a contribution to respectability. His 'princely man' was, in modern terminology, the 'perfect gentleman', characterized by 'kindness, sincerity, graciousness, loyalty, and self-denial'. He emphasizes the importance of virtue, propriety and correct ritual, while accepting the current religious beliefs in 'heaven' (*tien*) and in spirits, though his advice was to keep aloof from 'spiritual beings' (*shen*) about which he declined to express an opinion. His references to the deity are in impersonal terms. But he recognized this impersonal power as a sanction for moral conduct.

His interest was in this world rather than the next, though he showed a childlike pleasure in religious ritual as such. In common with most Chinese philosophers he probably believed in the inherent goodness of man, though this doctrine is first affirmed by Mencius. The innate sinfulness of man as taught in the Bible is a doctrine Chinese traditionalists have found it hard to accept. Man, said Confucius, can be virtuous if only he makes up his mind to it. 'What I do not wish others to do to me, that also I wish not to do to them' is his famous interpretation of *jen* – goodness or charity – a very different attitude from the positive 'Golden Rule' of the Sermon on the Mount, given five centuries later. But in fact, Confucius does give emphasis to helping others positively; for example, 'Wishing to stand yourself, help others to stand.' His philosophy was very simple: namely, virtue is the foundation of happiness.

Yet Confucius threw no new light on life's problems, was uncertain about God and was content to be ignorant of the after-life. He was concerned with living in society, and when his lifelong endeavours to bring about a permanent social reformation in his home state came to nothing, he spent his last days under a cloud of disillusionment.

'Confucianism,' says Dr Lin Yu-tang, 'unlike Christianity, is of the earth, earth-born. Strictly speaking, it is not a religion: it has a certain feeling towards life and the universe that borders on religious feeling, but it is not a religion.'[2]

Confucius can perhaps be compared to one of the Old Testament prophets for he was clearly raised up as a witness to moral values in a corrupt age.

Mencius

Meng-tzŭ or Mencius (371–289 BC), a contemporary of Plato and Aristotle, was even less interested in religion than his master. He made no attempt to make of the Confucian teachings a religious message and emphasized even more than Confucius the inherent goodness of man. His works give to Confucian ethics a more speculative form. 'Man's nature is good, as water flows down.' The corollary of this is that as water can flow uphill only by force, so man does evil only against his nature. Such a hypothesis, so contrary to the Christian doctrine of original sin, has had the incalculable effect of innoculating the Chinese educated classes against the acceptance of Christian teaching. When Mencius tried to guide rulers to govern wisely, only

[2] Lin Yu-tang, *My Country and My People* (Reynal & Hitchcock, New York, 1935), p. 99.

his disciples would listen and he became just as disillusioned as Confucius.

Later Confucianism

1. Its influence on the state

The cult of Confucius outlived all rival philosophies and the well-trained Confucians were the only men capable of handling public affairs. It was this scholar class that made Confucianism the cult of the state. After 631 AD the sole qualification for holding public office was a successful examination in the Confucian classics. Thus China until recent years was always ruled by scholars and gentlemen rather than by professional politicians and soldiers. It was their influence which lay behind the strong conservatism and opposition to progress which characterized China before the 1911 Revolution. With the fall of the empire in 1911, Confucianism suffered a severe blow. The old examination system was abolished and the imperial cult came to an end. In spite of periodic attempts to reinstate Confucian morals, there has been no come-back and Communists denounce Confucianism as pure feudalism and therefore a bar to progress. They have even attempted to break up the intense family loyalty which Confucius inculcated and have had a measure of success, at least temporarily.

2. The cult of the ancestors

As nowhere else, this cult has been developed in China and Japan. It goes back into antiquity and Confucius certainly did not invent it. But recognizing the importance of filial piety for the stability of society, he carried over this reverence to the dead as well as the living. He said that children should spend three years mourning for their departed parents and revived the elaborate ritual for the 'veneration of the dead', which, until the advent of Communism at least, was practised by every devoted son, often at a cost he could not afford which might involve him in debt for life. Mencius declared, 'One of the three great sins is to be without posterity, because then there is no-one to provide for the ancestral spirits.' Marriage was therefore a duty and concubinage inevitable whenever the legal wife had no male offspring.

After death, the important thing was to set up the tablet for the deceased in the guest-room cabinet together with all the other tablets of near ancestors. Such was the home altar around which the family ritual was concentrated – the burning of incense and paper money and the offering of food to the ancestors. Every spring, when a great family reunion took place, sacrifices were offered at the grave during the Spring Festival. Formerly ancestral halls used to be built for the use of the whole clan sharing a common name. Here the older tablets were laid up as they were replaced in the home by the tablets of the more recently dead. The halls were used for meetings of the clan leaders, regular family reunions and feasts and ceremonies for the departed reverently conducted. Professor K. S. Latourette says, 'Ceremonies for the departed constitute one of the most outstanding characteristics of Chinese culture.'

Dr Lin Yu-tang has stated that ancestor-worship is the real religion of China, and as such it constituted the greatest barrier to the progress of Christianity. For when an older son becomes a Christian, he can no longer indulge in ancestral worship and his heathen parents – as in Malaysia today – naturally feel that tradition and the long line of family loyalty have been broken by an alien faith – namely Christianity. In Japan, where the cult has not been universally regarded as idolatrous, a compromise has sometimes been made to enable Christians to maintain their traditional veneration of the family ancestors.

In the seventeenth century Matteo Ricci, the Jesuit missionary and scholar, in seeking to come to terms with Chinese culture, carefully studied the Confucian Rites and concluded that they were not idolatrous. Thus a Christian could conscientiously observe them. The Franciscans and Dominicans disagreed and the controversy was bitter. The emperor Kang Hsi supported Matteo Ricci, but the pope sided with his rivals. Consequently the Jesuit and Franciscan missionaries were expelled from China.

3. The 'yin-yang' principle

One important aspect of Chinese philosophy is the belief that the cosmos is governed by two opposing forces – *yin* and *yang*. *Yin* represents femininity, maternity, earth, cold, darkness, weakness and death. It is negative and passive. It is the north. *Yang* is masculinity, paternity, heaven, warmth, light, strength and life. It is positive and active. It is the south. The *yin* force contracts, while the *yang* force expands.

The origins of this fundamental dualistic outlook are uncertain and may not be earlier than the fourth century BC. The system was finally elaborated by both Confucianists and Taoists and the form, completed in the Sung Dynasty (AD 960–1217), was Neo-Confucianism. It was an endeavour to express the phenomena of nature. Under the Taoists, it grew to be more than a speculative theory as to the order of the universe. It became a science applied both to geomancy (*feng shui*) and to medicine, alchemy, *etc*.

The symbol of this system is the *pa kua* (eight trigrams), which comes from the appendices of *The Book of Changes* and is ascribed to Confucius, but may be of a later date. The trigrams are composed of combinations of a long dash (*yang*) and two short dashes (*yin*). Heaven, for instance, is totally male with three long dashes, while earth is totally female with six short dashes. The other six trigrams represent water, fire, wind, thunder, vapour and mountains. These are arranged around the central symbol of the two 'fish' (*yin* and *yang*) which was added in the Sung Dynasty. The fish complement each other and represent *T'ai chi* (primal matter). One version is included, incidently, in the Korean national flag.

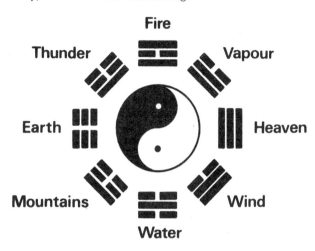

Confucianism and Taoism

While Confucius is a historical reality, Laocius is a shadowy and perhaps mythical figure of whom nothing is known except that he is the supposed author of the classic Taoist work, the *Tao-te Ching* or *Way and Moral Principle Classic*. While Confucianism is essentially down to earth, Taoism (pronounced 'Dowism') is an airy-fairy philosophy which might have been popular with the modern beatnik or hippie. For it advocated non-interference with the course of nature and a life free from all man-made restrictions. For the Taoist nothing stands still or is fixed. There are therefore no static standards or conventions.

The term *Tao* from which the religion derives its name is the same word used to translate both 'the Word' in chapter 1 and 'the Way' in chapter 14 of John's Gospel. The term is of great importance in Chinese thought. It means primarily the 'way' or the 'road' and thus 'the way of the Universe'. It is supposed to be the first principle, even preceding God – the 'universal cosmic energy behind the order of nature'. But it is so mysterious that 'they who know do not tell and they who tell do not know'. Man follows the laws of earth, earth follows the laws of heaven, heaven follows the laws of Tao and Tao follows the laws of spontaneity. Thus the original reign of Tao represents the ideal state of pristine perfection when men acted spontaneously in harmony with the laws of Tao and good and evil were unknown. The Taoist therefore aims at a return to this happy paradise by conforming to the Virtue (*Te*) of self-emptiness, seeking, like water, the lowest place and by returning to the absolutely simple life of nature. Taoist poetry expresses this mystical communion with unspoiled nature. The teaching of the *Tao-te Ching* has been compared with Greek thought in its development of neo-Platonism. Its quietism and passivity have influenced many Chinese minds and it has been called 'one of the prime ingredients of Chinese culture'.

Chuang-Tzŭ (b. 330 BC), a disciple of Laocius, was a contemporary of Mencius and one of the most brilliant writers of antiquity. He too stressed the uselessness of mere sense knowledge, emphasized the essential unity of all creation and spoke of the 'obliterating unity of *Tao*'. Man can return to his primitive innocence only by discarding all vaunted wisdom and an artificial way of life. In this Taoism is more akin to contemplative Buddhism than to Confucianism. Chuang-Tzŭ sometimes quoted from the *Tao-Te Ching* but hi version of Taoism is in some ways original.

Taoism was eventually corrupted from its early simplicity by the introduction of the magical side of philosophy. Its followers set out on a search for the elixir of immortality, and engaged in spiritism. And so Taoism quickly degenerated into what it is today – a polytheistic system of spiritualism, demonism and superstition.

Confucianism and Communism

The Communists in China practise Confucian morals but, on social and political grounds, object to the cult of ancestor-worship as perpetuating feudalism. It diverts people from loyalty to the state to a narrow clan loyalty. Initially the hierarchy sought to turn the people away from this narrow loyalty by persuasion, but in the face of repeated failures the cult of Mao was promoted. In some places ancestral shrines were dedicated to Mao. Everywhere the portrait or the bust of Mao became, for a while, an object of veneration. Chairman Mao Tse-tung is now the great father-figure and will no doubt become the venerated ancestor.

Bibliography

B. S. Bonsall, *Confucianism and Taoism* (Epworth Press, London, 1934).

F. T. Cheng, *China Moulded by Confucius* (Stevens and Son, London, 1947).

H. G. Creel, *What is Taoism? And Other Studies in Chinese Cultural History* (University of Chicago Press, Chicago, 1970).

E. R. Hughes, *Chinese Philosophy in Classical Times* (Dutton, New York, 1942).

K. S. Latourette, *The Chinese: Their History and Culture* (Macmillan,

New York, 1964).

James Legge, *The Religions of China* (Scribners, New York, 1881).

P. J. Maclagan, *Chinese Religious Ideas* (SCM Press, London, 1926).

H. F. MacNair (ed.), *China* (Books for Libraries, Freeport, New York, 1946).

W. E. Soothill, *The Three Religions of China* (Hyperion Press, Westport, Conn., repr. 1973).

Arthur Waley, *The Analects of Confucius* (Random, New York, 1938)

Richard Wilhelm, *Confucius and Confucianism* (Harcourt, Brace, Jovanovich, New York, 1971).

CHAPTER EIGHT

A Christian approach to comparative religion

Norman Anderson

The study of comparative religion, fascinating though it is, leaves many with a sense of bewilderment. Such diverse beliefs are held by multitudes whose sincerity cannot be questioned that the student may easily fall into the logical absurdity of wondering whether any ultimate truth exists in matters of religion, or into the resigned pessimism of doubting whether any firmly founded conviction in such matters can be attained by man. Should not all religions be regarded, then, as vain attempts to solve the insoluble or, alternatively, as different roads, however devious, to one grand but distant goal? Admittedly, most of the world's faiths seem to the unprejudiced enquirer to be a patchwork of good and bad, or at least of the desirable and the less desirable; but cannot the mind which eschews fanaticism accept the postulate which seems in some sense common to all, that there is a Principle or a Person beyond and behind the material universe, which to recognize, or whom to worship, meets some craving of the human heart? As for the rest – the details of dogma and worship – may not each individual work out for himself an eclectic faith chosen from what seems best in all the great religions?

There are, however, decisive reasons which preclude the Christian from adopting such an attitude. He will be vitally concerned, of course, with what millions of his fellow creatures believe, and their convictions will command not only his interest, but also his study and respect. More, he will find much in those who follow other religions which will rebuke, instruct and inspire him – as, for instance, the Muslim's fidelity in prayer and fast, the Buddhist's dignified self-discipline, and the Sadhu's detachment from the things of time and sense. But these things concern matters of observance rather than teaching, of practice rather than dogma, noble – and, in its context, valid – though much non-Christian dogma undoubtedly is. With the basic content of his faith, however, the Christian will neither want, nor dare, to meddle – although he will retain an insatiable longing to enter into a much deeper understanding of the revelation on which it rests and an ever richer experience of the God who thus reveals himself.

But how can the Christian be so confident that his faith does in fact rest on a uniquely authoritative self-revelation of God? The history of the Christian church is so darkened by the sin, intolerance, frailty and divisions of generations of its adherents that it is easy to understand the cynicism with which it is often regarded. Even the Christian religion, as it has been elaborated, expounded and embodied down the centuries, has been so fraught with human error that this, too, stands under the judgment of God. What is it, then, which gives the Christian his confident conviction in the essential truth and unique authority of the divine revelation which it is his duty and privilege to proclaim?

It is to Jesus himself that the Christian will continually return. Behind him, of course, stands the long history of Israel, and God's progressive revelation of himself through Abraham, Moses and a succession of prophets. But the Old Testament is always looking forward – whether through promise, prediction or prefiguration – to One who was to come. Then at last, as the apostle Paul puts it: 'When the time had fully come, God sent forth his Son, born of woman, born under the law, to redeem those who were under the law, so that we might receive adoption as sons' (Galatians 4:4, 5). And the whole New Testament bears witness to that unique event and its essential implications.

About the historicity of Jesus, about his basic teaching and the impact he made on his contemporaries, and about his death on a Roman gibbet, there can surely be no serious question. Nor is there any room for doubt that, after his death, something happened which transformed his little band of dejected and dispirited followers into a company of witnesses whom no persecution could silence, and who 'turned the world upside down'. One and all, moreover, they testified that what had happened was that the crucified Jesus had been raised from the dead and had appeared to them and many other witnesses. As Paul wrote to the Corinthians in a letter which is unquestionably authentic: 'I delivered to you first of all (or as a matter of first importance) what I also received, that Christ died for our sins in accordance with the scriptures, that he was buried, that he was raised on the third day in accordance with the scriptures, and that he appeared to Cephas, then to the twelve. Then he appeared to more than five hundred brethren at one time . . .' (1 Corinthians 15:3-5). Now Paul must himself have received this tradition, at least in outline, immediately after his own conversion, within between two and (at most) five years of the crucifixion; and he must certainly have received it in its fullness, with the appended list of the principal witnesses, on his first visit to Jerusalem (which he describes in the first chapter of his letter to the Galatians) just three years later. In all probability, then, he received it within five years of the alleged event. He tells us, moreover, that this was the common message of all the apostles (cf. 1 Corinthians 15:11). And he goes out of his way to assert that the majority of those five hundred witnesses to having

seen the risen Christ were still alive when he wrote to the Corinthians some twenty years later. As C. H. Dodd put it: 'No statement
could be more emphatic or unambiguous. In making it Paul is
exposing himself to the criticism of resolute opponents who would
have been ready to point to any flaw in his credentials or in his
presentation of the common tradition.'[1] So the addition of this
comment can only have meant: 'If you don't believe me, there are a
very large number of witnesses still alive to whom you can turn for
confirmation of what I say.'

It is perfectly true – as critics have not been slow to emphasize –
that there is no explicit reference to the empty tomb in this earliest
piece of historical evidence. But what oriental Jew of the first century
could possibly have written that Christ died (physically, of course),
that he was buried (physically, of course), and that he was later
'raised again on the third day' unless he had believed that *something*
had happened to the body which had been laid in the sepulchre?
When, from the very first, the early Christians – as C. H. Dodd again
insists – said that 'He rose again from the dead', they 'took it for
granted that his body was no longer in the tomb. If the tomb had
been visited it would have been found empty. The gospels supplemented this by saying, it *was* visited, it *was* found empty.'[2] And that
this was an authentic part of the original apostolic tradition seems to
me beyond any reasonable doubt.

But while it was the joyful certainty that Jesus was risen and still
alive which was, unquestionably, the dominant note in the earliest
apostolic proclamation, they soon began to put an equal emphasis on
his atoning death. It was in the same letter to the Corinthians that
Paul insisted that the gospel must be so preached that the cross of
Christ should not 'be emptied of its power. For the word of the cross
is folly to those who are perishing, but to us who are being saved it is
the power of God' (1 Corinthians 1:17, 18). And in his second letter
to the same church he explained this by saying, 'What I mean is,
that God was in Christ reconciling the world to himself, no longer
holding men's misdeeds against them, and that he has entrusted us
with the message of reconciliation' (2 Corinthians 5:19, NEB).
And the basis of this reconciliation was that, at the cross, God 'for
our sake . . . made him to be sin who knew no sin, so that in him we
might become the righteousness of God' (verse 21). This, indeed, was
the united testimony of the apostolic church, which they saw as the
fulfilment of the fifty-third chapter of Isaiah and other Old Testament
prophecies.[3]

It is for this reason that the Christian can allow no compromise,
syncretism or theological relativism to obscure the inevitable in-

---

[1] C. H. Dodd, "The Appearances of the Risen Christ," in *Studies in the Gospels*,
ed. D. E. Nineham (Allenson, Naperville, Ill., 1955), p. 28.

[2] C. H. Dodd, *The Founder of Christianity* (Macmillan, New York, 1970), p. 166.

[3] *Cf.* Mark 10:45; Luke 22:37; I Peter 2:24; *etc.*

tolerance – not in its spirit, but in its essential nature – of the gospel to which he is committed. It is not that he denies that there is any revelation of God's 'eternal power and Godhead' in the wonders of nature (*cf.* Romans 1:20) or in those glimpses of the truth which God has vouchsafed to many seeking souls. But if God could have *adequately* revealed himself in any other way, is it reasonable to suppose that he would have taken the almost incredible road to the incarnation and the passion? And if it had been possible to deal with the problem of man's sin and its consequences in any other way whatever, is it conceivable that God would not have 'spared his own Son' the physical, mental and spiritual agony of Calvary – an agony in which he himself was so intimately involved? Surely that would not make sense.

If, then, the basic Christian message is true – and for this the evidence seems wholly convincing – it must follow that, as Stephen Neill puts it:

'Simply as history the event of Jesus Christ is unique. Christian faith goes a great deal further in its interpretation of that event. It maintains that in Jesus the one thing that needed to happen has happened in such a way that it need never happen again. . . . Making such claims, Christians are bound to affirm that all men need the Gospel. For the human sickness there is one specific remedy, and this is it. There is no other. Therefore the Gospel must be proclaimed to the ends of the earth and to the end of time. The Church cannot compromise on its missionary task without ceasing to be the Church. If it fails to see and to accept this responsibility, it is changing the Gospel into something other than itself. . . . Naturally, to the non-Christian hearer this must sound like crazy megalomania, and religious imperialism of the very worst kind. We must recognise the dangers; Christians have on many occasions fallen into both of them. But we are driven back ultimately on the question of truth.'[4]

If many different groups of pathologists, let us suppose, were all seeking earnestly to discover the cause and cure of cancer, and one group – through no brilliance of their own – were to light upon the secret, would it constitute 'crazy megalomania' for them to share what they had found with their fellows? Would it not, rather, be criminal folly for them to keep the secret to themselves?

To what conclusion, then, does this lead us in regard to the attitude of the Christian to other religions as systems and to the eternal destiny of those who follow them? In regard to both these questions Christian opinion has been – and still is – widely divided. There have been many, all down the centuries, who have regarded most, if not all, of the non-Christian religions as a sort of *praeparatio evangelica* –

---

[4] S. C. Neill, *Christian Faith and Other Faiths* (OUP, New York, 1970), pp. 17f.

as, indeed, all Christians would say of Old Testament Judaism. Some of those who take this view find the secret of the elements of truth in other religions in terms of an original divine revelation, the traces and influence of which have never been wholly lost or forgotten – or even in some cross-fertilization of ideas from one religion to another. Others, again, discern in them the influence of the 'cosmic Christ' who, as the eternal Logos or revealer of the Godhead, is the 'light that enlightens every man'. This view was taken by Justin Martyr and the Christian philosophers of Alexandria in the early centuries of the Christian era, and was summed up by William Temple when he wrote: 'By the word of God – that is to say by Jesus Christ – Isaiah and Plato, Zoroaster, Buddha, and Confucius uttered and wrote such truths as they declared. There is only one Divine Light, and every man in his own measure is enlightened by it.'[5]

Other Christians have adopted, at times, a diametrically opposite attitude. Instead of giving prominence to the elements of truth to be found in other religions they have emphasized the darker side of their ethical teaching and the less persuasive of their theological tenets, and have concluded that they emanate from the devil, rather than from God. In particular, those who take this view insist that these other religions clearly deny, whether by explicit statement or implicit teaching, the unique claims of the 'Word made flesh' and the fundamental need for the atonement that he alone could – and did – effect. Those elements of truth which can unquestionably be found in these other religions should therefore be explained, they feel, in terms of the fact that even Satan himself not infrequently appears as an angel of light – as, indeed, he might be expected to do in any religion designed to capture, and hold, men's allegiance and to constitute a substitute for, or an alternative to, the Christian gospel.

Yet a third view regards these other religions as not emanating primarily from either God or the devil, but as representing a variety of human attempts to explain the phenomena of life, to reach out after ultimate reality and to construct some system of thought, behaviour and religious observance which will satisfy man's needs. Those who founded and developed these religions were, like the rest of us, a compound of good and evil, of sincere aspiration after truth and of self-seeking; and they were also exposed to supernatural influences – both from God and Satan. It is scarcely to be wondered at, then, that the non-Christian religions commonly represent such a diverse amalgam of truth and falsehood. All that is true must surely come from God, whether directly or indirectly; and all that is false must, presumably, owe its ultimate origin to the 'father of lies', although its immediate source can usually be found in the sincere, but mistaken, conclusions of some human teacher.

[5] W. Temple, *Readings in St. John's Gospel* (St. Martin's Press, New York, 1945), I, 10.

The Christian preacher, then, will not feel that he can commend the non-Christian religions (other than Old Testament Judaism) as divinely inspired preparations for the gospel – although he will frequently, like the apostle Paul, use some element in their teaching or practice as a bridge by means of which he can reach the minds and hearts of their followers and bring to them the message he longs to communicate in an intelligible way. Nor will he – normally, at least – feel at liberty to speak against (or, still less, to ridicule) what other men sincerely, if mistakenly, believe, although he may at times be forced to speak out plainly about some particular point. His characteristic stance, however, will be positive rather than negative; and his habitual message will be to plead with all men to consider – or, in some cases, to reconsider – Jesus Christ. But far from any personal sense of superiority he will freely and frankly acknowledge that he is himself no better than anyone else; and he will do his best to present the essential Good News in a way which is stripped bare of accretions derived from the thought and culture of his own race or background. The truth as it is revealed in Jesus will be his one criterion, and the need of all men, without exception, for the forgiveness, reconciliation and new life which Jesus died to bestow will be the message he lives to proclaim.

But this means that he must listen quite as much as he speaks, for he needs to learn how someone from another religion and culture sees things. It is only then that the Christian 'may be given access to the dark places of that stranger's world – the things that really make him ashamed or anxious or despairing'. And then, at last, he will see the Saviour and Lord of that other world, his own Lord Jesus, yet not as he has known him hitherto. Instead he will 'understand how perfectly he matches all the needs and all the aspirations and all the insights of that other world – He who is the unique Lord and Saviour of all possible worlds'.[6] For every man, whatever his religion, race or moral virtue, is a sinner; and sin always, and necessarily, alienates men from a holy God. So all of us alike need forgiveness, and all of us stand in need of a Saviour – since a sinful man can never save either himself or anyone else. It is precisely at this point, moreover, that the New Testament is at its most unequivocal, for Jesus himself is reported as saying, 'I am the way, and the truth, and the life; no one comes to the Father, but by me' (John 14:6) – or, in the Synoptic tradition, 'no one knows the Father except the Son and any one to whom the Son chooses to reveal him' (Matthew 11:27; cf. Luke 10:22). And the apostles in their turn reiterated this truth when they asserted that 'there is salvation in no one else, for there is no other name under heaven given among men by which we must be saved' (Acts 4:12).

Inevitably, however, this raises in an acute form the question of the

---

[6] J. V. Taylor, *The Go-between God* (Fortress, Philadelphia, 1973), p. 189.

eternal destiny of those who, for example, have never so much as heard the truth as it is in Jesus. This is usually through no fault of their own, but rather through the failure of Christians to take sufficiently seriously the commission to preach the gospel to every creature. But if all men are sinners, and alike stand in need of forgiveness; if sinful men can never save either themselves or one another; and if there is only one Saviour – then what hope can any man have? Does this mean that they are inevitably lost? That would, indeed, be an agonizing conclusion to those whose basic belief is that 'God is love'; but is there really any alternative?

It is at this point, as I see it, that the Old Testament throws a ray of light on our darkness, for who can doubt that Abraham, Moses, David and a host of others enjoyed both forgiveness and fellowship with God? Yet they did not know Jesus and the salvation he was to effect – except as a vague hope of the future which they proclaimed but only dimly understood. And what of that multitude of more ordinary Jews who, convicted of sin by God's Spirit, turned to him in repentance and faith, brought the prescribed sacrifices, and threw themselves on his mercy? Were they not, too, forgiven and accepted – not because they had merited salvation, for no man can do this; nor on the basis of their animal sacrifices, which could never atone for human sin; but, rather, on the basis of what the God of love was going to do in the unique 'Lamb of God' who was still to come, and of that atoning death to which all the Old Testament sacrifices were designed to point. For this supreme event, although it certainly – and necessarily – happened at one particular time and place in human history, is timeless in its divine efficacy. And that this alone was the ultimate ground on which the transgressions and sins of Old Testament believers were forgiven seems to be clearly taught by New Testament verses such as Romans 3:25 and Hebrews 9:15.[7]

May this not provide us with a guideline to the solution of the burning problem of those in other religions who have never heard – or never heard with understanding – of the Saviour? It is not, of course, that they can earn salvation through their religious devotion or moral achievements, great though these sometimes are – for the New Testament is emphatic that no man can ever earn salvation. But what if the Spirit of God convicts them, as he alone can, of something of their sin and need; and what if he enables them, in the darkness or twilight, somehow to cast themselves on the mercy of God and cry out, as it were, for his forgiveness and salvation? Will they not then be accepted and forgiven in the one and only Saviour? And if it be asked how this can be when they have never so much as heard of him,

---

[7] There are also, of course, many verses which refer to the pre-incarnate Christ, through whom all things were created and in whom they are held together, whose atoning death was an essential part of the eternal counsel of God.

then the answer must be that they will be accepted on the basis of what the God of all grace himself did in Christ at the cross; for it is on that basis, alone, that a God who is light as well as love, just as well as merciful, can welcome and forgive repentant sinners.

It cannot be claimed that this is the clear and unequivocal teaching of the New Testament, where the primary emphasis is on the Christian's duty to share the Good News of God's love with the whole world. But how else can we understand Peter's words in the house of Cornelius: 'I now see how true it is that God has no favourites, but that in every nation the man who is godfearing and does what is right is acceptable to him' (Acts 10:34, 35, NEB)? This cannot mean that the man who does his best to be religious and moral will earn salvation, for the whole of the New Testament, as we have seen, denies this possibility. But may it not mean that the man who realizes something of his need, and who casts himself on the mercy of God with a sincerity that shows itself in his life, will find that mercy where it is always available – at the cross where Jesus died?

If such a person should subsequently hear and understand the gospel, he would presumably be among the company of those (whom the Christian does meet, sometimes, in non-Christian lands) who accept it at once, and even say: 'Why didn't you come and tell me this before? It is what I have been waiting for all my life.' And if he never hears it in this life, then I believe he will wake up, as it were, on the other side of the grave to worship the One in whom, without understanding it, he had found the mercy of God.

This, it should be understood, is totally different from what has been termed the doctrine of the 'second chance'. In the latter it is the opportunity to choose, and the subsequent decision of faith, which are deferred to the after-life, while what I suggest happens to such a man beyond the grave is that he will come into the light of a joyful understanding of the salvation to which the Spirit of God has brought him through the repentance and faith which he inspired – faltering, it may be, and unenlightened, certainly – during the days of his earthly pilgrimage.

But if this is true – as I myself believe – then it certainly does not lessen the Christian's missionary responsibility. To begin with, his Master's last commission and command was that he should go and tell the Good News, and that should be quite enough. If, moreover, he reflects how he himself was brought to the point of no longer trying to earn salvation, but accepting it as a gift, he will almost certainly conclude that this was through hearing the gospel story and its implications; so how can he deny this privilege to others? Any who are enabled by the Holy Spirit to turn to God, in the twilight, in repentance and faith, would still, moreover, lack that assurance, conscious companionship and confident message which come only from a knowledge that Christ died to justify his people, rose again to manifest himself to them in the 'power of an endless life' and has commissioned them as his ambassadors to appeal to others to be reconciled to God. So it is our manifest duty to share this knowledge, and these privileges, with all mankind.

The question remains, however, whether the non-Christian religions may be said in any way to represent a 'saving structure' which serves to point men to the 'cosmic Christ'. This is certainly the contention of Raymond Panikkar, who believes that the 'good and *bona fide* Hindu is saved by Christ and not by Hinduism, but it is through the sacraments of Hinduism, through the message of morality and the good life, through the mysterion that comes down to him through Hinduism, that Christ saves the Hindu normally'.[8] Somewhat similarly, W. Cantwell Smith, writing of more than one non-Christian religion in the light of fellowship with their adherents, insists that we must recognize these religions as 'channels through which God Himself comes into touch with these His children'.[9] But it seems to me that both Panikkar and Cantwell Smith here go much too far. It is not through other religions as 'saving structures', as I see it, but rather through the basic fact of God's general revelation, vouchsafed in nature and in all that is true (including, of course, the truth there is in other religions), and the equally fundamental fact of our common humanity, that the Spirit of God, or the 'cosmic Christ', brings home to men and women something of their need. It is this, I think, which helps to explain what Lesslie Newbigin terms an 'element of continuity' which is 'confirmed in the experience of many who have become converts to Christianity from other religions. Even though this conversion involves a radical discontinuity, yet there is often the strong conviction afterwards that it was the living and true God who was dealing with them in the days of their pre-Christian wrestlings'.[1] This is naturally most clearly marked in Judaism, as in the case of the apostle Paul;[2] but I have also found that converts from Islam never regard the God whom they previously sought to worship as wholly false, but rather rejoice that they have now, in Jesus Christ, been brought to know, and have fellowship with, that God as he really is.

So, indeed, it is to Jesus Christ that we always, and inevitably, come back. 'A most sensitive, lonely man from Pakistan', John V. Taylor tells us, 'spoke at the New Delhi Assembly of the World Council of Churches about his conversion from Islam. All his longing was still for his own people, their language, their ancient culture; and in the factious and generally defeated church of that land he finds little consolation or fellowship. "I am a Christian", he confessed, "for

---

[8] R. Panikkar, *The Unknown Christ of Hinduism* (Humanities, New York, 1968), p. 54.

[9] W. Cantwell Smith, *The Faith of Other Men* (New American Library, New York, 1963), p. 124.

[1] L. Newbigin, *The Finality of Christ* (John Knox, Richmond, Va., 1969), p. 59.

[2] *Cf.* Acts 22:3f., 14f.; 24:14f.; Galatians 1:15f., *etc.*

one reason only – because of the absolute worship-ability of Jesus Christ. By that word I mean that I have found no other being in the universe who compels my adoration as he has done. And if ever some pundit or theologian should prove me wrong and show that, after all, the High God is not of the character which I see in Jesus, I, for one, would have to blaspheme and turn my back on any such god." [3]

The attitude of the Christian, then, is essentially that of positive, humble, but unashamed witness to Jesus. As Lesslie Newbigin puts it, he

'points to the one Lord Jesus Christ as the Lord of all men . . . The Church does not apologise for the fact that it wants all men to know Jesus Christ and to follow him. Its very calling is to proclaim the Gospel to the ends of the earth. It cannot make any restrictions in this respect. Whether people have a high, a low or a primitive religion, whether they have sublime ideals or a defective morality makes no fundamental difference in this respect. All must hear the Gospel.' [4]

[3] Taylor, *Go-between God*, p. 193.
[4] Newbigin, *op. cit.*, p. 59.

Index